Economic Well-Being of the Elderly

Public Policy and Social Welfare
A Series Edited by Bernd Marin

 European Centre Vienna

Volume 25

Tine Stanovnik, Nada Stropnik, Christopher Prinz (Eds.)

Economic Well-Being of the Elderly

A Comparison Across Five European Countries

Routledge
Taylor & Francis Group

LONDON AND NEW YORK

First published 2000 by Ashgate Publishing

Reissued 2018 by Routledge
2 Park Square, Milton Park, Abingdon, Oxon OX14 4RN
711 Third Avenue, New York, NY 10017, USA

Routledge is an imprint of the Taylor & Francis Group, an informa business

Copyright © European Centre Vienna, 2000

Publisher's Note
The publisher has gone to great lengths to ensure the quality of this reprint but points out that some imperfections in the original copies may be apparent.

Disclaimer
The publisher has made every effort to trace copyright holders and welcomes correspondence from those they have been unable to contact.

ISBN 13: 978-0-8153-9493-8 (hbk)
ISBN 13: 978-0-8153-8236-2 (pbk)
ISBN 13: 978-1-351-20875-8 (ebk)

Contents

Preface   7

Chapter 1
Introduction and Comparative Summary   9
Tine Stanovnik / Carl Emmerson / Christopher Prinz /
Zsolt Spéder / Nada Stropnik / Adam Szulc

TRANSITION COUNTRIES   51

Chapter 2
Hungary: Getting Better and Becoming Dissimilar   53
Zsolt Spéder

Chapter 3
Poland: Transition Gainers with an Uncertain Future   99
Adam Szulc

Chapter 4
Slovenia: Income Stability in a Turbulent
Period of Economic Transition   135
Tine Stanovnik / Nada Stropnik

Non-Transition Economies   181

Chapter 5
Austria: Do Trends in Income Distribution
Influence Policy?   183
Christopher Prinz

Chapter 6
Reforms in the UK:
Involving the Private Sector   233
Carl Emmerson / Paul Johnson / Gary Stears

List of Contributors   269

Preface

The research on which this book is founded was undertaken with support from the European Union's Phare ACE Programme 1996. It is an in-depth study of the economic well-being of the elderly in five European countries: Hungary, Poland, Slovenia, Austria and the United Kingdom, with national experts assuming responsibility for the country studies. These studies were all performed under a common methodology which made possible not only cross-country comparisons, but also comparisons in time – since the analyses for individual countries cover at least two years: one in the mid-1980s and one (or two) in the mid-1990s.

Many people were involved in the work on the research project and in the preparation of the book through administrative, technical and computing assistance. The authors would particularly like to thank Rita Hegedüs, Günther Nemeth, Jolanta Perek-Bialas, Marek Pęczkowski, Valentina Prevolnik Rupel, Marek Styczeń, Willem Stamatiou, Eva Thalhammer and István György Tóth. Michael Förster, Róbert Iván Gál and Winfried Schmähl provided valuable comments and suggestions on earlier drafts of the country papers, submitted at the Budapest workshop in 1998.

It is gratifying to reach the final goal, after a long, and at times difficult, journey. During this journey, a fine cooperative relationship developed among the researchers, which ultimately resulted in the joint authorship of the summary chapter. Finally, we can only hope that this book will be a welcome addition to the quite expansive research literature on the subject.

Tine Stanovnik / Nada Stropnik /
Christopher Prinz   Ljubljana – Vienna, March 2000

Introduction and Comparative Summary

Tine Stanovnik, Carl Emmerson, Christopher Prinz,
Zsolt Spéder, Nada Stropnik and Adam Szulc

1.1 Introduction

The reform of social security systems, in particular of public pension systems, will remain the focus of political debate for some years to come. The reasons for the high visibility of this issue are well-known: social security systems are increasingly having difficulties in financing current obligations and entitlements, not to speak of the subject of sustainability, i.e. their ability to honour obligations and entitlements in the long term. It seems as if these systems have been unable to adequately adapt to the enormous demographic, social and economic changes, which have occurred in the past decades. Two important factors eroding the foundation of many pension systems in industrialized countries are: (a) demographic trends, evident in increasing life expectancy and decreasing fertility rates, both of which result in population ageing; and (b) diminishing labour force participation rates among the older age groups.

As social security systems are effectively pay-as-you-go systems, current pensions and other social security entitlements are financed by the current revenues (contributions), which means that a diminishing number of active earners contributing to the system are paying for the social security benefits of an increasing number of pensioners and other recipients.

In all the countries of our study, Hungary, Poland, Austria, U.K. and Slovenia, financial difficulties, as well as the unsustainability of existing pension systems induced pension reforms in recent years. The scope and depth of these reforms varies widely among them: Hungary and Poland have opted for more radical variants by introducing mandatory saving schemes (i.e. a new second pillar). Slovenia, and to a lesser degree Austria, have introduced important changes in their public pension system (first pillar), whereas the reform in the U.K. has endeavoured to diminish the role of public pension provision. The effects of these reforms will be felt only very gradually, although it is worth mentioning that the political economy of pension reforms in the Central European transition countries is already the subject of lively debate (Augusztinovics, 1997; Müller, 1999; Nelson, 1999).

Our research was not concerned with pension systems as such, but rather with one of the outcomes of the system, i.e. the economic well-being of the elderly. True, the well-being of the elderly does not depend exclusively on the functioning of the pension system, and the elderly often have other sources of income besides pensions. The 'outcomes' could also be analysed in a more general manner by defining certain criteria and then evaluating pension systems according to these criteria. The criteria are (Milanovic, 1998; Deleeck et al., 1992):

- efficiency: measures how much of pension outlays is for poverty alleviation and how much goes to income enhancement, meaning raising the level of income above the poverty level;
- effectiveness: concerned only with the poorest segment of the population and measures the number of poor who escape poverty due to the social transfers received, in our case pensions.

One could very well add a third criterion, that is

- equity, which could be broken down into two separate criteria. The first is horizontal equity, meaning equal pension benefits for persons with an equal stream of contributions; the second is vertical equity, meaning different pension benefits for persons with different streams of contributions; this actually provides the rationale for greater income redistribution among the elderly.

All of these criteria are in fact quite complex; in discussing equity we would have to explore not only intragenerational equity, but also intergenerational equity. Intergenerational equity is methodically explored under the concept of "generational accounting".[1] This is particularly relevant in assessing the sustainability of pension systems and their long-term impact on fiscal deficits; older generations can shift their burden to younger generations, i.e. they do not 'pay their way'.

With regard to efficiency, pension systems in continental Europe were not designed to achieve the efficiency thus defined. They were conceived as social insurance systems and were (and still are) more concerned with income security and income maintenance in old age than with targeting and alleviating poverty. Thus, this 'narrow' concept of efficiency is somewhat alien to the continental European systems. Taking into account a broader view of efficiency, in which not only the efficiency of the pension system itself is evaluated, one might also ask the question of how social security systems influence the efficiency of other markets, in particular the labour market. In this case, strong empirical evidence (Gruber and Wise, 1998) suggests that the design of social security systems in many industrialized countries encourages the early exit from the labour force. In other words, it has a negative impact on the efficiency of labour markets. Ironically, social insurance systems were originally introduced with the intention to increase the efficiency of labour markets.[2]

Our research side-steps the broader issues of evaluating the performance of pension systems according to the above described criteria. Its aim seems to be more modest and is to provide an in-depth analysis of the economic well-being of the elderly. The research comprises five European countries, with the following experts assuming responsibility for the individual country studies: Zsolt Spéder (Hungary), Adam Szulc (Poland), Tine Stanovnik and Nada Stropnik (Slovenia), Christopher Prinz (Austria), and Carl Emmerson, Paul Johnson and Gary Stears (United Kingdom).

Obviously, our research has no claim to originality, and there is a now rich body of literature devoted to the comparative analysis of well-being. Understandably, these analyses vary according to the number of countries selected and the regional emphasis, the data sets and samples used, the time periods chosen, the attention given to particular population subgroups, as well as the aspects of well-being analysed. Smeeding et al. (1990) presented the first broad comparative research on income and income distribution in seven countries using the LIS data set. This has been followed by more specific uses of this data set, such as Mitchell (1991) who used the LIS data set to analyse the effects of income transfers in industrial countries, and Whiteford and Kennedy (1995) who analysed income and living standards of the elderly in industrial countries during the 1980s. Deleeck et al. (1992) used panel data for several countries to analyse the distribution and ad-

11

equacy of social transfers. Eastern Europe has also been a research target: Atkinson and Micklewright (1992) analysed income and income distribution in Eastern Europe in the pre-transition years; Milanovic (1998) extended this analysis to the transition years.

Our research differs from the aforementioned research in one important aspect, namely that the country data are analysed by country experts. This assures a more differentiated interpretation of the results, by providing a richer and more profound analysis of certain national phenomena. Of course, many of the conclusions we reached are quite in line with the conclusions of the aforementioned research.

The structure of the country studies is similar, though by no means uniform; a binding, fixed layout would have imposed unnecessary restrictions and impeded the presentation of certain country-specific features. On the other hand, a common methodological framework was the *conditio sine qua non* for meaningful cross-country comparisons. The research was thus based on a set of agreed-on definitions, methodology and core analyses to assure 'communality in diversity'.

Without attempting to duplicate the results and rich analytical background of each country's case-study, the introductory chapter presents a comparative analysis demonstrating important common features and the major differences among the countries under review. The structure of this comparative summary is as follows. In section 1.2, a brief overview of some macroeconomic and demographic trends, as well as of other developments that have an impact on the national pension systems is presented. Section 1.3 provides a short description of pension system reforms that are being implemented in the countries studied. Section 1.4 describes some basic definitions used throughout the country case-studies, provides an assessment of the data sets and discusses relevant methodological issues. Section 1.5 presents some comparisons of income trends and household income composition, whereas section 1.6 provides a broad overview of pensioners and their position within the society. In particular, the income position of various types of pensioner households is assessed, and the gender and age dimensions are explored. Section 1.7 is devoted to comparisons of inequality and poverty measures, while section 1.8 concludes the introductory chapter.

1.2 Demographic Trends, the Labour Market and Pension Expenditures

1.2.1 Demographic Trends

All of the analysed countries experienced a large increase in life expectancy during the past 10 to 15 years. During the same period, the total fertility rate (number of live births per woman) has been decreasing. These two trends predictably reinforced each other and have resulted in accelerated ageing, thus further reshaping what used to be the population pyramid. The relative impact of these two factors varies from country to country: for example, in Hungary it was the decline in the fertility rate that played a greater role in population ageing rather than the increase in life expectancy. The most recent values of two demographic indicators, life expectancy and the share of the population under age 15, are presented in Table 1.1.

Table 1.1: Demographic Indicators

Country	Life expectancy at birth			Share of population aged 0-14 in total population	
	Year	Men	Women	Year	Share in %
Hungary	1995	65.3	74.5	1997	17.7
Poland	1996	68.1	76.6	1996	21.9
Slovenia	1995-1996	70.8	78.3	1997	17.0
Austria	1998	74.7	81.0	1995	17.5
U.K.	1993-1995	73.9	79.2	1995	19.4

Source: Country case-studies.

1.2.2 The Labour Market, GDP and Pension Expenditures

Demographic trends are secular, and exert their influence on pension systems gradually. Another secular trend, which had a strong structural component, particularly among the transition countries, is the decreasing labour force participation, mostly among the older age groups. In developed countries the early exit from the labour force was caused by an increase in indi-

Tine Stanovnik / Carl Emmerson / Christopher Prinz /
Zsolt Spéder / Nada Stropnik / Adam Szulc

vidually accrued benefits from both public and private pension schemes; in countries in transition they were caused by the 'transformation depression'. Rather than risk socially disruptive high unemployment rates, the state offered many employees the option to retire under fairly generous, early retirement schemes; the pension system was thus used to solve the problems of the labour market. In some countries disability criteria were also relaxed and the number of disability pensioners increased considerably; this occurred in Slovenia, Hungary and Poland, but also in non-transition countries such as in Austria. While the pension system was solving labour market problems at the upper end of the age distribution, i.e. among the active population in the older age groups (50 years and above), for younger age cohorts and for younger potential entrants into the labour market there was no 'systemic' solution. Thus, the number of unemployed in the three countries in transition increased dramatically, particularly among the young and particularly in the first years of transition (Table 1.2).

Table 1.2: Unemployment; 1988, 1992 and 1996

Country	Number of unemployed (in 000)		
	1988	1992	1996
Hungary	28	556	485
Poland	10	1670	2507
Slovenia	21	103	120
Austria	159	193	231
U.K.	2341	2678	2292

Note: The figures for the U.K. refer to unemployed according to the ILO definition; for other countries, the data refer to registered unemployed.

Source: Milanovic (1998) (for Hungary and Poland); Annual reports of the Employment Office of Slovenia; OECD, Quarterly Labour Force Statistics, various years (for Austria and the U.K.).

The large increase in pensioners and unemployed in the three countries in transition has to be viewed against the backdrop of the initial sharp decrease in GDP, with GDP surpassing the pre-transition levels in Slovenia and Poland only in the mid 1990s, as shown in Table 1.3.

Table 1.3: Changes in Real GDP

Country	Change in real GDP	
	1992	1996
Hungary (1987 = 100)	82	86
Poland (1987 = 100)	86	105
Slovenia (1990 = 100)	86	101
Austria (1987 = 100)	121	129
U.K. (1987 = 100)	101	114

Source: Milanovic (1988) (for Hungary and Poland); Statistical Yearbook, Statistical Office of Slovenia, 1997 and 1999; Österreichs Volkseinkommen 1997, Statistik Österreich; Office for National Statistics, London.

In the five countries, pensioners represent between 19 and 26% of the total population, as shown in Table 1.4.

Table 1.4: Share of Pensioners in Total Population

Country	Hungary (1996)	Poland (1996)	Slovenia (1993)	Austria (1995)	U.K. (1995)
Pensioners as % of all persons	25.6	19.2	19.9	21.2	24.9

Note: According to the definition of pensioners in Section 1.4.1.
Source: Country case-studies; data refer to the most recent year.

The continuous increase in the number of pensioners and the related heavy shifts in labour force participation rates produced quite predictable consequences on the values of pension system parameters. Thus, the ratio between active contributors and pensioners decreased, particularly in transition countries. In Slovenia in 1989, the year prior to transition, this ratio was 2.75, while in 1997 it was 1.73; in Poland, it was 2.69 in 1989 and dropped to 1.72 in 1996; in Hungary it was 2.09 in 1993 and 1.84 in 1996. Of course, the change was more gradual in Austria, where this ratio decreased from 1.92 in 1980 to 1.62 in 1996, whereas in the U.K. it has remained stable. In countries where the replacement rate (i.e. ratio between average pension and average wage) has

15

not changed much, the contribution rates and/or government transfers to social insurance funds increased. The latter was evident in Slovenia and Poland, where government transfers to the social security pension fund currently represent some 25% of the funds' total revenue.

As shown in Table 1.5, pension outlays, expressed in percentage of GDP, increased in most of the countries under review.

Table 1.5: Contributors to Pensioners Ratio and Pension Expenditure as a Percentage of GDP

Country	Contributors/pensioners ratio			Pension expenditure as % of GDP		
	Year	Ratio	Changes in the 1990s	Year	%	Changes in the 1990s
Hungary	1996	1.84	decrease	1996	8.9	small decrease
Poland	1996	1.72	large decrease	1996	15.2	increase
Slovenia	1997	1.73	large decrease	1996	14.5	large increase
Austria	1996	1.62	decrease	1995	14.3	increase
U.K.	1988	1.80	no change	1996/97	4.2	no change

Source: Country case-studies.

Using pension expenditure measured as a percentage of GDP as our criterion, we could classify three countries in the same group: Slovenia, Poland and Austria are 'high' spenders, with their pension outlays amounting to 14-15% of GDP. Hungary is an 'average' spender, with pension outlays amounting to about 9% of GDP, while the United Kingdom is a 'low' spender, with pension expenditure amounting to some 4% of GDP. Of course, such high or low shares do not directly translate into high or low levels of economic well-being for the elderly. In spite of high spending on pensions, there are many elderly persons who might not be eligible for pension benefits and therefore, only have a low level of income. Moreover, in spite of low spending on pensions, many elderly might have other income sources besides pensions, and thus they might not experience poverty. The income position of the elderly will be explored in section 1.6.

1.3 A Brief Description of Pension System Reforms in the 1990s

All of the three transition countries (Poland, Hungary and Slovenia) had certain 'soviet' elements in their social security systems, such as an early legal retirement age, privileged retirement schemes for a vast array of occupations, a strong solidarity in disability insurance, etc. Nevertheless, the welfare systems in these countries may be described as corporatist Bismarckian systems. This observation is based on the fact that they do not have a national ('universal') minimum pension; also, in order to be eligible for pension benefits a minimum number of contribution years is required: 15 years in Slovenia, 20 years for women and 25 for men in Poland, and (currently) 10 years in Hungary.

Changes and reforms of the pension systems are described in greater detail in each of the country case-studies. In the past few years, Poland and Hungary have paved the way for the introduction of the second pillar, i.e. a nation-wide mandatory pension saving scheme. The 1999 Slovenian Pension Act enacted a thorough reform of the first pension pillar (public pay-as-you-go system). The Austrian pension system has undergone a number of changes in the 1990s, particularly in 1993 and in 1997, though it still contains strong characteristics of a Bismarckian corporatist system. The United Kingdom is in many respects a European outlier, since pension benefits from the public pension system are modest by continental standards.

Slovenia
In Slovenia, a new Pension Act was passed in 1999. Among its more important features are: a gradual increase in the contribution period used for calculating one's pension (from best 10 years to best 18 years) and an increase in the legal retirement age for women from 53 to 58. The full insurance period will be 40 years for men and 38 years for women. Also, accrual rates have been reduced, while the incentives for later retirement and disincentives for early retirement are much stronger. A mandatory second pension pillar is planned to be introduced, though it will be mandatory only for certain occupations. Indexation (on growth of net wage) has been retained, though the pension adjustments will be less frequent.

Poland and Hungary

Both Poland (starting in 1995) and Hungary (in 1997) introduced extensive pension reforms aimed at providing the institutional framework for a three-pillar system, where the second pillar is to be a mandatory funded system, based on individual contributions. Hungary also introduced a series of measures for reducing pension costs: in 1991 the rise in pensions was linked to the rise in net wages, in 1997 the retirement age was increased to 62 (for both men and women) and the required contribution period increased from 10 to 20 years.

Austria

Austria has also introduced some measures for stabilizing the growth of pension outlays during the 1990s. Schemes for different occupational groups (mainly for civil servants) are to be gradually harmonized. As regards particular measures, the period relevant for the calculation of pension benefits has been extended from the best 5 to the best 15/18 years, the benefit indexation rate has changed from gross wage growth to growth of gross wages net of contributions. Austria has also tightened conditions for early retirement. Due to the generosity of the pension from the first pillar, the second pillar, i.e. occupational pension schemes, is still not very developed.

United Kingdom

State pension provision in the United Kingdom is comprised of two parts: a basic state retirement pension and a state earnings-related pension scheme (SERPS). The basic state retirement pension is price-indexed and is not universal, but is conditional on having sufficient insurance contributions. Contribution years for men and women were equalized, and are now 44 years. Insured persons (employees) can opt out of the second part (SERPS) and transfer their accumulated sums to private pension funds; many of them have actually done so in the past. The long-term sustainability of the public pension system is not in doubt, judging from the low replacement ratio and the low pension expenditure/GDP ratio presented in Table 1.5. Nevertheless, the low level of benefits and further reductions in benefits (because of price indexation) will simply mean that retirees without private sources of income will be substantially poorer. Currently, one fifth of those over retirement age are eligible for means-tested benefits, and this share might increase even further.

1.4 Definitions, Data and Methodological Issues

1.4.1 Definitions

In assessing economic well-being, the *disposable household income* is used as the measure of resources. This definition of income includes earnings, self-employment income, property income, pensions, other social transfers and private transfers (gifts, inter-family transfers, remittances from abroad, etc.). It does not include benefits in kind, such as a household's own consumption of agricultural produce or imputed rent. Also, it does not include savings withdrawals or loans received. It is after taxes, meaning that direct taxes and social security contributions are subtracted. By opting for this measure of resources, we circumvent the discussion of other possible measures of economic well-being, such as expenditures or consumption. Data on consumer expenditure are missing in the Austrian database, so this welfare measure could not be taken into account. Though tenure status, housing quality and ownership of consumer durable goods are analysed, household wealth and assets are not explicitly taken into account.

19

The term *pension* includes old-age, disability and survivor pension; not all survey data permitted a disaggregated approach with regard to pensions, i.e. it did not allow for a separation of the three pension types.

The term *pensioner* is used to denote a person, aged 50 or over, who has declared himself or herself a pensioner. The status is thus based on self-declaration. We abstain from the use of the term *retired person*, since this denotes a complete withdrawal from the active population, and this is somewhat more difficult to ascertain. A pensioner may basically receive a pension, while participating at the same time in some way or other in the labour market, either as a temporary worker or part-time worker, etc.

Pensioners live in various household types. In order to evaluate the pension system in terms of its ability to maintain income for the elderly population, it is necessary to devote particular attention to one type of household, i.e. *pensioner households.* These are households with at least one pensioner and none of the other household members being employed, self-employed or unemployed. A pensioner household can therefore have the following composition: a single pensioner, a pensioner couple, or a pensioner living with other pensioner(s) and/or non-pensioner(s) who is (are) *not* active earner(s). We note that this definition of pensioner household is not the one commonly used; for example the OECD (1998) defines pensioner households as households whose head of household is older than 42 years and main income is from pension.

A *non-pensioner household* is a household that is not a pensioner household. Obviously, this type of household can include pensioners. Households containing a pensioner and an active earner fall into this category.

1.4.2 The Data

The idea was to present at least one pre-transition year and one transition year for post-communist countries, and to select similar years for non-transition countries as well. As regards the transition countries, the Polish Household Budget Survey seems to be relatively highly developed.[3] The longstanding household survey covers a large number of households and is carried out on an annual basis. There was some difficulty with the Hungarian data. The Household Income Survey constituting the database for the 1980s was replaced in the 1990s by the Household Panel, which seems to be of good quality. However, it consists of a much smaller sample of households. As far as Slovenia is concerned, the database covering the Yugoslav period (precisely, 1983) was credible and comparable to the 1993 data, as all member republics of the Yugoslav federation carried out mostly independent surveys, but within a unified framework. It should be noted, however, that the 1988 data were found to be unreliable by the country experts (due to high inflation and the poor training of the interviewers) and it could therefore not be taken into account in this study.

In Austria, the household survey started only in 1994-95 (and was not accessible before 1998). To ensure that the 1985 statistics were comparable to the recent ones, Microcensus data were used for the purpose of this research. In spite of the large sample size, such income data, which are not collected through diary books, tend to be underestimated. Notwithstanding very high non-response rates in the Microcensus (note that answering the income questions is voluntary), the reasonable quality of the Microcensus data was confirmed by comparisons with other Austrian data sources (e.g. tax sheets). The British Family Expenditure Survey obviously represents the highest standard both in terms of data quality and stability.

It is not surprising that economic and political changes taking place in all post-communist countries also have had serious impacts on the official statistics. The specific reasons were different in each case, however, the final effect was apparently the same: none of the 1980s surveys remained unchanged. Furthermore, Hungarian panel studies show entirely different results in the 1990s than the previous household income surveys. However, it must be stated that a comparison by Atkinson and Micklewright (1992) shows the income data of the 1987 survey to be of high quality. Of course, comparisons between two conceptually different surveys can always be problematic due to differences in sampling design, data collection and sample size (though for panel studies, even a small sample allows a relatively precise estimation of changes during the investigated period). A similar problem, though probably to a lesser extent, affected the Polish data which cover 1987, 1993 and 1996. In 1992, the Statistical Office switched household rotation from quarterly to monthly and waived random control of income declarations. As a result, 1993 and 1996 incomes seem to be underreported as compared to those of 1987. Ironically, the Slovenian data set appears to be the most stable among the transition countries; the extremely important political changes did not result in changes in official statistics, at least in terms of household surveys. In the comparative summary, we have used as our point of reference the pre-transition year 1983 for Slovenia, and 1987 for Poland and Hungary.

21

Different methods of data collection suggest that some reservations would be appropriate regarding cross-country comparisons of absolute measures, especially the poverty and inequality indices. Obviously, surveys based on monthly rotation should not be compared directly to those based on quarterly and annual rotation. Unfortunately, this is the case in our study. For example, in the Slovenian survey, households are observed throughout the whole year. At the other extreme, the British, Hungarian and Polish (the two 1990s surveys only) surveys provide monthly data. It is well known that inequality calculated from monthly data is higher than when using quarterly or annual data (Szulc, 1999).

Ideally, all the statistics should be calculated for the same years. However, this was not possible. For example, the Slovenian survey is carried out on a five-year basis. On the other hand, the Hungarian and the Polish surveys allowed a selection of two transition years, thus capturing quite profound changes. It would be possible to do this also with the Austrian and the British data, but there was no such need. Both economies are stable enough to assume a lack of significant changes during short periods of time.

Table 1.6 summarizes the country databases.

Table 1.6: Statistical Sources and Some Data Problems

Country	Survey	Years	Sample size (households)	Data problems
Hungary	Household Income Survey (1987 only), Hungarian Household Panel	1987	19,623	Change in the survey
		1992	2,059	
		1996	1,857	
Poland	Household Budget Survey	1987	26,434	Household rotation
		1993	32,108	changed from quarterly
		1996	31,907	to monthly in 1992
Slovenia	Household Expenditure Survey	1983	3,992	Low (5-year)
		1993	3,270	frequency
Austria	Microcensus	1985	29,000[1]	High non-response
		1995	29,000[1]	rate for income
U.K.	Family Expenditure Survey	1989	7,000[1]	
		1995	7,000[1]	-

Note: [1] Approximate values.

Source: Country case-studies.

1.4.3 Equivalence Scales

Irrespective of the type of individual welfare measure applied, equivalence scales had to be defined to allow comparisons across households of different size and composition. In general, the scales may be normative or empirical. The first type is based on the judgements of experts who decide by what proportion, e.g. a two-person household, should increase its expenditures in comparison to those of a one-person household to attain the same standard of living. As regards normative scales, this question is usually answered for each commodity group separately. The empirical scales are based on econometric models of consumption or subjective income questions. All methods mentioned caused numerous methodological difficulties, albeit each of a different type.

We opted for a normative scale, which is the most popular 70/50 formula conceived by OECD experts and named by researchers as the "standard OECD scale" (OECD, 1982). The first adult in the household is assigned the value 1, all other adults 0.7 and each child (below 16 years of age) is assigned the value 0.5. The sum of values for household members produces the number of equivalent adults. Thus, for two adults it amounts to 1.7, for two adults and two children 2.7, etc. Our choice is founded mainly on practical criteria. Scales of this type are very easy to calculate and have been utilized in numerous studies covering both developed and less developed countries. They are sometimes criticized for overestimating the elasticity of the costs of living with respect to the number of persons in a household. The consequence of a steep scale, which infers relatively less economies of scale for larger households, is a lower equivalent household income for persons in larger households and hence a relatively lower income for children in general as compared to persons in one-person households (see, for instance, Förster, 1994). It seems that parameters 0.7 and 0.5 of a standard OECD scale are not adequate for prevailing consumer patterns in most developed countries. For example, Atkinson et al. (1995) employed much flatter scales when calculating inequality measures for the European Union countries and the USA. In their study, the equivalence scale is defined as the square root of the number of persons in the household. Thus, the scale for two adults with two children is 2.[4]

Nonetheless, for countries like Poland or Hungary, a 70/50 scale does not seem to be too steep. Szulc (1995) calculated econometric equivalence scales for Poland and obtained results close, on average, to the standard OECD scale. Similarly, Hancock and Pudney (1997) found it acceptable for Hungary. On the other hand, the standard OECD scale obviously underestimates economies of scale for Austria and the U.K., and probably also for Slovenia (whose GDP per capita is almost double that of Poland). It was decided, however, to keep the scale the same in all countries, to avoid the possible effects of methodological differences. This approach seems acceptable, as the focus is mainly on trends within countries rather than on comparisons of absolute measures between countries.

An individual is the primary object of concern in welfare analysis. By contrast, the unit of analysis in the household expenditure (budget) surveys, is the household. For the purpose of this study it is assumed that all individuals in the household share their incomes equally. Consequently, an individual's income is obtained by dividing the household income by the appropriate number of equivalent adults, as resulting from the equivalence scale applied.

1.4.4 Poverty Lines

Selecting a poverty line is a central point in any study on poverty. There is no agreement among economists whether it should be absolute or relative. In the former case, poverty is conceived as the non-ability to purchase a given bundle of goods which should be fixed over a certain time period. In accordance with the other view, poverty lines should adapt to changes in standards of living (not necessarily at the same pace). If the relative poverty line concept is used, the poor are those in the bottom income percentiles.

We decided to employ a relative concept of poverty for both practical and theoretical reasons. Setting an absolute poverty line is debatable even for a single country. For five different countries it would be almost impossible to agree upon a common poverty line, even if exact purchasing power parities were available. For example, a poverty line appropriate for Poland would be completely unsuitable for Austria or the U.K., and vice versa.

In most studies, the relative poverty line is related to the median rather than to the mean equivalent income. This is because the first parameter is more immune to the under- or overestimation of incomes, which is the most significant at the low and top extremes. It is also difficult to decide what proportion of median equivalent household income should constitute the 'correct' poverty threshold. To circumvent this problem, four proportions, from very low (40%) to very high (70%), are employed.

1.4.5 Income Inequality Measures

Three income inequality measures are employed in our analysis: the Gini coefficient and two percentile ratios (90/10 and 75/25). The first compares the income of the person (or household) 10% from the top of the income distribution to the income of the person (or household) 10% from the bottom; it is sometimes also referred to as the 'decile ratio'. The second ratio is sometimes referred to as the 'quartile ratio'. These three measures jointly provide the information necessary for a more qualified description of income inequality. The Gini coefficient is an aggregate measure and we use all incomes for its computation; the 90/10-percentile ratio measures the extremes of the income distribution whereas the 75/25-percentile ratio measures incomes more toward the 'middle' of the income distribution.

1.5 Household Income and Income Structure

Table 1.7a shows the structure of income sources in the mid-1990s in four of the five countries. Earnings are still the prevalent income source for all households, though their share in total household income has decreased considerably over the 10-year period, as shown in Table 1.7b. Pensions represent the second most important income source in all four countries, and their share in household income has increased, particularly in Slovenia and Hungary. Not surprisingly, the share of other social benefits has also increased during this 10-year period.

Obviously, the changes are more pronounced in the three transition countries, and this is doubtlessly due to the large increase in the number of pensioners and unemployed persons, and a decrease in the number of employees. The large changes in the socio-economic structure of households thus had a predictable impact on the structure of household income.

Table 1.7a: **Structure of Household Income Sources (percentage of disposable household income)**

Income sources	Hungary (1996)		Poland (1996)		Slovenia (1993)		U.K. (1995)	
	All households	Pensioner households	All households	Pensioner households	All households	Pensioner households	All households	Pensioner households
Earnings	50.2	6.7	45.8	0.0	60.3	4.9	58.9	3.4
Pensions[1]	24.1	80.8	29.6	82.0	20.7	86.4	14.7	59.5
Other social benefits	10.7	2.6	7.7	3.2	4.1	2.5	12.5	20.8
Other[2]	15.0	9.9	16.8	14.8	15.0	6.2	13.8	16.2

Notes: [1] Pensions include occupational pensions (relevant for the U.K.).

[2] 'Other' includes self-employment income, income from capital, gifts and interfamily transfers.

Source: Country case-studies.

Tine Stanovnik / Carl Emmerson / Christopher Prinz /
Zsolt Spéder / Nada Stropnik / Adam Szulc

Table 1.7b: **Changes in the Share of Income Sources (in percentage points)**

Income sources	Hungary (1987-96)		Poland (1987-96)		Slovenia (1983-93)		U.K. (1989-95)	
	All households	Pensioner households	All households	Pensioner households	All households	Pensioner households	All households	Pensioner households
Earnings	-12.5	-2.3	-15.2	-8.9	-12.7	-3.8	-3.2	1.2
Pensions	8.7	11.4	-0.5	0.3	6.1	7.2	1.7	-3.8
Other social benefits	3.1	1.1	0.0	-3.7	1.8	-1.2	3.4	5.3
Other	0.7	-10.2	15.6	12.4	4.9	-2.3	-2.0	-2.7

Source: Country case-studies.

Obviously, for pensioner households pensions are the prevalent source of income. The relatively low share of pensions in the household income of pensioner households in the U.K., as compared to other countries, is due to the fact that many of these households are beneficiaries of means-tested benefits. Social benefits in the U.K. are quite an important source of income considering their share was 20.8% of pensioner household income in 1995. The U.K. also stands out in another respect: income from capital represents an important income source for pensioner households. As for Slovenia, Hungary and Poland, a certain 'homogenization' has been taking place among pensioner households, since the share of earnings has decreased. This is a consequence of a tightening of the labour market and diminishing opportunities for pensioners to earn income.

Table 1.8: Trends in Real Income (index; base year = 100)

Country	Period	Real equivalent income of all households	Real equivalent income of pensioner households
Hungary	1992-1996	100	113
Poland	1987-1996	101	104
Slovenia	1983-1993	86	100
Austria	1985-1995	130	133
U.K.	1989-1995	107	122

Source: Country case-studies.

What were the changes in real income? Although the time period in which the comparisons are performed differs among countries, it still does seem that the real equivalent income of pensioner households has increased more than the real equivalent income of all households; this is particularly pronounced for Hungary and the U.K. (Table 1.8). In Slovenia, the real equivalent income of pensioner households in Slovenia remained unchanged, whereas the real equivalent income of all households decreased considerably.[5]

1.6 Elderly and their Position in Society

1.6.1 Households in which Pensioners Live

Most pensioners live in one-person and two-person households. This is shown in Table 1.9.

Table 1.9: Population Living in One-person and Two-person Households

Country	Hungary (1996)	Poland (1996)	Slovenia (1993)	Austria (1995)	U.K. (1995)
All persons (%)	26.0	19.8	20.0	45.0	39.2
Pensioners (%)	66.8	60.7	59.4	92.3	77.7

Source: Country case-studies.

In evaluating the income position of pensioners, it seems logical to take into account the various types of households in which pensioners live. In such an analysis, one household type is of particular interest: pensioner households, defined as households with at least one pensioner and with no other active household members (employed, self-employed or unemployed). This type of household is pertinent because our aim is to see how well the pension system maintains income and alleviates poverty among the elderly. Therefore, the analysis of pensioner households and their subtypes – such as single female pensioner household, single male pensioner household, couple pensioner household and other pensioner household – are relevant. Of course, pensioners live in other types of households as well (such as households with a pensioner and an active earner, for instance), and one also might wish to further subdivide the non-pensioner households.[6]

Table 1.10 shows the share of pensioner households as a percentage of all households in each of the five countries; in Poland 23% of all households are pensioner households, whereas in Hungary this share is as high as 35.7%. The table also presents the shares of each of the four types of pensioner households. Single female pensioner households and couple pensioner households are obviously the two pensioner household types that have by far the largest shares.

Table 1.10:   Share of Pensioner Households in All Households

Country	% of pensioner households in all households				
	Single male	Single female	Couple	Other	All pensioner households
Hungary (1996)	3.1	12.7	13.7	6.2	35.7
Poland (1996)	1.5	8.1	8.6	4.7	23.0
Slovenia (1993)	2.1	9.9	9.4	4.8	26.2
Austria (1995)	2.9	13.9	12.0	1.6	30.4
U.K. (1995)	4.3	11.4	12.9	2.7	31.3

Source: Country case-studies.

Table 1.11:   Share of Pensioners, Pensioners Living in Pensioner Households and Persons Aged 60 and Over in the Total Population (percentage)

Country	% of all persons		
	Pensioners	Pensioners in pensioner households	Persons aged 60 and over
Hungary (1996)	25.6	18.3	19.6
Poland (1996)	19.2	10.2	15.1
Slovenia (1993)	19.9	11.8	17.7
Austria (1995)	21.2	15.9	21.0
U.K. (1995)	24.9	19.9	21.4

Source: Country case-studies.

Most pensioners live in pensioner households. As illustrated in Table 1.11, in 1995 pensioners represented 24.9% of the U.K. population, whereas the corresponding percentage for pensioners living in pensioner households was 19.9%; in other words, 4 out of 5 pensioners lived in pensioner households.

1.6.2 The Income Position of Pensioners and Pensioner Households

The income position of all pensioners, regardless of the type of household they live in, is analysed below. Tables 1.12a and 1.12b show the share of pensioners situated at the lower and upper end of the income distribution, at the two points in time (the mid-1980s and mid-1990s). The lower end is taken to be the bottom three income deciles, and the upper end as the top three income deciles (the reasons for this choice are given on the next page).

Table 1.12a: Share of Pensioners in Bottom Three Income Deciles   29

Country	Share of pensioners (%)		Difference
	mid-1980s	mid-1990s	(in percentage points)
Hungary (1987-1996)	40.7	20.7	-20.0
Poland (1987-1996)	28.6	16.6	-12.0
Slovenia (1983-1993)	38.7	31.4	-7.3
Austria (1985-1995)	27.3	25.4	-1.9
U.K. (1989-1995)	61.7	53.9	-7.8

Note: Persons are included with their equivalized household income. In the U.K., only heads of households are considered with their equivalized benefit unit income.

Source: Country case-studies.

Obviously, pensioners have improved their relative income positions in all of the five countries studied, though the extent varies greatly. Hungary experienced the greatest improvement since in 1987, 40.7% of all pensioners were situated in the bottom three deciles, and in 1996, their share dropped to 20.7%. The improvements were modest in the case of Austria and also, relatively speaking, in the U.K., where in 1995 a share of 53.9% of all pensioners were still situated in the bottom three deciles.

Tine Stanovnik / Carl Emmerson / Christopher Prinz /
Zsolt Spéder / Nada Stropnik / Adam Szulc

Table 1.12b: Share of Pensioners in Top Three Income Deciles

Country	Share of pensioners (%)		Difference
	mid-1980s	mid-1990s	(in percentage points)
Hungary (1987-1996)	20.9	23.8	+2.9
Poland (1987-1996)	27.6	36.7	+9.1
Slovenia (1983-1993)	23.7	26.9	+3.2
Austria (1985-1995)	27.7	30.7	+3.0
U.K. (1989-1995)	9.6	11.7	+2.1

Note: Persons are included with their equivalent household income. In the U.K., only heads of
            households are considered with their equivalent benefit unit income.

Source: Country case-studies.

In accordance with expectations, the gains at the upper end of the distribution were not as great as the improvements at the lower end of the distribution. Poland is the only exception, since in 1987 27.6% of all pensioners were situated in the top three income deciles, and in 1996 their share increased by some 9.1 percentage points to 36.7%. The gains in other countries were modest and amounted to some 2 to 3 percentage points.

Overall, it appears that pensioners have improved their relative income position. Could this also be said for the income position of pensioner households? Table 1.13a presents the share of various pensioner household types in the bottom three income deciles; here we rank households according to their equivalent household income, whereas in Tables 1.12a and 1.12b, we ranked individuals according to their equivalent household income. The use of the first (bottom) three deciles as the lower end of the income distribution is justified on the following grounds. Due to various social benefits, such as means-tested supplements in Austria, means-tested benefits in the U.K., means-tested supplements in Slovenia, many pensioner households are not placed within the bottom decile and are more concentrated in the second and third deciles. Thus, using only the first decile might not be appropriate in describing their income position.

The share of all types of pensioner households in the bottom three deciles has decreased in all countries except Austria, where during the time period studied, this share increased for two types of pensioner households (single male and single female). The decreases in shares were in most cases substantial, thus in Slovenia in 1983, 46.6% of all couple pensioner house-holds were situated in the bottom three income deciles, whereas the corre-sponding figure for 1993 is 28.0%; even sharper decreases occurred in Hun-gary and Poland. Table 1.13a shows certain regularities in the ranking of various types of pensioner households according to their share in the bot-tom income deciles at both points in time. If ranking is in descending order, i.e. from worst to best, the couple pensioner household ranks fourth (i.e. best), in Slovenia, Poland and the U.K., and third in Hungary. The category of other pensioner households ranks first (i.e. worst) in four countries: Slovenia, Hungary, Poland and the U.K.; these households are non-couple households with at least one pensioner and dependent. Needless to say, their number is in most countries quite small, as shown by Table 1.10. In Slovenia, Hungary, Poland and the U.K. single female pensioner households rank second among pensioner households, only in Austria these households ranked first (i.e. worst).

Table 1.13a: **Share of Pensioner Households in the Bottom Three Income Deciles, by Pensioner Household Type**

Country	Pensioner household type				
	Single male	Single female	Couple	Other	All pensioner households
	1980s				
Hungary (1987)	50.2	69.7	45.7	61.0	57.8
Poland (1987)	30.8	50.5	22.9	45.5	41.8
Slovenia (1983)	(50.8)	55.5	46.6	61.7	52.8
Austria (1985)	17.0	41.5	37.8	38.9	37.8
U.K. (1989)	53.6	60.5	48.2	52.3	53.8
	1990s				
Hungary (1996)	(10.9)	45.9	14.4	60.0	33.3
Poland (1996)	20.0	24.8	8.7	42.6	22.0
Slovenia (1993)	(36.2)	42.8	28.0	54.2	39.0
Austria (1995)	20.3	45.0	35.8	32.3	38.4
U.K. (1995)	40.9	43.0	38.9	47.4	41.4

Note: Brackets denote small sample size.

Source: Country case-studies.

A more complete assessment of the changing income position of pensioner households can be obtained by looking at Table 1.13b, which shows their share in the top income deciles as well.

Table 1.13b: **Share of Pensioner Households in the Top Three Income Deciles, by Pensioner Household Type**

Country	Pensioner household type				
	Single male	Single female	Couple	Other	All pensioner households
			1980s		
Hungary (1987)	15.9	6.2	14.4	7.4	10.5
Poland (1987)	21.7	11.3	20.8	17.6	16.3
Slovenia (1983)	(17.5)	10.4	19.0	9.3	14.0
Austria (1985)	40.0	15.9	18.7	14.8	19.0
U.K. (1989)	8.2	7.6	12.9	12.3	10.2
			1990s		
Hungary (1996)	(28.3)	6.7	22.3	9.5	15.1
Poland (1996)	34.8	22.1	38.5	14.7	27.5
Slovenia (1993)	(25.7)	16.1	26.4	15.2	20.4
Austria (1995)	37.6	15.3	21.2	25.3	20.2
U.K. (1995)	16.5	9.2	17.8	11.5	13.9

Source: Country case-studies.

Table 1.13c: **Differences over Time in the Share of Pensioner Households (a) in the Bottom Three Deciles, (b) in the Top Three Deciles; in percentage points, by country**

Country	Bottom three deciles	Top three deciles
Hungary (1987-1996)	-24.5	4.6
Poland (1987-1996)	-19.8	11.2
Slovenia (1983-1993)	-18.8	6.4
Austria (1985-1995)	0.6	1.2
U.K. (1989-1995)	-12.4	3.7

Table 1.13c summarizes the results from Tables 1.13a and 1.13b, by computing for each country the differences in the share of pensioner households in the bottom three and top three deciles, respectively, between two points in time.

Notwithstanding the fact that we are dealing with different time periods, the relative income position of pensioner households improved markedly in most countries under review. Thus, the share of pensioner households situated in the bottom three deciles decreased in Hungary by 24.5 percentage points between 1987 and 1996 and similar large improvements occurred in Poland and Slovenia. A somewhat smaller improvement occurred in the U.K., whereas there was virtually no change in Austria. While one can see the 'aggregate' improvement in the income position of pensioner households in Table 1.8,[7] the decile analysis based on a more detailed subdivision of pensioner households shows the extent of this improvement. What were the causes for this improved relative income position of pensioner households? In Hungary, Poland and Slovenia, the most important causes were large shifts in the labour market coupled with indexation rules. With a sharp drop in employment and an increasing number of persons receiving unemployment and other social benefits, the income position of non-pensioner households deteriorated, since there were less earners per household. On the other hand, since pension indexation was based on the growth of the average net wage, the income position of pensioner households improved, virtually by default, in comparison to non-pensioner households. In these three countries there were also some country specific factors at work. In Hungary, the decrease in the real value of social benefits (such as unemployment benefits, family benefits, etc.) further deteriorated the income position of non-pensioner households. In Slovenia, the increase in the proportion of women having pension entitlements additionally improved the income position of pensioner households. Pensioner households in the U.K. also improved their relative income position, though due to entirely different causes: the level of private pension income increased considerably, and social security benefits also experienced real increases.[8]

1.6.3 Age Groups and Income Position

Income follows certain life-cycle stages: it starts from low levels in the beginning of one's active life, increases until the fifties, and then starts decreasing in the sixties.[9] We are, of course, not as interested in the whole life-cycle, but mostly in its upper end, i.e. persons aged 60 and over. In order to ascertain the relative income position of the elderly, in Table 1.14a we present the proportion of persons in the bottom three deciles for three age groups, and in Table 1.14b the proportion of persons in the top three deciles for the same age groups.

Table 1.14a shows a near regularity of income positions decreasing with increasing age. We use the term near-regularity, because there are several deviations from this postulation. In 1987 in Poland, the share of persons aged 80 and above situated in the bottom three deciles was smaller than the share of persons in the age group 70-79 situated in the same deciles. When considering only the elderly population (aged 60 and above), the explanation for decreasing income with increasing age may be tautologically described by the fact that younger cohorts tend to be richer than older cohorts. This actually appears to be a general phenomenon with some country-specific explanations. Johnson and Stears (1998) have shown that in the U.K. younger cohorts receive substantially higher occupational pensions. In an analysis of the elderly in Slovenia, Stanovnik (1997) has shown that the younger age groups have attained higher levels of education than the older age groups. This, of course, corresponds to expectations; it actually means that younger age groups have more human capital and thus a greater capacity to generate income; in a Bismarckian social security system this means that younger age groups have higher income (and pensions) than older age groups. Among the elderly, young elderly (i.e. the age group 60-69) in some countries are much better off than those aged 70 and above. This is to a certain degree caused by a shift in the gender structure; the proportion of women above age 70 is much higher than the proportion of men, and women typically have smaller pension entitlements.

It is evident from Table 1.14a that in both Slovenia and the U.K., there is a fairly large share of elderly persons situated in the bottom three deciles. For the U.K., this result is simply a consequence of the public pension system based on a flat-rate state pension. This also explains the very small share of the elderly (age groups 70-79, and 80 and over) in the top three deciles. In Slovenia, the large share of elderly persons in the bottom three deciles can be explained by the large number of elderly dependants (mostly women) and the fact that many farmers receive quite low pensions.[10]

34

Table 1.14a: Share of Persons in the Bottom Three Income Deciles, by Age Group

Country	Age group		
	60-69	70-79	80+
		1980s	
Hungary (1987)	36.4	56.4	58.4
Poland (1987)	28.1	36.4	29.3
Slovenia (1983)	46.0	52.7	55.6
Austria (1985)	24.6	33.4	31.0
U.K. (1989)	49.6	70.7	79.4
		1990s	
Hungary (1996)	17.4	20.4	28.4
Poland (1996)	18.5	18.8	19.0
Slovenia (1993)	37.4	48.7	52.7
Austria (1995)	26.3	29.5	30.5
U.K. (1995)	43.7	63.3	63.5

Note: Persons are included with their equivalent household income. In the U.K., only heads of
            households are considered with their equivalent benefit unit income.
Source: Country case-studies.

35

Table 1.14b: Share of Persons in the Top Three Income Deciles, by Age Group

Country	Age group		
	60-69	70-79	80+
		1980s	
Hungary (1987)	21.5	11.9	12.4
Poland (1987)	34.7	20.2	24.0
Slovenia (1983)	20.4	15.2	15.0
Austria (1985)	30.4	21.7	21.6
U.K. (1989)	14.2	6.8	5.5
		1990s	
Hungary (1996)	23.4	20.8	14.0
Poland (1996)	38.0	33.8	37.0
Slovenia (1993)	23.9	17.9	16.4
Austria (1995)	30.5	26.4	27.3
U.K. (1995)	15.0	7.1	7.8

Note: Persons are included with their equivalent household income. In the U.K., only heads of
            households are considered with their equivalent benefit unit income.
Source: Country case-studies.

Table 1.14b shows that the U.K. has the lowest share of the elderly in the top three deciles. However, it must be noted that in the 1990s, the elderly were still underrepresented in the top three deciles in all of the countries studied, with the sole exception of Poland.

Table 1.14c: Country Differences over Time in the Share of Persons (a) in the Bottom Three Deciles, (b) in the Top Three Deciles; in percentage points

Country	Age group		
	60-69	70-79	80+
	Bottom three deciles		
Hungary (1987-1996)	-19.0	-36.0	-30.0
Poland (1987-1996)	-9.6	-17.6	-10.3
Slovenia (1983-1993)	-8.6	-4.0	-2.9
Austria (1985-1995)	1.7	-3.9	-0.5
U.K. (1989-1995)	-5.9	-7.4	-15.9
	Top three deciles		
Hungary (1987-1996)	1.9	8.9	-1.6
Poland (1987-1996)	3.3	13.6	13.0
Slovenia (1983-1993)	3.5	2.7	1.4
Austria (1985-1995)	0.1	4.7	5.7
U.K. (1989-1995)	0.8	0.2	2.3

The changes which have occurred in the income position of the elderly between two points in time are illustrated in Table 1.14c. For each age group, the share of persons situated in the bottom three deciles decreased, the only exception being the age group 60-69 in Austria. Similarly, the share of persons situated in the top three deciles increased in all countries and for all age groups. Poland, in particular, experienced a very substantial income improvement, not only in pensioner households (see Table 1.13c), but also of the elderly in general. This improvement occurred at both ends of the income distribution, i.e. at the bottom and the top. Explanations for this remarkable improvement are: the increase in the minimum pension in 1991 and an increase in the pension upper limits. Slovenia's elderly experienced modest improvements in their income position, but improvements were somewhat more pronounced in the age group 60-69; in our view, this was caused by the decrease in the number of dependants in this age group. Unlike Poland, where the change in the level of benefits occurred in all of the elderly age groups, the improved income position in Slovenia was more cohort-specific. More people born in 1924-1933 (who were 60 to 69 years old in 1993) had pension entitlements than their preceding age cohort born in 1914-1923.

Hungary stands out as a country where the elderly experienced the largest relative income gains in the bottom three deciles, but rather modest income gains in the top three deciles. As shown by Table 1.13c, this conclusion is also valid for pensioner households.

1.6.4 Gender and Income Position

Gender differences in the income distribution of the elderly population reproduce the gender differentials in educational attainment, in labour force participation and in income from work. Essentially, these gender differences indicate the extent to which differences in the distribution of paid and unpaid work during adult life translate into income differences in older age.

Looking at the same two indicators as before – the proportion of persons (respectively households) in the bottom and the top 30% of all persons (respectively households) – three different groups are compared by pairs: (a) single male vs. single female pensioner households, (b) male vs. female pensioners, and (c) men vs. women aged 60 and over.

The first comparison (a: "pensioners who live alone") is one of a relatively small group, at least as far as men are concerned (Table 1.15a). This is the most direct comparison of gender differences, since household incomes considered here only consist of a male or of a female (pension) income.

The second comparison (b) includes all persons over the age of 50 classifying themselves as pensioners, i.e. drawing an old-age, a survivor or a disability pension (Table 1.15b). Here, equivalent incomes take the income of an available partner into account. Another way of looking at the gender divide is through comparisons of income positions of (i) single female pensioner households and female pensioners and (ii) single male pensioner households and male pensioners. If, for example, female pensioners are in a much better income position than single female pensioners, and male pensioners in a worse income position than single male pensioners, that would be proof of important gender differences in pension income.

The third comparison (c) looks at all elderly persons above age 60 (Table 1.15c). In this case as well, the income of an available partner is taken into account. The main difference to the second comparison is that now persons without income or pension entitlements (such as housewives) are included directly, hence, a large difference to the second comparison would indicate a high proportion of the elderly totally dependent on another person's income.

Among men, differences between the three groups – single pensioners, pensioners and persons aged 60 and over – are small in all of the countries studied. In three countries – Austria, Hungary, and the U.K. – single pensioners are slightly better off, also because they do not have to share their income with other persons with potentially lower incomes. Compared across countries and focusing on the mid-1990s, men in Hungary, Poland and Austria are in the best position. In Hungary, for example, only 11% of single pensioners are found in the bottom three income deciles (15% of all men over age 60 and 17% of all pensioners). Only in Austria and Poland are men, at the same time, overrepresented in the top three deciles; 38% and 35% of single pensioners, respectively (Table 1.15a). Among all three groups (single pensioners, all pensioners, all persons aged 60 and over), men in the U.K. are in the worst position, i.e. their share in the bottom three deciles is by far the largest among the five countries compared.

Between the two points in time, the income position of all three male groups improved significantly, both with a much lower proportion in the bottom three and a higher proportion in the top three income deciles. In terms of time trends, Austria is the only exception: the position of male pensioners and men aged 60 and over improved only slightly and the position of single male pensioners even worsened between 1985-1995.

Table 1.15a: Gender Perspective A: Share of Single Pensioner Households in the Bottom Three and in the Top Three Income Deciles (percentage), and Gender Difference (percentage points)

Country (year)	Single female		Single male		Gender difference	
	Bottom three	Top three	Bottom three	Top three	Bottom three	Top three
Austria (1985)	42	16	17	40	25	-24
Hungary (1987)	74	6	54	16	20	-10
Poland (1987)	51	11	32	23	18	-11
U.K. (1989)	68	7	60	8	8	-1
Slovenia (1983)	55	10	51	18	4	-7
Hungary (1996)	46	7	11	28	35	-22
Austria (1995)	45	15	20	38	25	-22
Slovenia (1993)	43	16	36	28	6	-12
Poland (1996)	25	22	20	35	5	-13
U.K. (1995)	45	9	43	16	2	-7

Note: Sorted by column gender difference in bottom three deciles.
Source: Country reports.

Table 1.15b: Gender Perspective B: Share of Pensioners in the Bottom Three and in the Top Three Income Deciles (percentage), and Gender Difference (percentage points)

Country (year)	Female pensioners		Male pensioners		Gender difference	
	Bottom three	Top three	Bottom three	Top three	Bottom three	Top three
U.K. (1989)	65	9	58	11	7	-2
Poland (1987)	24	25	21	27	4	-2
Hungary (1987)	43	20	40	22	3	-2
Austria (1985)	27	27	26	29	1	-2
Slovenia (1983)	34	27	44	20	-10	+8
Hungary (1996)	23	20	17	29	6	-9
U.K. (1995)	56	10	51	13	4	-3
Poland (1996)	17	35	16	39	1	-4
Austria (1995)	26	30	25	32	1	-3
Slovenia (1993)	31	27	32	27	-1	0

Note: Sorted by column gender difference in bottom three deciles.
Source: Country reports.

Table 1.15c: Gender Perspective C: Share of Persons Aged 60 and over in the Bottom Three and in the Top Three Income Deciles (percentage), and Gender Difference (percentage points)

Country (year)	Women 60+		Men 60+		Gender difference	
	Bottom three	Top three	Bottom three	Top three	Bottom three	Top three
U.K. (1989)	69	8	56	12	12	-4
Hungary (1987)	52	14	43	20	9	-6
Poland (1987)	33	24	27	30	6	-6
Austria (1985)	31	23	26	30	5	-7
Slovenia (1983)	50	17	48	18	2	-1
Hungary (1996)	25	19	15	28	10	-9
U.K. (1995)	59	9	51	13	8	-4
Austria (1995)	31	26	24	33	6	-7
Slovenia (1993)	45	19	39	23	6	-4
Poland (1996)	19	36	18	40	0	-3

Note: Sorted by column gender difference in bottom three deciles.

Source: Country reports.

The situation among women is different with the exception of the trend between the two time periods, which was very much the same as the trend for men. As expected, the three groups of women (single pensioners, pensioners and persons aged 60 and over) are in different situations, and these differences also vary from country to country. Three countries, Hungary, Poland and Austria, show a similar pattern.

There is only little difference between female pensioners and all women aged 60 and over, though the first group is always slightly better off (Tables 1.15b and 1.15c). One explanation for this small difference is the relatively low proportion of women without pension entitlements in these countries. In Austria, where almost every second married woman does not have any pension entitlement, the difference is possibly larger and is compensated by two counteracting factors. First, due to enormous war losses among men, married women are still a minority among the age groups 60 and over; the majority of them are widowed, reducing the overall proportion of elderly women without pension entitlements to around 18%. Second, married women without pension entitlements tend to live with partners earning incomes above the average; on the other hand, working class women always had relatively higher labour force participation rates and, hence, draw individual pensions.

Single female pensioners, however, are in a much worse position in all three countries, because they depend entirely on their own pension income (Table 1.15a). In the mid-1990s, both in Hungary and in Austria, around 45% of this group of pensioner households were positioned in the bottom three income deciles, compared to only around 25% of all female pensioners. Due to smaller gender differences in income, the difference is smaller in Poland.

The two other countries show (slightly) different patterns. The U.K. is the only country where single female pensioners are better off than the two other groups, a fact that can be explained by the flat-rate benefit system; pensioners who live in larger pensioner households or with non-pensioners have lower equivalent incomes, both among men and among women. Slovenia is the only country where women 60 and over are in a significantly less advantaged position than female pensioners. This is explained by a particularly large proportion of women without a pension entitlement (40% in 1983 and 31% in 1993), which is to some extent a consequence of the relatively higher proportion of married women among the age group 60 and over (59% in 1983 and 54% in 1993, e.g. compared to only 37% in Austria in 1995).

In all countries except Poland, differences among the three groups of women are smaller when looking at the top three income deciles, and the same when looking at the bottom three deciles. Compared across countries, again focusing on the mid-1990s, the results for women aged 60 and over and for female pensioners resemble the results found for men (Tables 1.15b and 1.15c). Women in Poland are in the best position (overrepresented in the top three and significantly underrepresented in the bottom three deciles) followed by Hungary and Austria (in both countries female pensioners and women aged 60 and over are underrepresented in the bottom three deciles). In the other two countries there is an overrepresentation (and in the U.K. even a very sharp one) in the bottom income deciles. Comparing only single female pensioner households (Table 1.15a), these differences between countries largely disappear except for Poland which keeps its leading position. In all other countries, the share in the bottom three income deciles was around 45%; some differences, however, remain in the extent of underrepresentation in the top deciles.

Looking at the mid-1990s, differences between men and women are the largest in Hungary, irrespective of the groups compared, while in the previous decade the gender difference was largest in Austria (when comparing single pensioner households) and in the U.K. (when comparing persons aged 60 and over or pensioners). In general, gender differences are the most pronounced among single pensioner households, the group which exclusively depends on its own income. Hungary and Austria are striking examples of the particularly large gender difference for this group: the difference in the proportion of single pensioner households positioned in the bottom three income deciles was 35 percentage points in Hungary (45% of female, but only 10% of male single households) and 25 percentage points in Austria (45% of female, 20% of male), suggesting that in these two countries gender differences in income are particularly large and also not significantly reduced by compensation measures for unpaid work done by women (Table 1.15a). In Poland and Slovenia due to significantly smaller gender differences both in working and in pension income, gender differences among single pensioner households are small. The UK is the only country where gender differences are smallest among single pensioner households (where no other incomes intervene), again a direct consequence of the flat-rate benefit system. Gender differences are generally much smaller among the group of persons aged 60 and over (Table 1.15c), and very small or almost negligible among pensioners (Table 1.15b).

Gender differences at the top of the income distribution only partly reflect those at the bottom. Among single pensioner households (Table 1.15a), gender differences at high income levels are substantial and at a comparable level in Poland (21% of single female households and 45% of single male households placed in the top three income deciles), Austria (15% women, 38% men) and Hungary (7% of women, 28% of men), and they are larger than at the bottom in Poland, Slovenia and the U.K.. Trends in the gender difference during the last decade also diverge among countries. At the top of the income distribution, gender differences tend to increase (the only exception being Austria), while at the bottom they have either increased (in Austria and in Slovenia) or decreased (in Hungary, Poland and the U.K.).

To conclude, the gender analysis shows a strong similarity among Hungary, Poland and Austria, three countries with a hitherto Bismarckian pension system (but with structural reforms in Hungary and Poland recently), a certain difference in Slovenia (notwithstanding the closeness of the Austrian and the Slovenian pension system), and a totally different pattern in the U.K., with its characteristic, largely flat-rate pension system.

1.7 Poverty and Inequality

1.7.1 *Poverty*

Poverty is defined in relative terms, i.e. as a given percentage of the median household equivalent income. In the country case-studies, the poverty lines are set at 40%, 50%, 60% and 70% of median household equivalent income. Table 1.16 presents poverty incidence based on the poverty line set at 50% and 70% of median household equivalent income.

Table 1.16: **Poverty Incidence (percentage of persons) Based on 50% and 70% Median Household Equivalent Income**

Household	Hungary	Poland	Slovenia	Austria	U.K.
			50% poverty line		
All persons	3.9	11.4	7.3	9.6	14.0
	8.3	**8.4**	**7.1**	**8.5**	**15.6**
Pensioners	5.1	8.7	9.2	7.6	16.8
	2.3	**2.7**	**6.7**	**4.6**	**12.1**
Pensioners in	8.3	10.3	10.7	8.2	20.9
pensioner households	**2.2**	**1.1**	**7.3**	**5.5**	**14.2**
Persons aged 60	7.0	9.7	15.8	8.6	40.7
and over	**2.0**	**3.1**	**12.6**	**5.5**	**28.7**
			70% poverty line		
All persons	16.4	24.2	20.5	29.1	32.0
	22.3	**21.8**	**20.6**	**26.3**	**33.6**
Pensioners	24.2	21.5	28.5	26.4	49.3
	13.6	**10.6**	**20.5**	**22.6**	**38.1**
Pensioners in	36.3	26.8	36.4	29.0	59.9
pensioner households	**15.7**	**7.5**	**22.7**	**26.8**	**44.0**
Persons aged 60	30.3	23.5	38.2	28.8	48.6
and over	**14.3**	**10.7**	**31.4**	**25.3**	**38.0**

Legend: Data in first rows mostly refer to the 1980s, and data in second rows (bold type) refer to the 1990s. Hungary: 1987 and 1996, Poland: 1987 and 1996, Slovenia: 1983 and 1993, Austria: 1985 and 1995, U.K.: 1989 and 1995.

Source: Country case-studies.

In assessing the poverty incidence for the whole population, we note that in Slovenia, the U.K. and Austria it did not change appreciably during the observed time period, whereas the changes in Poland and Hungary were somewhat more pronounced. Thus, the proportion of persons having household equivalent incomes below 50% of the median household equivalent income has decreased in Poland from 11.4% in 1987 to 8.4% in 1996, and increased in Hungary from 3.9% in 1987 to 8.3% in 1996.

Poverty incidence among pensioners has decreased in all of the five countries. The poverty incidence for this group is as a rule lower than that of the whole population, in some cases quite drastically. In Hungary, the poverty incidence for the total population in 1996 was 8.3% and for pensioners only 2.3%; in Austria in 1995 it was 8.5% for the total population and only 4.6% for pensioners.

Since none of the members of pensioner households are employed, self-employed or unemployed, and their income sources consist mostly of pensions and social benefits, one would expect that the poverty incidence for this subgroup of pensioners would be larger than that for the whole group of pensioners. In three or four of the countries (depending on the poverty line) this actually turns out to be the case. In Hungary, Poland and the U.K. the poverty incidence for pensioners in pensioner households has decreased significantly in the observed time period, whereas in Slovenia and Austria the decrease was not as large, but still greater than 2 percentage points. Similarly, persons aged 60 and over have improved their relative position, and the poverty incidence for this group has decreased in all of the countries. It is interesting to observe that in Slovenia the poverty incidence for this group is higher than the poverty incidence for the whole population: this is caused by the still rather large number of dependants older than 60 years.

The decile analysis of pensioner households (see section 1.6.2) and elderly age groups (see section 1.6.3) revealed a marked improvement in the income position of various types of pensioner households as well as of the elderly. In other words, the decrease observed in the poverty incidence for pensioners in pensioner households and for persons aged 60 and over was to be expected. Qualitatively similar conclusions are reached whether setting the poverty line at 50% or 70% of the median household equivalent income. Namely, in Slovenia, Hungary, Poland and the U.K. all three subgroups: (a) pensioners, (b) pensioners in pensioner households and (c) persons aged 60 and over experienced large decreases in poverty incidence. In

Austria, poverty incidence for these three subgroups also decreased, though not as much.

In spite of the changes that occurred in the observed time period, poverty incidence is still quite high in the U.K., particularly when compared to the other countries presented in our study. In the U.K., the high poverty incidence is characteristic not only for the three population subgroups, but also for the whole population. For the other countries, one could say, slightly exaggerating, that "... poverty is not a problem of pensioners anymore, and income poverty is not the most significant problem that pensioners face" (Hungarian case-study).

1.7.2 Income Inequality

Three income inequality measures – the Gini coefficient and two percentile ratios: 90/10 and 75/25 – are presented in Table 1.17.

The Gini coefficient for the total population (taking individuals with their household equivalent income) has increased considerably in Hungary, Slovenia and Poland, and has remained unchanged in the U.K. and decreased in Austria. It appears that the incomes of certain social groups (mainly entrepreneurs and the self-employed) have increased vigorously in this period of transition and this has caused the increases in the three transition countries.

The ranking of subgroups with regard to inequality measures (particularly the Gini coefficient) is similar to the ranking based on poverty incidence. Thus, the computed Gini coefficient for pensioners is consistently lower than the Gini coefficient for the whole population. The values of the Gini coefficient for pensioners decreased somewhat in the U.K., Austria and Poland and remained virtually unchanged in Hungary and Slovenia. In full agreement with our expectations, the Gini coefficient for pensioners in pensioner households is lower than the Gini coefficient for all pensioners: income in pensioner households is more homogeneous and consists mostly of pensions, which are more equally distributed than other income sources. The Gini coefficient for persons aged 60 and over is in most, but not all cases the greatest among the three subgroups; this again is in line with the results based on the poverty analysis.

Broadly speaking, the ranking of the 75/25-percentile ratio for the three subgroups is similar to the ranking of the Gini coefficient. In other words, the value of this inequality measure in the most recent year is, for all the countries observed, consistently lower for pensioners than for the whole population, and consistently lower for pensioners in pensioner households than for all pensioners.

Table 1.17:   Inequality Measures (using household equivalent income)

Country	Hungary	Poland	Slovenia	Austria	U.K.
			Gini coefficient		
All persons	0.228	0.278	0.237	0.250	0.35
	0.286	**0.309**	**0.275**	**0.234**	**0.35**
Pensioners	0.217	0.255	0.242	0.233	0.30
	0.219	**0.249**	**0.241**	**0.210**	**0.29**
Pensioners in		0.230	0.236		0.28
pensioner households		**0.218**	**0.241**		**0.27**
Persons aged 60	0.220	0.251	0.265	0.240	0.29
and over	**0.206**	**0.260**	**0.263**	**0.215**	**0.28**
			75/25 percentile ratio		
All persons	1.64	1.88	1.74	1.9	2.31
	1.82	**1.88**	**1.82**	**1.8**	**2.17**
Pensioners	1.63	1.76	1.80	1.7	1.81
	1.51	**1.72**	**1.76**	**1.7**	**1.82**
Pensioners in		1.56	1.82	1.7	1.73
pensioner households		**1.60**	**1.74**	**1.7**	**1.76**
Persons aged 60	1.62	1.69	1.83	1.7	1.88
and over	**1.46**	**1.68**	**1.89**	**1.7**	**1.86**
			90/10 percentile ratio		
All persons	2.69	3.72	2.94	3.1	4.67
	3.48	**3.62**	**3.32**	**2.9**	**4.45**
Pensioners	2.56	3.12	3.01	2.8	3.21
	3.57	**2.79**	**3.00**	**2.6**	**3.27**
Pensioners in		2.99	2.97	2.8	3.10
pensioner households		**2.60**	**3.02**	**2.5**	**3.13**
Persons aged 60	2.52	3.02	3.42	2.9	3.41
and over	**2.35**	**2.85**	**3.40**	**2.5**	**3.22**

Legend: Data in first rows refer to the 1980s, and data in second rows (bold type) refer to the 1990s. Hungary: 1987 and 1996, Poland: 1987 and 1996, Slovenia: 1983 and 1993, Austria: 1985 and 1995, U.K.: 1989 and 1995.

Source: Country case-studies.

The 90/10-inequality measure was more volatile in the analysed time periods, but even this inequality measure exhibits a certain regularity: its value for pensioners has been consistently lower than that for the whole population. The very high values of this inequality measure in the U.K. (1995) for the three subgroups are not surprising. For richer pensioners, public pensions represent only a fraction of the total income; actually, for pensioners in the upper income stratum, private pensions and investment income appear to be very important. All in all, the U.K. has high income inequality for the whole population as well as for the three subgroups, whereas Austria has consistently low values. The trends in inequality among pensioners, pensioners in pensioner households and persons aged 60 and over appear to be generally more favourable and also more stable than inequality trends for the whole population.

1.8 Concluding Remarks

During the 1990s, pensioners and – more generally – the elderly have improved their relative income position in all of the five countries compared. The extent of this improvement has been explored through the analysis of different types of pensioner households and different age groups. The gender divide was also analysed in detail, and it has been shown that the gender income gap has been narrowing, particularly at the lower end of the income distribution scale. The measurements of poverty incidence and income inequality provided additional and clear evidence about improved income positions. This of course does not mean that relative income gains for the elderly population have been uniform. The elderly population is still mostly heterogeneous; although in all of the five countries, income differentiation among the whole population is greater than among the pensioner population.

The income position is only one, albeit the most important, dimension of economic well-being. We have not touched on other aspects such as the wealth position, accessibility of health care and long-term care; these are also quite relevant in assessing the overall economic well-being of the elderly. The wealth position of the elderly was actually analysed in the country studies, showing that they are not in a particularly disadvantaged position. True, pensioner households have lower ownership levels of durables and a lower quality of housing than the general population. However, they tend to have much higher ownership levels of the most important asset, namely, housing. This observation is valid particularly for the U.K.

Four of the five countries presented in our comparative analysis have introduced important pension reforms in recent years. Although the primary aim of these reforms was to stabilize the growth of pension expenditure and assure sustainability of the pension systems, their success will also have to be judged on how the reformed pension systems perform their basic task of providing income security for the elderly.

Notes

1   For a review of the premises and relevant methodology, see Auerbach, Gokhale and Kotlikoff (1994).

2   This argument is developed in greater detail in Atkinson (1995).

3   This opinion is expressed by Atkinson et al. (1995: 19).

4   This solution, contrary to that applied in OECD scales, does not discriminate between adults and children in terms of costs of living. Therefore, it does not seem to be appropriate for studies which focus on specific demographic groups, like children or the elderly (who frequently live in households without children).

5   Slovenia's households achieved pre-transition income levels only in 1996.

6   Such a subdivision was actually carried out in the Hungarian study.

7   Except Poland, where pensioner households seemingly experienced only modest income growth. In fact, as seen from Table 3.12, with the exception of 'other pensioner households', all other pensioner household types in Poland experienced quite large increases in real equivalent household income.

8   This is shown in Table 6.16.

9   A more recent strong empirical verification of these life-cycle stages is provided in Whiteford and Kennedy (1995); their analysis is based on the LIS data files.

10 These pensions could almost be labelled as non-contributory benefits, since the contributions that farmers pay are negligible in proportion to the benefits (albeit small) that they receive.

References

Atkinson, A.B. (1995) *Incomes and the Welfare State*. Cambridge: Cambridge University Press.

Atkinson, A.B./ Micklewright, J. (1992) *Economic Transformation in Eastern Europe and the Distribution of Income*. Cambridge: Cambridge University Press.

Atkinson, A./ Rainwater, L./ Smeeding, T. (1995) *Income Distribution in European Countries*, DAE Working Papers, MU 9506. The Microsimulation Unit, Department of Applied Economics, University of Cambridge.

Auerbach, A./ Gokhale, J./ Kotlikoff, L.J. (1994) 'Generational Accounting: a Meaningful Way to Evaluate Fiscal Policy', *Journal of Economic Perspectives*, vol. 8, no. 1: 73-94.

Augusztinovics, M. (ed.) (1997) *Pension Systems and Reforms – Britain, Hungary, Italy, Poland, Sweden*, Final Report, European Commission's Phare ACE Programme 1995, Research Project P95-2139-R.

Deleeck, H./ Van den Bosch, K./ De Lathouwer, L. (1992) *Poverty and the Adequacy of Social Security in the EC*. Aldershot: Avebury.

Förster, M. (1994) Measurement of Poverty and Low Incomes in a Perspective of International Comparisons, *OECD Labour Market and Social Policy Occasional Paper* no. 14, Paris.

Gruber, J./ Wise, D.A. (eds.) (1998) *Social Security and Retirement around the World*. Chicago: The University of Chicago Press.

Hancock, R./ Pudney, S. (1997) 'The Welfare of Pensioners During Economic Transition: an Analysis of Hungarian Survey Data', *Economics of Transition*, vol. 5, no. 2: 395-426.

Johnson, P./ Stears, G. (1998) 'Why are Older Pensioners Poorer?', *Oxford Bulletin of Economics and Statistics*, vol. 60, no. 3: 3-22.

Milanovic, B. (1998) *Income, Inequality and Poverty during the Transition from Planned to Market Economy*. Washington, D.C.: The World Bank.

Mitchell, D. (1991) *Income Transfers in Ten Welfare States*. Aldershot: Avebury.

Müller, K. (1999) *The Political Economy of Pension Reform in Central-Eastern Europe*. Cheltenham Glos: Edward Elgar Publishing.

Nelson, Joan (1998) *The Politics of Pension and Health Care Delivery Reforms in Hungary and Poland*, discussion paper no. 52, Collegium Budapest.

OECD (1982) *The OECD List of Social Indicators*. Paris.

OECD (1998) *Maintaining Prosperity in an Ageing Society*. Paris.

Smeeding, T./ O'Higgins, M./ Rainwater, L. (1990) *Poverty, Inequality and Income Distribution in Comparative Perspective. The Luxembourg Income Study*. New York: Harvester Wheatsheaf.

Stanovnik, T. (1997) 'Dohodki in socialni položaj upokojencev', *IB revija*, vol. 31, no. 5-6: 23-39.

Szulc, A. (1995) 'Towards a Balanced Consumer Market: an Equivalence Scale Exercise for Poland', paper presented at the 7th World Congress of the Econometric Society, Tokyo, 22-29 August.

Szulc, A. (1999) 'Economic Transition, Poverty, and Inequality: Poland in the 1990s', Invited and Contributed Papers of the 12th World Congress of the International Economic Association, Buenos Aires, 23-27 August 1999 (available on CD-ROM).

Whiteford, P./ Kennedy, S. (1995) *Incomes and Living Standards of Older People*. London: HMSO.

49

References

Part I

Transition Countries

CHAPTER 2

Hungary: Getting Better and Becoming Dissimilar

Zsolt Spéder

2.1 Introduction: Why Is It Important to Address the Situation of the Elderly?

An Unintended Consequence of Transition

Policy-makers and those who define social goals have more or less agreed on the basic goals of transition from a more redistributive socialist society to a democratic political system and a market economy based on private ownership. However, there have been significant differences of opinion with respect to the sequence and rhythm of the concrete steps to be taken in this transition. One should only recall the dispute on shock therapy versus gradualism (Balcerowicz, 1996). Political discourse was dominated by the nature of the political decisions. The majority of the participants in that discussion measured the appropriateness of the decisions by the extent to which they helped to achieve the social goals defined. Even when negative consequences were mentioned, such as poverty, inequality, or unemployment, it was usually the attributes and functions of these negative phenomena, as known from developed industrial societies, that were discussed. Little was said about the possible extent to which these phenomena could affect society, or the probability of these phenomena and their interrelationships being quite different from the dynamics in Western Europe. It seems that the almost 30% increase in the number of pensioners was an unplanned consequence of transition (more precisely, of the restructuring of the economy). Its significance was not only underestimated but also recognized rather late by policy-makers, although there is an obvious explanation for this trend. It is important to stress that the process was not recognized by the players concerned until it was too late, and that the high growth in the number of pensioners within such a short period of time has resulted in adverse long-term consequences.

The budgetary and institutional consequences derive from the fact that transition means a temporary ('transitory') socio-economic situation, whereas retirement tends to be a permanent situation on the level of the individual, and has consequences on the level of society as a whole also, which can only be changed gradually.

Table 2.1: Distribution of the Population by Economic Activity, 1980, 1990 and 1996

Year	Employed*	Unem-ployed	Inactive income receiver**	Dependant	Total
			Total population		
1980	47.3	-	20.6	32.1	100
1990	43.6	1.2	25.6	29.5	100
1996	34.2	4.7	32.5	28.5	100
			Active-age population groups		
1980	79.5	-	8.7	11.8	100
1990	75.2	2.1	10.3	12.3	100
1996	56.8	8.0	18.6	16.7	100

Note: * In Hungarian statistics: active earner.

          ** In Hungarian statistics: "inactive earner"; mainly pensioners.

Source: KSH, 1997: 16-17.

As a result of the "transformational recession" (Kornai, 1992), "de-industrialization" and the "reduction of the possibilities in the agrarian sphere", many hundreds of thousands were crowded out of the labour market. In Hungary in 1980, 47.3% of the entire population were active earners, whereas by 1996 the figure was only 34.2%, as shown in Table 2.1.[1] Restructuring becomes even more visible if the active-age population is considered on its own. The proportion of active earners fell from 79.5% to 56.8% between 1980 and 1996. According to initial schemes, unemployment insurance and unemployment benefits were supposed to 'take care' of the negative consequences. However, the figures show that unemployment benefits alone could not solve the social problems resulting from the strong decline in labour market activity.

Table 2.1 also highlights the fact that the reduction of the labour market and the parallel rise in the number of inactive earners started in the 1980s, and the transformation substantially speeded up the rate of change. The majority of inactive earners are either pensioners or pensioners' spouses, but the number of dependants among the active age group has also grown.

Goal of the Study

The present study does not intend to present and analyse the above processes in detail but reference will be made to them if this adds to our goal. The basic goal is to analyse *the welfare situation of pensioners* and to find out *if their social position has changed (and if so, in what direction).* It is also interesting to know how *differentiated the society of pensioners is,* and what the factors are that explain the internal differentiation. Some indicators will refer to the living conditions of pensioners and to changes in these conditions.

Differentiating and Homogenizing Processes

Internal differentiation of pensioners is just as important as the assessment of their situation within society.

The lifelong occupational career and occupational status before retirement should be specifically mentioned as one of the *differentiating factors* among pensioners. The resources available to pensioners are accumulated during their working life. The size of one's pension also depends on the number of years employed and on the wages received during the final working period. *Demographic factors* such as household type and gender cannot be disregarded either. Studies have shown that poverty is not independent of the individual's family type. The household context may strengthen or deteriorate the individual's advantages. The same applies to disadvantages: a family environment full of risk factors deepens an individual's disadvantages, whereas an advantageous family context can 'absorb' their (negative) consequences (Spéder, 1999). All these factors presum-

55

ably hold true for pensioners as well – one should only think of life events such as becoming widowed, or moving in with one's children. It is worth recalling a conclusion of Vogel's comparative study (Vogel, 1997). In his analysis, there were significant differences between various generations in the European countries. According to Vogel's approach, 'family regimes' could be responsible for the inequality among the generations in different countries; for example, whether or not the various generations lived together (then the differences are smaller) or in separate households (Vogel, 1997). Therefore, it is important to study in more detail the specific *types of households* in which pensioners live. Many authors also assume that there is a difference between *male and female pensioners*. Elderly women living alone are the often quoted examples in papers on poverty (Glendiding and Millar, 1992).

Of the *homogenizing factors*, the most important is the formula for the preservation of the value of pensions. If pensions are not indexed appropriately in an inflationary environment,[2] the real value of pensions decreases, along with the income differences among pensioners. These degression elements used in the calculation of pensions also encourage homogenization. The social policy measures applied in the case of minimum pensions act to homogenize the income levels of low-income pensioners.

These hypotheses are investigated more closely in section 2.5. Section 2.2 provides a discussion of the major conditions determining the financial well-being of pensioners, including both institutional and macroeconomic factors. Section 2.3 describes the data used in the empirical analysis. Section 2.4 deals with one of the central issues of this study – how the relative position of pensioners has changed in the society during the period under review. Section 2.5 investigates the stratification of the pensioner population using bi- and multivariate analysis methods. The living conditions of pensioners are presented in section 2.6. Section 2.7 presents the conclusions.

2.2 Institutional Conditions and Demographic Characteristics Relevant for the Economic Well-Being of Pensioners

The income position of pensioners is determined mainly by the nature of the welfare state. In particular the state pension and health insurance systems are of outstanding importance, but social support programmes may also play a significant role. Naturally, market resources also constitute part of the pensioners' income structure, but as the studies conducted thus far show, their proportion is relatively low. This section presents the major features of the pension system, which basically determine the material situation of pensioners, and also describes the demographic processes that constitute the framework of the pension system.

The Basic Features of the Pension System[3]

While the Hungarian pension system has been constantly adapted since the mid-1980s, its pay-as-you-go structure did not change until 1994. The separation of the pension system and the social assistance system started in 1989, and in 1991, the indexing of pensions underwent significant changes. In 1992, the system of social insurance was split into two separate entities: health and pension insurance. During the 1990s, the country shifted toward a three-pillar pension system. Private insurance companies began offering savings programmes aimed at old-age social security. Reliable macro statistics are available only from 1992 onwards; hence, data before and after 1992 are not always comparable.[4]

57

The *enormous increase in the number* of inactive persons, and of *pensioners* among them, is considered as an important factor driving pension reform. The changes in the number of pensioners were caused by several factors, but the framework was set by demographic trends.

Demographic Structure

Like in other European countries, the second part of the 20th century was marked by a change in the age structure of the Hungarian population. From the viewpoint of this study, it is the rise in the proportion of the elderly population that is very crucial. While the ageing of the population of Western European countries is the result of two parallel processes, which are almost equal in significance, in Hungary, the significance of the two processes differs. The decline in the number of births plays a greater role in ageing than the improvement of the mortality rates. While the proportions with respect to births have changed similarly to the European ones, there has been no significant change as regards mortality. This is reflected in the changes in the age composition of society, as well as in the changes in life expectancy.

Retirement Age

It may contain incentives and counter-incentives concerning retirement and activity, but ultimately, it is the pension system which determines at which age the active period of life may be concluded. During the socialist period, the retirement age was set relatively low: women could retire at the age of 55 and men at the age of 60.[5] It was possible to retire before the prescribed age limit if one became disabled (these pensions were disability, not old-age pensions). In Hungary, the retirement age changed in 1997, when the age limit was raised to 62 for both genders.[6] Another precondition for old-age retirement is a required length of employment or service period, or in other words, a minimum contribution record (until 1980 it was 10 years, and after that 20 years).

Retirement During the Transition[7]

58   As indicated earlier, the number of pensioners increased more rapidly during the transition period than could be expected from demographic and health trends. The pension system was used to 'absorb' the negative consequences of transition. Partly, the existing forms of retirement were used for dismissals (disability pensions) and partly, new forms of pension appeared. The largest growth was recorded in the number of disability pensioners. Between 1989 and 1996, their number grew from 500,000 to almost 850,000, as shown in Table 2.2. Clearly, the 'loosening' of the eligibility guidelines for disability pensions may have been one of the reasons for this increase (ONYF, 1997).[8] Two new forms of early retirement have also emerged. One may retire five years before the statutory age, if the pension is financed by the employer until the person reaches that age. Likewise, *pre-retirement* became available to those who had been unemployed for six months or more. Their pension is paid by the unemployment fund.

The large majority of pensioners in Hungary are old-age and disability pensioners. In addition, there are a noteworthy number of persons entitled to survivor pensions and beneficiaries of the separate pension scheme for agricultural workers. Individuals falling into these categories only appear in Table 2.2 if they receive a pension on the grounds of being widowed or if they are receiving an agricultural annuity.[9]

Table 2.2: Change in the Number of Pensioners between 1989 and 1996,
by Pensioner Status (000)

	1989	1992	1994	1996	'96/'89
Old-age pensioner	1371	1542	1589	1621	1.18
Disability pensioner (above age limit)	298	342	377	393	1.32
Disability pensioner (under age limit)	204	389	313	352	1.72
Subtotal	1873	2273	2279	2366	1.26
Survivor pensioner	x	268	254	241	x
Early retiree	x	64	57	45	x
Pre-retiree	x	7	43	53	x
Agricultural annuity	x	52	41	31	x
(Total)*	x	(2594)	(2674)	(2736)	x

Note: * There may be some very small overlap between the different categories.

Source: Statistical Yearbooks, Yearbooks of the ONYF.

Table 2.2 shows that the number of pensioners grew by about 25 to 30%
within a relatively short period of time. The transition was clearly the driving force behind this increase, as well as strong incentives and a broader
range of options. In addition, the tightening of the labour market created a
more difficult situation for the labour force population. Working beyond retirement age was also limited by the changes in the political system. In fact,
whether on their own initiative or because they were forced to in the beginning of the 1990s, the political as well as power elites also chose to retire.

The Value of Pensions

One of the most important components of material well-being of pensioners is the pension level, which depends on two factors: the initial level, and,
particularly relevant during periods of high inflation, the indexation method.
Two principles guide the *determination of new pensions*: the payment of contributions and the principle of solidarity. The importance of the two principles relative to each other has changed over time. From the early 1990s onwards, it was the principle of the payment of contributions which gained
importance, but in the case of low-income groups the principle of solidarity
has always been present. The former principle was represented by the con-

tribution period and the wages in the last years of employment (contribution level), whereas the latter was represented by the existence of a minimum pension. Until 1992, the calculation of the pension was based on the three best income years. Starting in 1992, the basis for calculating the initial pension was the monthly average of net wages from 1988 onwards.

During the period under review there were several changes[10] in the method of indexing pensions, caused mainly by political decisions. Consequently, pensions increased more or less in line with net wages, with the exception of 1994 when they rose higher than other incomes (ONYF, 1997: 32). Table 2.3 shows the value of pensions as a share of average wages. The respective proportions were around 60% in the 1990s. Pensioners were in the best position in 1990-1991, when an average pension attained around 65% of average net wages.

Table 2.3: Average Replacement Rate in Hungary 1985-1996

Average pension / average wage (in %)	1985	1990	1991	1992	1993	1994	1995	1996
(old)*	61.2	66.2	64.2	62.7				
(new)				60.1	59.8	59.5	61.1	58.9

Note: * As related to the institutional changes introduced in 1992.

Source: ONYF, 1997: 9.

Some Macro-economic Interrelationships

The growing number of pensioners entitled to guaranteed pensions is causing expenditure to rise. For active earners, in a pay-as-you-go system, this means a growing burden of contributions. Table 2.4 presents some characteristics of this interrelationship. The second column shows that the proportion of people in the inactive and active age segments has hardly changed. This confirms the earlier conjecture that demographic change does not explain the growing financial burden of the Hungarian pension system. The decrease in the proportion of insured persons versus pensioners shown in column 4 is due to the change in the retirement patterns described above. There was also a substantial drop in activity rates among working-age individuals, as shown in column 3.

Table 2.4: Relations between Activity and Retirement in Hungary 1985-1996

Year	Population of inactive/active age**	Active earners/population of active age**	Active insured persons/pensioners*
1985	40.4	86.9	
1990	41.8	86.4	
1991	41.9	81.3	
1992***	41.7	73.7	
1993	41.4	68.3	2.09
1994	41.1	65.8	2.04
1995	40.9	64.7	1.96
1996	40.7	64.0	1.84

Note: *   Calculated on the basis of Statistical Yearbooks from the National Insurance Office.
       **   ONYF, 1997.
       *** Institutional changes were introduced in 1992.

The proportion of pension expenditures in the GDP (Table 2.5) is an indicator used worldwide to illustrate the financial burden of pension systems, although in this study this controversial issue of public finance is not further elaborated.[11] Ten per cent of GDP is not very large compared to other countries.

Table 2.5: Pension Expenditure as a Percentage of GDP

Year	Expenditure on pensions (as % of GDP)
1992	9.8
1993	9.7
1994	10.0
1995	9.3
1996	8.9

Source: ONYF, 1997: 7.

This section has set out some demographic, socio-political and economic factors that could influence the economic well-being of the elderly. Two main points have surfaced. First, in Hungary, as in many other countries in transition, it is not predominately the ageing of society, but the structural crisis of the economy and the political adjustment to this situation that are the most important factors behind the growing pensioner society. Second, transition is not only an adjustment of the economic system, but it is also the process of rebuilding institutions and the welfare system (Nelson, 1998). The pension system and programmes securing the well-being of the elderly were – and still are – constantly changing. The following sections describe and analyse the population of pensioners in society.

2.3 The Data

The material well-being of pensioners and changes in this status are studied by comparing three points in time, starting with 1987. The income data used are from the Household Income Survey conducted by the Central Statistical Office in 1987. This report contains the income data for almost 20,000 households and 56,000 household members. The data characterizing and presenting the material well-being in two years of the 1990s come from considerably smaller data sets: they were prepared on the basis of the first and fifth waves of the Hungarian Household Panel (HHP).[12] In 1992, the sample consisted of 2,600 households containing around 7,500 adults. The sample overrepresented Budapest, therefore the data are weighted; as a result, there were 2,059 households and 5,744 persons figuring in the 1992 analysis. Panel mortality is a characteristic of every panel survey, which had to be corrected by weighting. On the other hand, the HHP used a far more detailed questionnaire than the HIS, which provides further analysis options.

It is important to assess whether the two data sets are comparable or not. On the one hand, it is known that the two samples are representative; both had the aim to collect information on all of the income sources of households. On the other hand, the questions were formulated differently in the two questionnaires; in addition, the HIS contains monthly incomes, whereas the HHP yearly incomes. Sample sizes are different as well, and it could be the case that the staff of the Statistical Office is perceived differently than the employees of a public opinion research institute. Although all of these factors may play a minor role in the different analyses, it is believed that the income ranking of the sample population is well covered in both cases. Hence, a careful comparison should be possible.

2.4 The Relative Well-Being of Pensioners

The 1990s were a period of fairly large growth in income inequality and poverty (Andorka, Ferge and Tóth, 1997; Förster and Tóth, 1997; Flemming and Micklewright, 1997; Vecernik, 1996; Spéder, 1998). Differences are great among researchers regarding the extent of growth (Andorka, Ferge and Tóth, 1997). This is mainly due to three distinct factors. First, inequality measures are sensitive to income changes in various parts of the income distribution; some are sensitive to changes in the medium part, and some are sensitive to those at the extremes. Second, it was not always sufficiently clear what constituted the sampling unit in the survey (all individuals, all adults or households) and what was the income basis for calculating the individual indices. Third, though there were many methods of data collection applied in the early 1990s, sample sizes, representativeness and survey questionnaires differed significantly from those of the surveys conducted in the mid- and late 1980s. Thus, little of the data collected in the 4-year period between 1988 and 1992 can be reliably compared.[13] This analysis will not be able to overcome that deficiency, either. The difference in size between the two databases, the Household Income Survey of the Central Statistical Office and the Hungarian Household Panel, as well as the different questionnaires (what was asked and how the questions were phrased) suggest that one should be careful with comparisons. However, comparability is enhanced by the fact that a detailed survey of incomes was the primary objective of both surveys, thus the adjustment of the questionnaires to the changing situation may have had a positive effect on the validity of the data collected. The data presented below should be interpreted in view of all these caveats.

63

The percentiles in Table 2.6 clearly show that inequality has been continuously increasing in society during the ten years under review. The increases were larger at the extremes, as seen from the 90/10-decile ratio; the increases in the 75/25-quartile ratio were less pronounced. Obviously, the incomes of a significant social group have grown strongly. Changes in inequality among pensioners differ from those for the whole population. On the one hand, the ratio between the equivalent incomes of the richest and the poorest pensioners has increased, as has the one for the whole population. On the other hand, the inequality among those pensioners who were not in an extreme position (i.e. the 75/25-ratio) has not changed. If one looks at the Gini coefficient more closely, the picture is somewhat more confused.

The coefficient increased between 1987 and 1992 for all three categories, but from 1992 to 1996 the category of pensioners and category of the elderly experienced a large decrease in this measure of inequality. The explanation for this divergent development of the inequality measures is unclear, since the Gini coefficient is more sensitive to changes in the middle part of the income distribution (Coulter, 1989: 53). Elsewhere it has been argued that behind an unchanged Gini coefficient there may be changes not only in the 90/10-ratio, but also in other measures of inequality (Spéder and Habich, 1999).

Table 2.6: Income Inequality Measures; 1987, 1992 and 1996

Inequality measure	1987	1992	1996
	Equivalent income of the population		
90/10	2.7	3.1	3.5
75/25	1.6	1.7	1.8
Gini	.23	.28	.28
	Equivalent income of pensioners		
90/10	2.6	2.5	2.6
75/25	1.6	1.5	1.5
Gini	.22	.24	.22
	Equivalent income of persons aged 60 and over		
90/10	2.5	2.5	2.3
75/25	1.6	1.5	1.5
Gini	.22	.24	.20

2.4.1 Basic Trends in the Material Well-Being of Individuals

Another traditional method used to study inequalities is the analysis of the decile distribution. As the average size of households is not equal, both individuals and households have been distributed by decile, and both decile distributions are used in the respective analyses.[14] Thus, the following analysis investigates:

– where, i.e. in which decile are pensioners overrepresented, and
– has the relative position of pensioners changed, and if so, how?

Table 2.7a shows that in 1987 pensioners were overrepresented in the lowest income decile. Three tenths of them were located in the lowest two deciles. Many researchers consider the lowest two deciles – more exactly the lowest quintile – as below the poverty line. This means that pensioners had an above average risk of poverty in 1987. Five years later, while the proportion of pensioners in the lowest decile was somewhat below average, the presence of pensioners in the four highest deciles had also fallen, as shown in Table 2.7b. The majority was concentrated in the lower and lower middle part of the income distribution; 56.5% of pensioners were located in the income deciles 2 to 5. Table 2.7c shows that again four years later (in 1996) a concentration of pensioners was observed around the median income deciles. Almost half of the pensioners (44.4%) could be found in the middle of the income distribution and only very few of them (3.3%) were found in the lowest income group. While the share of those in the upper income deciles has grown somewhat, they still remain underrepresented.

Summing up, it may be stated that pensioners have gradually climbed upwards in the hierarchy of incomes. While in the late 1980s they were exposed to an above average risk of poverty, by the mid-1990s they constituted the bulk of the middle income class. This does not mean that their situation has improved in absolute terms, as one could witness a general deterioration of living standards during the period surveyed. But their situation has deteriorated less than that of the general population.

Taking only persons aged 60 and over into consideration, a similar summary statement can be made (Tables 2.7a-c). Their situation has also improved in relative terms. It should also be noted that the improvement within this group somewhat lags behind that of all pensioners. One reason, though not very frequent, is that there are some elderly who do not have income from social insurance. On the other hand, young pensioners (between the age of 50 and 60) usually have some labour income. There is, however, a significant number of disability pensioners who receive a lower pension. Of the three social groups, it is pensioners living in pensioner households who are in the most disadvantaged financial situation. It is understandable, that those pensioners who live together with active earners have, on average, higher equivalent incomes than those of pensioners living in pensioner households. The following section looks at the degree to which the household types influence the well-being of pensioners.

Table 2.7a: Distribution of Persons by Income Decile (vertical distribution), 1987

Income deciles (all individuals)	Pensioners	Pensioners living in pensioner households	Persons aged 60+	Total population
Lowest	14.9	23.5	19.5	10.0
2	14.4	19.4	16.4	10.0
3	11.4	12.7	12.0	10.0
4	11.1	11.6	10.9	10.0
5	9.8	8.6	9.0	10.0
6	9.1	6.1	8.2	10.0
7	8.5	6.2	7.4	10.0
8	8.2	4.7	6.6	10.0
9	7.0	4.1	5.4	10.0
Highest	5.7	3.1	4.6	10.0
All	20.5	11.0	18.4	100
N=	11578	6208	10383	56435

Table 2.7b: Distribution of Persons by Income Decile (vertical distribution), 1992

Income deciles (all individuals)	Pensioners	Pensioners living in pensioner households	Persons aged 60+	Total population
Lowest	9.2	11.3	10.9	10.0
2	15.3	19.2	16.6	10.0
3	15.5	18.6	16.0	10.0
4	12.7	13.7	12.1	10.0
5	13.1	14.1	13.3	10.0
6	8.5	6.5	8.0	10.0
7	7.6	5.2	6.8	10.0
8	6.9	4.9	5.7	10.0
9	6.3	4.0	5.1	10.0
Highest	4.9	2.3	5.5	10.0
All	23.4	16.9	21.4	100
N=	1296	938	1186	5539

Table 2.7c: Distribution of Persons by Income Decile (vertical distribution), 1996

Income deciles (all individuals)	Pensioners	Pensioners living in pensioner households	Persons aged 60+	Total population
Lowest	3.8	4.0	3.7	10.0
2	7.3	8.4	7.3	10.0
3	9.6	10.5	10.1	10.0
4	16.1	20.0	17.2	10.0
5	14.0	16.0	15.5	10.0
6	14.3	15.5	14.1	10.0
7	11.1	9.1	11.1	10.0
8	8.8	5.9	8.0	10.0
9	8.0	5.5	7.7	10.0
Highest	7.0	5.1	5.1	10.0
All	25.6	18.3	19.6	100
N=	1253	899	962	4901

67

2.4.2 Basic Trends in the Material Well-Being of Households

Before we analyse household income distribution, it is important to examine how much the size and composition of the households in which pensioners live have changed during the period 1987-1996. On the basis of the macro data presented in section 2.2, the number of pensioners grew 25-30%. In 1996, the proportion of pensioners has reached 25.6%. It should be kept in mind, however, that in the three samples mentioned above, only those over 50 are considered pensioners.

Although the number of pensioners has significantly changed, there was no significant change in the size of households in which pensioners lived. Almost half of them lived in two-person households, one fifth lived in single households, and 15-17% in three-person households. Others lived in larger households. To test the hypothesis outlined in the first section, we considered the types of households shown in Figure 2.1.

During the period surveyed there was a slight change in the composition of pensioner households, namely an increase in the proportion of both single female pensioner households and pensioner couple households. The proportion of pensioner households consisting of pensioners living together with other inactive persons and dependants has also grown, whereas the proportion of households of pensioners and active earners living together has decreased.

Figure 2.1: The Typology of Households where Pensioners Live

General	Specific
Pensioner households	• female pensioner living alone
	• male pensioner living alone
	• pensioner couple[15]
	• pensioner and other inactive or dependant household members
Non-pensioner households	• pensioner and economically active household members
	• other households without pensioners

The income position of *pensioner* and *non-pensioner* households is considered in columns six and nine of Tables 2.8a-c. Characteristics and changes in the well-being of individuals, identified earlier, can be observed for households as well. At the end of the 1980s, more than four tenth of pensioner households were located in the lowest two deciles, whereas one decade later it was only two tenth of them, as shown in Tables 2.8a and 2.8c. Over the past ten years, the concentration of pensioner households moved from the lower end towards the lower-middle section of the income distribution. Changes in the income position of non-pensioner households went in the opposite direction. Although they were overrepresented in the top income deciles in all of the three years observed, the situation has changed considerably in the lowest income deciles. In 1987, the representation of non-pensioner households among the poorest was far below the average, whereas ten years later they are overrepresented in the lowest income decile.

The welfare situation of *female pensioners living alone* was rather critical throughout the period surveyed. In 1987, more than half of them belonged to the lower two deciles, and ten years later, a little more than one fourth, as shown in columns 2 of Tables 2.8a-c. This follows the general trend among pensioners. There is only one type of pensioner household whose position has not improved over the period surveyed. The relative position of *pen-*

sioners living together with other inactive people and/or dependants deteriorated in 1992, as compared to their situation five years earlier. Their position then improved slightly over the next four years, as shown in column 5 of Table 2.8c. This curious trend has left people living in this type of household in a worse situation than that of female pensioners living alone. As far as households without active earners are concerned, it is the *pensioner couples* who are in the relatively best situation, as shown in columns 4 of Tables 2.8a-c.[16] In 1996, only a little more than one tenth of the couples was found in the lowest three deciles. Ten years earlier, 45% of pensioner couples belonged to the lowest three deciles. By the mid-1990s couples were strongly concentrated in the middle position of the income distribution. Column 3 of Table 2.8c shows that more than one-third of them can be found in the fifth and sixth deciles. Those pensioners who lived in households with at least one economically active person were clearly located in the upper income distribution levels, as shown by column 6 of Table 2.8c.

Table 2.8a: **Distribution of Different Household Types by Income Decile (vertical distribution), 1987**

Income deciles	Type of pensioner household					Type of non-pens. hh.		
	Single female	Single male	Couple	Other	All	With pens.	Without pens.	All
Lowest	33.8	16.7	15.5	20.1	23.7	4.1	6.3	5.6
2	21.8	20.0	16.5	22.3	19.6	7.2	6.8	6.9
3	14.6	13.5	13.7	18.6	14.5	9.0	8.3	8.5
4	10.7	10.8	12.5	11.4	11.5	10.9	8.9	9.5
5	6.2	9.8	11.4	7.2	8.7	11.3	10.0	10.4
6	4.2	6.9	8.3	7.2	6.4	13.1	10.3	11.2
7	2.7	6.3	7.7	5.7	5.3	12.0	11.3	11.5
8	2.5	5.5	5.8	3.5	4.2	12.5	11.6	11.9
9	1.8	4.9	5.4	2.2	3.5	10.9	12.6	12.1
Highest	1.9	5.5	3.2	1.7	2.8	9.0	13.8	12.3
Total	10.2	2.5	9.6	2.1	24.3	23.2	52.5	75.7
N=	2015	490	1884	412	4768	4552	10302	14854

Table 2.8b: Distribution of Different Household Types by Income Decile (vertical distribution), 1992

Income deciles	Type of pensioner household					Type of non-pens. hh.		
	Single female	Single male	Couple	Other	All	With pens.	Without pens.	All
Lowest	22.6	(6.7)	1.3	31.4	15.4	4.0	8.1	7.2
2	26.3	(21.3)	9.3	15.8	17.7	3.5	6.9	6.2
3	23.4	(11.1)	15.0	13.4	17.2	5.1	6.7	6.4
4	8.5	(16.2)	18.6	9.2	12.9	10.0	8.1	8.5
5	6.6	(9.2)	17.6	9.8	11.4	11.9	8.5	9.3
6	6.2	(8.3)	14.7	5.9	9.0	10.9	10.4	10.5
7	1.7	(5.7)	8.7	3.2	4.9	14.5	12.1	12.6
8	2.4	(6.7)	7.6	3.5	4.9	14.6	12.0	12.6
9	1.0	(8.9)	5.7	3.8	4.0	12.8	13.1	13.0
Highest	2.1	(6.0)	1.5	4.8	2.7	12.8	14.0	13.7
Total	11.6	3.2	11.9	7.0	33.7	15.0	51.3	66.2
N=	231	63	236	139	670	298	1020	1318

Table 2.8c: Distribution of Different Household Types by Income Decile (vertical distribution), 1996

Income deciles	Type of pensioner household					Type of non-pens. hh.		
	Single female	Single male	Couple	Other	All	With pens.	Without pens.	All
Lowest	7.8	0	0.5	19.6	6.4	4.9	14.4	11.9
2	19.4	(4.0)	4.2	24.4	13.1	4.6	9.6	8.3
3	18.7	(6.9)	9.7	16.0	13.8	7.0	8.2	7.9
4	22.3	(19.6)	13.4	7.9	16.1	7.1	6.5	6.7
5	11.7	(14.2)	18.1	8.3	13.8	0.0	7.8	7.9
6	7.1	(15.3)	18.5	8.0	12.3	11.3	7.8	8.7
7	6.4	(11.8)	13.2	6.4	9.5	14.2	9.1	10.4
8	2.5	(5.7)	9.1	4.0	5.6	16.9	10.8	12.4
9	2.4	(13.0)	8.1	1.0	5.3	13.7	12.4	12.7
Highest	1.8	(9.6)	5.1	4.5	4.2	12.2	13.5	13.1
Total	12.7	3.1	13.7	6.2	35.7	16.5	47.6	64.1
N=	223	54	240	109	625	289	834	1123

Although the trend of the improving relative well-being of pensioners is similar for each type of household, different household types rather strongly differentiate the group of pensioners. It is unclear, however, whether these results would persist if other variables (such as age, occupational status before retirement, etc.) were also included in the analysis. The influence of the household context will be analysed in more depth in section 2.5.

To conclude the overview of basic trends in inequalities among pensioners, changes in poverty rates are analysed, using relative income measures.[17] Table 2.9 shows four poverty thresholds defined as percentages of the median income, to identify the different 'grades' of poverty.

Table 2.9: Poverty Rates by Social Group, Using Different Poverty Thresholds; 1987, 1992 and 1996

Poverty threshold	Total population	All pensioners	Pensioners in pensioner households	Persons aged 60+
1987				
40% of median	1.2	1.1	1.8	1.6
50% of median	3.9	5.1	8.3	7.0
60% of median	8.8	13.2	20.9	17.2
70% of median	16.4	24.2	36.3	30.3
1992				
40% of median	2.3	1.1	1.4	1.0
50% of median	5.0	5.3	4.4	3.6
60% of median	10.4	9.8	12.0	11.6
70% of median	17.8	20.2	25.5	21.4
1996				
40% of median	3,9	1.1	1.1	1.0
50% of median	8.3	2.3	2.2	2.0
60% of median	14.7	6.2	6.6	6.5
70% of median	22.3	13.6	15.7	14.3

Source: CSO, 1987, HHP. Waves 1 and 5, author's calculations.

The table shows that during the ten years under review the proportion of poor among the total population has vigorously increased as measured by all poverty thresholds (Table 2.9). Growth had been significant between 1987 and 1992, and this trend accelerated in the early and mid-1990s. *Contrary to the trend for the total population,* poverty declined for both pensioners and the elderly. While in the late 1980s, poverty was a problem of pensioners and the elderly, ten years later, pensioners were far underrepresented at all poverty threshold levels. Thus poverty is not a problem of pensioners anymore, and income poverty is not the most significant problem that pensioners face.

2.4.3 What is Behind the Relative Improvement of the Situation of Pensioners?

There are several factors behind the relative improvement in the income position of pensioners. One of the most important factors is that, although pensions were unable to preserve their real value, they have more or less kept up their relative position as compared to average wages. Average pensions amounted to about 60% of the average wage during the entire 10-year period. In 1990 it was even more generous. In other words, *pensions have not deteriorated when compared to earnings.* The composition of pensioners' income clearly suggests that pensions as a source of income play a central and increasingly important role in determining pensioners' financial situation, as shown by Tables 2.10a-c. While pensions accounted for 70% of the income of pensioner households in 1987, this proportion had grown to 80% by 1996 (Table 2.10c). This is one of the most significant changes.

All this, of course, and if all other conditions remain unchanged, only explains why the situation of pensioners has not deteriorated further. A reason for the relative improvement in the pensioners' standard of living is that many working-age individuals left the labour market (or never entered it). These persons who do not have an income from work live mostly in active (non-pensioner) households. This is partly manifested in Tables 2.10a-c, which present the income composition of non-pensioner households. In 1987, income from work accounted for 70% of their total income, by 1992 this share had declined to 55%, and at the end of the period surveyed it was 61%. There is more or less reliable information about some other factors as well. For instance, it is known that the level of unemployment benefits decreased between 1992 and 1996. In 1992, it was 68% of the net average wage, while in 1996 it was only 53% (Laky, 1998: 62, 85). This had a clear impact on non-pensioner households. Similar conclusions may be drawn from the data of the Social Policy Databank of TÁRKI (TÁRKI, 1998, Supplement I/Table 6). Moreover, information is available on the changes in various other social benefits. Family allowance has lost most of its value as compared to other social benefits. In 1996, its real value was equal to only 40% of its 1990 value (Supplement I/Table 6).[18] The most vigorous erosion of these benefits took place in 1995 as a result of the Bokros austerity programme (TÁRKI, 1998). Finally, it should be mentioned that the proportion of earnings in the income of non-pensioner households may have decreased as the result of capital income growth.

Table 2.10a: The Structure of Household Income Sources, 1987*

Income source	All households	Non-pensioner households	Pensioner households
Earnings	63	70	9
Pensions	15	8	69
Social assistance	8	8	2
Other**	14	14	20
All incomes	100	100	100
HUF	14703	17143	7097

Note: * Monthly income.

** Income from part-time agricultural production, capital income, joint household income.

Table 2.10b: The Structure of Household Income Sources, 1992*

Income source	All households	Non-pensioner households	Pensioner households
Earnings	47	55	6
Pensions	18	7	78
Social assistance	11	12	1
Other	24	26	15
All incomes	100	100	100
HUF	346278	435197	167080

Note: * Income of March 1991 to April 1992, i.e. annual income.

73

Table 2.10c: The Structure of Household Income Sources, 1996*

Income source	All households	Non-pensioner households	Pensioner households
Earnings	51	61	7
Pensions	24	10	81
Social assistance	11	13	3
Other	15	16	10
All incomes	100	100	100
HUF	582122	714471	337089

Note: * Income of March 1995 to April 1996, i.e. annual income.

There is yet another factor that played a role in the improvement of the relative income position of pensioners. It is known that young pensioners generally have higher pensions than older pensioners. Therefore, as a result of 'natural replacement', the average pension would grow even if it was not indexed. In addition to this demographic phenomenon, during the period under review, the 'rejuvenation' of the average pensioner was promoted also by retirement caused by the transformation process (Tables 2.11a-c). Despite the fact that pensioners who retired earlier than the age limit (pre-retirement, early retirement, disability pensioners) did not receive a full pension, their pension is still likely to be higher than that of deceased pensioners. Hence, this has also contributed to the improvement of the relative well-being of pensioners.

Summing up, it may be stated that it is the relative stability of the value of pensions, the 'rejuvenation' of pensioners, the easing of the negative consequences of the labour market on pensioner households and the decrease in the value of family benefits that are behind the improvement of the relative financial and welfare situation of pensioners.

Table 2.11a: **Distribution of Persons in Different Age Groups by Income Decile (vertical distribution), 1987**

Income deciles (all individuals)	Age groups		
	60-69	70-79	80+
Lowest	11.0	24.6	27.9
2	13.9	18.5	19.0
3	11.5	13.3	11.5
4	12.3	10.8	8.2
5	11.2	7.3	7.6
6	9.3	7.6	7.2
7	9.4	6.0	6.2
8	8.5	5.1	5.5
9	7.3	3.4	4.3
Highest	5.7	3.4	2.6
Total	100	100	100
N=	5139	2810	1068

Table 2.11b: **Distribution of Persons in Different Age Groups by Income Decile (vertical distribution), 1992**

Income deciles (all individuals)	Age groups		
	60-69	70-79	80+
Lowest	9.2	10.7	17.4
2	13.8	19.7	21.0
3	14.5	21.1	11.9
4	11.0	13.9	12.7
5	16.8	8.8	9.5
6	9.2	6.1	7.1
7	8.0	4.8	6.1
8	6.3	4.6	5.7
9	5.5	5.0	4.0
Highest	5.9	5.2	4.4
Total	100	100	100
N=	654	347	185

Table 2.11c: Distribution of Persons in Different Age Groups by Income Decile (vertical distribution), 1996

Income deciles (all individuals)	Age groups		
	60-69	70-79	80+
Lowest	2.7	3.4	5.9
2	7.4	5.5	7.3
3	7.3	11.5	15.2
4	16.8	18.3	17.1
5	15.4	16.4	14.5
6	15.6	15.1	10.9
7	11.4	9.2	15.0
8	9.1	8.5	4.9
9	8.3	7.7	5.9
Highest	6.0	4.6	3.2
Total	100	100	100
N=	479	321	115

2.5 Factors Differentiating the Society of Pensioners

In the introduction, reference was made to those processes and structural interrelationships that point towards the internal differentiation among pensioners. This section will examine the various hypotheses suggested by the analysis thus far. It has been shown that the type of household strongly influences the financial situation of pensioners; this leads to the question of whether or not the other factors mentioned earlier – such as one's career in the labour market before retirement, gender, age, or type of settlement – also have an effect.

In order to answer these questions, a simple model was used, and the effects of each of the five predictors (*type of household, occupational status before retirement, education, gender, type of settlement*) were evaluated separately using (a) equivalent income and (b) individual income as the dependent variables. The best indicator of the material well-being of individuals, and hence of pensioners, is *equivalent income*, whereas *individual income* expresses the individual's past and present ability to earn an income.

2.5.1 Bivariate Analysis

The relationship between income and the five stated predictors was analysed using the technique of Multiple Classification Analysis (subsequently:
MCA, Andrews et al., 1973). MCA is similar to multiple regression analysis
using dummy variables, and also similar to the analysis of variance; the interpretation of the results is somewhat simpler.

Tables 2.12 to 2.16 show the effect of each predictor on the dependent
variables, starting with *type of household.* The dependent variables are individual income and equivalent income; it is shown that in 1992 the majority
of factors (i.e. predictors) had no influence on individual incomes, and only
in some instances on the economic well-being of pensioners (equivalent income). Four years later, in 1996, almost every factor (predictor) showed visibly significant effects on equivalent income(s). This all suggests that, as a
result of the effects of transition, pensioners *were strongly differentiated* during the period under review with respect to income indicators. The effects
of the individual factors are considered in greater detail in the following.

In 1992, the well-being of pensioners was significantly influenced by
the type of the pensioner household, as shown in Table 2.12. The effects seem to
have been stronger in 1996, and have partly changed since then. Female pensioners living alone had the worst economic situation during the entire
period surveyed. The situation of pensioners living together with other inactive individuals was also considerably below the average.[19] The situation
of a male pensioner living alone was similar to the average well-being of all
pensioners. This is also the case of pensioner couples. Pensioners with the
highest level of well-being were those who lived together with active
earner(s) (Table 2.12). It seems understandable that the type of household
does not show any significant influence on individual income.

Table 2.13 shows that the *occupational status before retirement*[20] decisively
determines individual income after retirement, and – though with slightly
less strength and in a milder form – also the material well-being of the individuals (i.e. equivalent income). Those who belonged to the white collar stratum before retirement, and in particular former managers and intellectuals,
are found considerably above the average. It is rather difficult to judge the
situation of the self-employed because of the small number of cases, but it
should be borne in mind that there is a large proportion among them who
worked 'privately' under very unfavourable conditions during socialism.
The income position and the well-being of pensioners who were skilled

Table 2.12: Average Income of Pensioners, by Type of Household, as Percentage of Average Income of All Pensioners, 1992 and 1996

Type of Household	1992		1996	
	Individual income	Equivalent income	Individual income	Equivalent income
Female living alone	95.0	78.4	93.1	79.1
Male living alone	100.6	96.3	125.2	105.9
Two (and more) pensioners	92.0	90.9	99.7	101.4
Pensioner with other inactive person	98.9	83.1	99.1	83.7
Pensioner with active person	113.9	134.6	101.2	116.4
Average (%)	100	100	100	100
(Ft)*	109981	141916	211909	264106
N=	1315	1296	1305	1253
eta	NS**	0.19	0.11	0.30

Notes:
    *   Due to different sample sizes, the average is not the same in all tables.
    **   NS = the relationship is not significant.
    eta^2 in the case of only one predictor represents the ratio between (a) the sum of squares explained by the predictor (and is identical to the between-group sum of squares in the one-way-analysis of variance) and (b) the total sum of squares.

Table 2.13: Average Income of Pensioners, by Occupational Status before Retirement, as Percentage of Average Income of All Pensioners, 1996

Last job	Individual income	Equivalent income
Manager	163.5**	147.8**
Intellectuals	153.9**	129.2**
Routine non-physical	110.6	114.4
Lower manager + foreman	122.7*	109.6*
Self-employed	98.90**	106.7**
Skilled worker	107.3	102.0
Semi-skilled and unskilled worker	84.3	88.9
Peasant/ Agricultural worker	84.1	89.3
Average (%)	100.0	100.0
(Ft)	206703	254017
N=	980	828
eta	0.48	0.37

Notes:
    *   Number of elements below 100.
    **   Number of elements below 50.
    eta^2:   see explanation in Table 2.12.

workers in their active life are somewhat above the average, whereas the semi-skilled and unskilled workers occupy the lower positions in pensioner stratification. Peasants and agricultural workers are also more likely to be found among those who are in an unfavourable welfare situation after retirement. The education variable is often used as a proxy for the occupational status before retirement. For 1996, this variable indeed tends to show the same pattern as occupational status, whereas in 1992 the strength of the relationship was not as strong as four years later. Those with higher educational status had much higher individual incomes and a privileged economic welfare position (equivalent income).

Table 2.14: **Average Income of Pensioners, by Education, as Percentage of Average Income of All Pensioners, 1992 and 1996**

Type of Household	1992		1996	
	Individual income	Equivalent income	Individual income	Equivalent income
Less than 8 primary	91.0	92.7	85.0	83.7
8 primary classes	85.8	92.7	86.4	94.0
Lower vocational	102.6	95.4	107.5	104.3
Secondary	128.9	118.3	128.7	126.1
Higher	149.2	127.2	175.9	153.3
Average (%)	100	100	100	100
(Ft)	109981	141916	211909	264106
N=	1315	1296	1305	1253
eta	NS	0.12	0.48	0.43

Note: NS = the relationship is not significant; eta^2: see explanation in Table 2.12

Poverty among *women*, and elderly women in particular, is often stressed in the literature as the 'feminization of poverty' (cf. Glendiding and Millar, 1992). Earlier analyses reached the conclusion that there is practically no gender difference with respect to poverty risks (Spéder, 1997). However, an interesting question is if the same interrelationship exists when studying not only the poor, but the entire population, and the pensioners within it? As far as individual income is concerned, women have a significantly lower income than men, and from 1992 to 1996 this interrelationship became significantly stronger. At the same time, with respect to welfare (i.e. equivalent income), there was a rather weak interrelationship in 1996, and there was no connection whatsoever between the average welfare situation and gender in 1992 (Table 2.15).

Table 2.15: Average Income of Pensioners, by Gender, as Percentage of Average Income of All Pensioners, 1992 and 1996

Type of Household	1992		1996	
	Individual income	Equivalent income	Individual income	Equivalent income
Female	85.6	98.0	88.0	96.8
Male	120.7	102.8	119.7	105.3
Average (%)	100	100	100	100
(Ft)	109981	141916	211909	264106
N=	1315	1296	1305	1253
eta	NS	NS	0.29	0.09

Note: NS = the relationship is not significant; eta^2: see explanation in Table 2.12

Table 2.16: Average Income of Pensioners, by Type of Settlement, as Percentage of Average Income of All Pensioners, 1992 and 1996

Type of Household	1992		1996	
	Individual income	Equivalent income	Individual income	Equivalent income
Village	83.4	90.2	86.4	90.9
Town	90.5	92.4	96.5	93.4
County capitals	149.3	130.3	105.1	101.2
Budapest	117.8	112.4	131.7	103.7
Average (%)	100	100	100	100
(Ft)	109981	141916	211909	264106
N=	1315	1296	1305	1253
eta	0.11	0.12	0.32	0.33

Note: eta^2: see explanation in Table 2.12

Finally, as regards the factor (predictor) of *settlement*, its effect gained strength in the 1990s, as has also been shown by other studies. In 1992, the place of residence did not differentiate pensioners, whereas in 1996 the income and

welfare situation of pensioners varied significantly across the various settlements, as shown in Table 2.16. This effect corresponds to the hierarchies
of settlements. Income and material well-being are the lowest in villages and
the highest in Budapest.

2.5.2 *Factors of Differentiation of Pensioners – A Multiple Classification Analysis (MCA)*

After having individually surveyed the factors which might influence the
two chosen dependent variables, an interesting question arises as to whether
the effects studied above would also occur in a multivariate analysis; again,
we use the Multiple Classification Analysis (Andrews et al., 1973) to explore
the relationship between the dependent variable(s) and all of the predictors.
This method provides the *eta* statistics produced in the previous bivariate
analysis; these statistics are appropriate for assessing the simple bivariate
relationship between the predictor and dependent variable. The column of
unadjusted deviations from the mean shows the effect of each predictor on
the dependent variable, before taking into account the effects of all the other
variables (predictors). The *betas* in the last column of Figure 2.2 show the
effect of each predictor, once the impact of the other predictors is controlled
for. The *betas* can be compared to each other: the higher the beta the stronger
the effects.[21] They differ in value from the *etas* because predictors correlate
among themselves. If predictors did not correlate among themselves, the
betas and *etas* would be the same. The column of adjusted deviations takes
into account this interrelationship among the predictors.

    The following section shows the results of the MCA in which the three
most important predictors – the type of household, the occupational status
before retirement and the type of pensioner's settlement – can be compared.

    On the basis of the results shown in Figure 2.2, it may be stated that
the *pensioner household type* still has an impact on the welfare position in a
multivariate model. The pensioners in the worst position are pensioners who
live together with other inactive persons, and women living alone. Their
well-being, measured in equivalent incomes, was considerably lower than
the average equivalent income of pensioners (which was some HUF 264
thousand). Men living alone were also found to be in a disadvantaged position. The situation of pensioner couples is close to average while those
pensioners who live in households with an active earner were in the best

situation. They had an income higher by HUF 56 thousand than the average in 1996 (Figure 2.2).

As seen from Figure 2.2, the strongest factor was found to be the *occupational status before retirement*. Pensioners who were in an advantageous position earlier, or who were intellectuals, have an equivalent income much above the average. The situation of lower level management and clerical workers was above average among the pensioners. The situation of skilled workers was around the average, while semi-skilled and unskilled workers were found to be in the worst situations. Thus the MCA has not modified the interrelationships shown in the bivariate analysis, but allowed measuring the strength of the influencing mechanisms. With respect to this factor (predictor), doubts justly emerge, as it was mentioned previously that approximate data was used whereas the number of missing values cannot be disregarded either. Therefore, it is worth studying a model where the occupational status before retirement was substituted for education; this is presented in Figure 2.3. The interrelationships continue to exist: education has the strongest effect, as measured by the *betas*, followed by the type of household, and finally, the type of settlement.

There is no good explanation for the persistence of the *type of settlement* when the factors mentioned above are controlled for. It might be that in Budapest it is possible to receive a greater remuneration for the same work than in the countryside, and its effect plays a role when the pension is calculated. Further, it is possible that residents of the capital may have a longer career in the labour market; also, in the capital there are greater opportunities to access supplementary incomes. However, these are only suppositions not confirmed by the data. But the result fits well into the observation according to which *the possibilities of life have been vigorously differentiated both regionally, as well as by types of settlement after the systemic change* (Andorka and Spéder, 1996).

The question may also arise as to whether there are any *significant joint effects* of the pairs of predictors. This was investigated only in the model containing education, because the number of missing values was too high in the first model; however, none of the pairs of predictors had a significant influence on the independent variable.

During the course of the analysis, *several different models* were tested. The *type of pension* showed a significant effect in addition to the factors mentioned above, together with the gender of the pensioner; however, the explanatory power of the model did not improve. Also investigated was the effect of *age* (unfortunately the date of retirement was not available), but no significant effect was found. Models were also established using individual income as the dependent variable. It is here that the gender effect is reflected, while the type of household has no significant influence.

In conclusion, it may be stated that the society of pensioners is decisively influenced by three factors. The most important is the *occupational status before retirement*, which was further strengthened by systemic change. Differences emerging during the period of employment do not disappear after retirement. *With whom the pensioner lives* also has a very strong effect, suggesting that households may 'reshape' the sources of well-being defined by the individual's resources. In other words, the events taking place at the end of the family cycle (becoming a widow, remarrying, or moving in together) and patterns of coexistence of generations (living together with adult children, moving back in with children) may be considered as very important factors of stratification. Therefore, pensioners who remain alone, or live together with individuals who have been crowded out of the labour market, are likely to find themselves in below-average welfare positions. The third differentiating factor is *settlement*. The dividing line is between Budapest and the 'countryside' (cf. Sík, 1996), which may be due to some of the reasons discussed above.

Figure 2.2: The Analysis of Pensioners' Economic Well-Being, in Hungary, in 1996 – MCA-Model* (Occupational Status before Retirement)

* * * M U L T I P L E   C L A S S I F I C A T I O N   A N A L Y S I S * * *

	EQJ5L	Equivalent income
by	TEL5TIP	Type of settlement
	TIP5D2	Household type
	NYU96R	Occupational status before retirement

Grand Mean = 264017,03

Variable + Category	N	Unadjusted Dev'n	Eta	Adjusted for Independents Dev'n	Beta
TEL5TIP					
1 Village	355	-21413,87		-13430,22	
2 Smaller town	245	-8466,73		-11305,16	
3 County capital	90	2348,59		1159,58	
4 Budapest	139	68207,76		53577,95	
			.28		.22
TIP5D2					
1 Single female pensioner	105	-44728,34		-49874,82	
2 Single male pensioner	31	4026,06		-13125,49	
3 Pensioner couple	344	-959,52		-4747,87	
4 Pensioner+other inactive	98	-30442,09		-17120,79	
5 Pensioner+active	250	31443,51		35707,49	
			.23		.24
NYU96R					
1 Manager	43	126221,05		111126,61	
2 Intellectual	35	77090,79		60618,36	
3 Clerical worker	92	38146,36		27304,33	
4 Lower supervisor	51	25453,95		20492,75	
5 Self-employed	10	17789,86		40884,83	
6 Skilled worker	126	5519,87		-3190,12	
7 Semi-skilled worker	344	-29388,62		-25306,88	
8 Peasant	128	-28134,59		-13102,28	
			.37		.31

Multiple R Squared	.227
Multiple R	.476

Note: The differences between former etas and those in this figure are because of the different sample sizes.

Figure 2.3: The Analysis of Pensioners' Economic Well-Being, in Hungary, in 1996 – MCA-Model (Level of Education)

MULTIPLE CLASSIFICATION ANALYSIS

	EQJ5L	Equivalent income
by	TEL5TIP	Type of settlement
	TIP5D2	Household type
	ISK5	Level of education

Grand Mean =264106,04

Variable + Category	N	Unadjusted Dev'n	Eta	Adjusted for Independents Dev'n	Beta
TEL5TIP					
1 Village	524	-26315,53		-12966,95	
2 Small town	345	-17282,08		-19062,12	
3 County capital	147	3072,85		-1774,18	
4 Budapest	237	81277,44		57386,84	
			.33		.23
TIP5D2					
1 Single female pensioner	223	-55205,08		-52765,56	
2 Single male pensioner	54	15520,31		2080,13	
3 Pensioner couple	489	3771,50		567,62	
4 Pensioner+other inact.	133	-42982,29		-30685,99	
5 Pensioner+active	354	43330,03		43641,08	
			.30		.28
ISK5					
1 less than 8 classes	412	-42899,78		-27811,76	
2 8 classes	435	-15818,89		-17397,64	
3 secondary training	166	11565,52		4383,16	
4 secondary general	157	68992,53		55668,44	
5 tertiary	84	140782,40		113980,07	
			.43		.33

Multiple R Squared	.301
Multiple R	.548

2.6 Some Characteristics of the Living Conditions of Pensioners

Thus far, this study has concentrated on the income situation of pensioners. Naturally, including other features that indicate the living conditions of pensioners would contribute to the explanation of the pensioners' relative situation and how this situation changes over time. It should also be borne in mind that it is probably not very characteristic for the elderly and pensioners to change their way of life, as people are unwilling to change their routines which have evolved over the course of decades. In other words, even if the possibilities are available (e.g. income resources), major investments are rare during pension age.

Comparing living conditions over the course of time is made difficult because there were relatively few indicators of living conditions in the 1987 HIS survey. It is thus not possible to address the issue of whether the improvement of the relative position of pensioners is reflected in changes in their living conditions. The major part of the analysis will therefore concentrate on the differences between pensioners.

While data for 1987 are scarce, the changes are quite impressive; for example, the proportion of those pensioner households who do not have a bathroom decreased by half. Between 1992 and 1996 all the other indicators improved, but that improvement was still much smaller than what could have been expected given the changes in the pensioners' relative income (Table 2.17). To conclude, *the living conditions of pensioners have improved, but the same is true for non-pensioner households. In other words, the relative income advantages of pensioners were not converted into advantages in living conditions.* There may be several explanations as to why this did not occur. Partly, there is the behavioural component mentioned above, namely 'routine'. After many years, an individual may find it difficult to change his or her way of living. It is also possible that the improvements in income were not significant enough to be converted into advantages of wealth. If this is the case, then any improvement in living conditions may be viewed as 'adequate'. It is less probable that the relative improvement of the situation allowed only for the preservation of existing living standards, since in this case there should have been a decline in the living standard among non-pensioner households.

Table 2.17: Living Conditions of Pensioner and Non-pensioner Households in 1987 and 1996

Living Conditions	Pensioner households			Non-pens. households		
	1987	1992	1996	1987	1992	1996
Size of the dwelling (m²)	60	66	71	71	77	79
No bathroom	43.1	26.9	22.0	19.4	11.2	10.5
No WC		33.6	31.8		14.5	13.4
No colour TV		57.2	33.0		30.5	16.5
No expensive goods*		89.8	90.7		74.0	73.3

Note: * They are the following: sewing machine, second car, second house, paintings, alarm on the house.

Table 2.18 shows that no improvement occurred in an indicator of individual life style – namely holidays – or in the case of satisfaction with the living standard. The proportion of pensioners spending money on holidays has slightly decreased. It may be understandable given the changes in the real income, as this is the item of consumption which people most easily give up, or, in case of pressure, are able to give up. It is surprising however, that the proportion of pensioners dissatisfied with their living standard has not decreased, and the proportion of pensioners satisfied has not increased. Perhaps it could be that, when assessing satisfaction by the standard of living, individuals compare themselves to others; however, if this were the only component of satisfaction, then the satisfaction of pensioners should have improved. A possible reason why this was not so may be the fact that individuals compare their present position to their past one, and in this case, the pensioners may have a negative balance. In other words, the pensioners were 'not any happier' because others fared worse.

Table 2.18: Holidays and Satisfaction of Pensioners and Non-pensioners in 1992 and 1996

	Pensioners		Non-pensioners	
	1992	1996	1992	1996
No holiday	87.0	91.4	72.6	76.6
Dissatisfied with the level of living	35.7	35.6	34.2	31.1

Now we turn to assess the impacts of three structuring factors 'elaborated' by the survey of incomes: type of household, last job and type of settlement. In other words, the aim is to see whether these structural factors point to any serious differences among pensioners' living conditions. Once again the 1996 data are analysed.

The indicators of living conditions mostly support the earlier findings. Those who had a favourable *occupational status* at the time of their employment, those who live in *more favourable family conditions* with regard to income, and those who *live in Budapest* tend to have more advantageous living conditions in respect to all the objective indicators: having a bathroom and a WC in their flats, possessing a colour TV set, possessing objects of high value, and going on holidays more often than the average (Tables 2.19-2.21). Individuals that fall under the following categories typically have housing conditions that are much worse than the average pensioner: those who were semi-skilled or unskilled workers at the time of their last employment, peasants, pensioners who live together with other inactive individuals or who live alone, and those who live in rural areas. Many of them lack basic durable goods such as colour TV, and they almost never go on holidays. As regards the objective indicators, former managers and intellectuals[22] live in much better conditions than the average, whereas the semi-skilled and unskilled workers as well as the agricultural labourers live under much worse conditions (Table 2.19). As far as the family context is concerned, there seems to be a strong dividing line: those who live alone or with other inactive person(s) are on the one side of the line, whereas the retired couples, and pensioners living with active individuals are on the other (Table 2.20). The type of settlement also matters (Table 2.21). Living conditions and the subjective perception of well-being by pensioners increase as we move from rural to urban settlements.

The above interrelationships can also be identified using indicators of subjective well-being (for example, a shortage of cash at the end of the month, or satisfaction with living standards), though their strength seems to be weaker. People of a 'lower' occupational status more frequently have liquidity difficulties. As far as the type of settlement is concerned, the effect of the subjective indicators changes; there are less dissatisfied people in small settlements and proportionately fewer pensioners get into financial difficulties regularly at the end of the month. Such results, namely that the subjective indicators of welfare show somewhat different interrelations from those based on objective indicators, are not rare. The exploration of the interrelationships would require a longer study. It is not possible to totally discard the hypothesis that pensioners in villages and towns 'catch up' with their income disadvantages using the household strategy of subsistence economy, and hence they are more satisfied with their living standards and less likely to get into financial difficulties with monthly regularity.

The indicators of living conditions corroborate and the indicators of subjective welfare somewhat weaken the results obtained during the course of the income analysis. The effects of family type and of the occupational status before retirement are confirmed with respect to all the indicators, whereas the effect of the type of settlement changes direction in the case of the subjective indicators.

Table 2.19: **Living Conditions and the Subjective Well-Being of Pensioners by Occupational Status before Retirement, 1996**

Occupational status	No WC in the flat	No bathroom	No colour TV	Frequent shortage of money	Dissatisfied with living standards	Went on holidays	Has valuable property
Top leader	7.3	7.3	0	20.2	27.0	19.7	37.4
Intellectual	0	0	9.9	15.6	22.0	12.5	35.1
Office worker	9.0	1.0	11.5	23.9	36.7	13.3	17.0
Lower leader + foreman	18.6	13.0	9.5	23.2	27.7	11.6	6.9
Skilled worker	15.9	10.1	22.1	31.6	43.7	8.0	22.2
Semi-skilled worker	31.6	20.2	27.9	33.5	40.4	5.1	14.3
Peasant	42.2	21.3	39.0	24.3	36.8	0.8	11.6
Total	25.5	15.0	23.3	28.5	37.7	7.3	17.1

Table 2.20: **Living Conditions and the Subjective Well-Being of Pensioners by Household Type, 1996**

Household type	No WC in the flat	No bathroom	No colour TV	Frequent shortage of money	Dissatisfied with living standards	Went on holidays	Has valuable property
Single female pensioner	35.2	29.0	40.9	25.7	47.5	5.5	6.7
Single male pensioner	39.8	24.1	33.3	16.2	25.7	2.9	8.2
Pensioner couple	27.2	14.9	24.7	20.2	34.2	6.8	15.2
Pens. with other inactive	41.9	31.0	41.6	48.7	48.6	3.8	12.4
Pensioner with active	17.2	10.7	12.9	25.8	31.3	15.8	27.4
Total	27.9	18.4	26.1	26.5	37.1	8.8	16.5

Table 2.21: Living Conditions and the Subjective Well-Being of Pensioners
by Type of Residence, 1996

Residence type	No WC in the flat	No bathroom	No colour TV	Frequent shortage of money*	Dissatisfied with living standards	Went on holidays	Has valuable property
Rural	38.2	25.6	35.6	28.9	36.4	5.4	14.1
Town	24.4	13.3	25.9	28.7	32.5	5.6	16.1
County capitals	11.2	9.6	18.1	15.1	38.5	11.3	15.3
Budapest	8.4	8.4	9.1	24.5	44.4	19.7	23.4
Total	27.9	18.4	26.1	26.5	37.1	8.8	16.5

Note: * "Never" recurrently: 28.9; 40.4;53.9; 44.5.

2.7 Summary: Getting Better and Becoming Dissimilar

As a result of transition, the number of employees was reduced and the proportion of pensioners, unemployed and other inactive and dependant persons has grown. This study has focused on the situation of pensioners. Their economic situation continuously improved in the period under review. They are now much more concentrated around the middle rather than at the bottom of the income distribution, as was the case in 1987. At the same time, a process of differentiation has also taken place. More precisely, a differentiated society of pensioners exists at the end of the period under review (in 1996). The most important differentiating factors among pensioners are the nature of co-habitation (household type), the legacy of their occupational career (occupational status before retirement) and the type of settlement. In other words, there is no homogeneous group of pensioners, but a society of pensioners unambiguously differentiated. The results of the analysis of living conditions, using a small number of indicators, should be interpreted with care. In absolute terms, there was an improvement in living conditions of pensioners; however their relative position is not better than before.

Notes

1   It should be noted that a small portion of inactive income recipients do have a job, as well. Taking this into consideration, the proportion of the employed increased from 34.2 to 35.0% in 1996 (KSH, 1997: 22).

2   Inflation was generally high during the period covered by this study.

3   The presentation of the pension insurance system is based on ONYF (1997).

4   It is not our objective to give a comprehensive description of the institutional and organizational transformation of the pension system, but to present the major characteristics that affect changes in the well-being of pensioners.

5   In the case of certain dangerous occupations (e.g. armed forces), it was possible to retire even earlier.

6   This is to be phased-in by 2010.

7   Unfortunately, as a result of the change in the financing of pensions and registration of pensioners, there are no consistent data series that include every type of pension over the entire period. It should also be noted that the data from various sources (Central Statistical Office and National Directorate of Pension Insurance) differ and are continuously changing (cf. ONYF, 1997; Nyitrainé, 1997; Laky, 1998). Nevertheless, the data included may still adequately reflect the scale and dynamics of change.

8   It is difficult to say to what degree the individual cases of disability retirement were justified by health reasons. While the number of disability pensioners has grown visibly, at the same time it is known that the health status of people is relatively poor in Hungary, as indicated by the mortality rates. The moral consequences of such a practice, i.e. the utilization of an existing institution for a purpose not in line with its function, are not discussed here.

9   For instance, provisions for orphans were not considered.

10   For those who are interested in this topic, see ONYF.

11   The relevant analysis can be found in ONYF, 8.ff.

12   For a more in-depth discussion see Tóth, 1995.

13   Naturally, there are always exceptions, e.g. Kolosi and Róbert (1992).

14   It should be noted that the distribution of the two deciles unambiguously corresponds, i.e. individuals are located in the same decile in both distributions.

15   A small number of households containing three pensioners were also classified under this heading.

16   It could be the case that the situation of male pensioners living alone is in fact even better, but due to small sample sizes it is not possible to draw well-founded conclusions.

17   For a discussion of the concepts of poverty see, for example, Andorka and Spéder (1996).

18   According to the TÁRKI data bank, the real net average wage decreased by 24% during the same period (TÁRKI, 1998: 60.)

19   Average here always means the average of pensioners' income situation and the average of the whole population.

20   The Hungarian Household Panel contains the occupational status before retirement for people who retired after 1992, but no such data are available for those who retired before 1991. Because of this, we studied the effect of the strata only using the 1996 data. For the sake of avoiding mistaken conclusions because of the data deficiency, we used the variable *education* (which is available for almost all pensioners) in addition to the occu-

pational status before retirement as a kind of proxy variable. The relationship between the two variables is very strong (Cramer's V = 0.4). Thus, if our interrelationships point towards the same direction of both variables and are of nearly the same strength, then our findings concerning the last job may be extended over the entire sample.

21   The *etas* show the effect of the individual variables for a bivariate case. These have already been presented and interpreted during the dispersion analysis.

22   And also the self-employed, though the sample sizes are rather small.

References

Andorka, R./Ferge, Zs./Tóth, I.Gy. (1997) 'Valóban Magyarországon a legkisebbek a jövedelmi egyenlőtlenségek?', *Közgazdasági Szemle*, no. 2: 90-112.

Andorka, R./Spéder, Zs. (1996) 'Poverty in Hungary', *Review of Sociology*, Special Issue, 3-28.

Andrews, F./Morgan, J.N./Sonquist, J./Klem, L. (1973) *Multiple Classification Analysis*, second edition. Michigan: Institute for Social Research, University of Michigan.

Atkinson, A.B. (1989) *Poverty and Social Security*. Hempstead: Harvester.

Balcerowicz, L. (1996) *Socialism, Capitalism, Transformation*. Budapest: Central European University Press.

Berger, R., *Multiple Klassifikationsanalyse, Sonderforschungsbereich 3, Mikroanalytische Grundlagen der Geselschaftspolitik*. Frankfurt and Mannheim: J.W. Goethe Universität Frankfurt and Universität Mannheim.

Bokor, Á. (1985) *Depriváció és szegénység*. Budapest: Társadalomtudományi Intézet.

Coulter, P.B. (1989) *Measuring Inequality: A Methodological Handbook*. Boulder: Westview.

Czibulka, Z./Lakatos, M. (1994) 'Az időskorúak életkörülményei és egészségi állapota', *Statisztikai Szemle*, vol. 74, no. 2: 143-165.

Flemming, J./Micklewright, J. (1997) 'Income Distribution, Economic System and Transition', paper presented at the conference "Inequality and Poverty in Transition Economics". London: EBRD.

Förster, M./Tóth, I.Gy. (1997) *Szegénység és egyenlőtlenségek Magyarországon és a többi visegrádi országban*. Budapest: TÁRKI Társadalompolitikai Tanulmányok.

Glendiding, C./Millar, I. (eds.) (1992) *Women and Poverty in Britain the 1990s*. London: Harvester.

Kolosi, T./Róbert, P. (1992) 'Munkaerőpiac és jövedelmek', pp. 8-24 in Andorka, R. et al. (eds.), *Társadalmi Riport 1992*. Budapest: TÁRKI.

Kolosi, T./Szívós, P./Bedekovics, I./Tóth, I.J. (1996) 'Munkaerőpiac és jövedelmek', pp. 7-27 in Sík, E./Tóth, I.Gy. (eds.), *Társadalmi páternoszter. Jelentés a Magyar Háztartás Panel V. hullámának eredményeiről*. Budapest: Department of Sociology, Budapest University of Economics and TÁRKI.

Kornai, J. (1992) 'Transformational Recession. A General Phenomenon Examined through the Example of Hungary's Development'. Collegium Budapest Institute of Advanced Study Discussion Paper Series No. 1, Budapest.

KSH (1997) *A foglakoztatás alakulása 1980-1996*, Mikrocensus 1996, Budapest.

Laky, T. (1998) *Main Trends in Labour Demands and Supply*. Budapest: Labour Research Institute.

Nelson, J. (1998) 'The Politics of Pension and Health Care Delivery Reforms in Hungary and Poland', Collegium Budapest, Institute of Advanced Study, Working Paper Series 56, Budapest.

Nyitrainé, F. (1997) *A nyugdíjasok helyzete.* Budapest: KSH.

ONYF (1997) *A nyugdíjkiadások alakulása és a nyugdíjrendszer változása a kilencbvenes években.* Budapest: Országos Nyugdjbiztosítási Főigazgatóság.

Parker, J.L./Smeeding, T.B./Torrey, T. (1988) *The Vulnerables.* Washington D.C.: The Urban Institute Press.

Ruggles, P. (1994) *Drawing the Line.* Washington D.C.: The Urban Institute Press.

Rendtel, U./Wagner, G. (eds.), (1991) *Lebenslagen im Wandel: Zur Einkommensdynamik in Deutschland seit 1984.* Frankfurt: Campus.

Sík, E. (1996) 'Budapest is "vidéke" ', in Sík, E./Tóth, I.Gy. (eds.), *Társadalmi páternoszter. Jelentés a Magyar Háztartás Panel V. hullámának eredményeiről.* Budapest: Department of Sociology, University of Economics and TÁRKI.

Sík, E./Tóth, I.Gy. (1996) *Az ajtók záródnak!? Jelentés a Magyar Háztartás Panel V. hullámának eredményeiről.* Budapest: Department of Sociology, University of Economics and TÁRKI.

Smeeding, T.M. (1988) 'Generations and the Distribution of Well-Being and Poverty: Cross National Evidence for Europe, Scandinavia and the Colonies', Luxembourg Income Study Working Paper No. 24.

Smeeding, T.M./Torrey, B.B. (1988) 'Poor Children in Rich Countries', Luxembourg Income Study Working Paper No. 16.

Spéder, Zs. (1999) 'The Twin Faces of Poverty in Present-day Hungary', pp. 66-103 in Spéder, Zs. (ed.), *Hungary in Flux.* Hamburg: Krämer.

Spéder, Zs. (1998) 'Poverty Dynamics in Hungary During the Transformation', *The Economics of Transition,* vol. 6, no. 1: 1-21.

Spéder, Zs. (1997) Szegény nők és férfiak, pp. 121-138 in Lévai, K./Tóth, I.Gy. (eds.), *Szerepváltozások.* Budapest: TÁRKI-Munkaügyi Minisztérium.

Spéder, Zs./Habich, R. (1999) 'Income Dynamics in Three Countries. An Investigation of Social Dynamics Using "Old" and "New" Types of Social Indicators', Wissenschaftszentrum Berlin, Working paper FS III 99-402, Berlin.

TÁRKI (1998) Gazdasági aktivitás vagy szociális támogatások? A jóléti újraelosztás megváltozott keretfeltételei, Budapest.

Tóth, I.Gy. (1995) 'The Hungarian Household Panel: Aims and Methods', *Innovation,* vol. 8, no. 1: 106-22.

Tóth, I.Gy. (1996) 'A háztartások jövedelmi szerkezete: a munkaerőpiac és a szociálpolitika szerepe', pp. 55-67 in Sík, E./Tóth, I.Gy. (eds.), *Az ajtók záródnak!? Jelentés a Magyar Háztartás Panel V. hullámának eredményeiről.* Budapest: Department of Sociology, Budapest University of Economics and TÁRKI.

UNICEF (1995) *Poverty, Children and Policy. Responses for a Brighter Future,* Economies in Transition Studies, Regional Monitoring Report No. 3.

UNICEF (1994) *Crisis in Mortality, Health and Nutrition,* Economies in Transition Studies, Regional Monitoring Report No. 2.

UNICEF International Child Development Centre (1993) *Public Policy and Social Conditions,* Regional Monitoring Report no. 1.

Vecernik, J. (1996) 'Tschechische Haushalte nach 1989: Einkommen und die Bewältigung schwieriger finanzieller Bedingungen', pp. 111-142 in Glatzer, W. (ed.), *Lebensverhältnisse in Osteuropa.* Frankfurt: Campus.

Vogel, J. (1997) 'Living Conditions and Inequality in the European Union 1997', Eurostat, Working Paper E/1997-3, Luxembourg.

Zapf, W./Schupp, J./Habich, R. (eds.) (1996) *Lebenslagen in Wandel: Sozialberichterstattung im Längschnitt.* Frankfurt: Campus.

93

Appendix

Table 2A1: **Share of Population in Different Age Cohorts**

Year	0-14 years	15-59 years	60-74 years	75- years	Total
1970	21.1	61.8	13.6	3.5	100.0
1980	21.8	61.1	12.5	4.6	100.0
1990	20.5	60.5	13.3	5.6	100.0
1995	18.3	62.3	14.6	4.8	100.0
1996	18.0	62.6	14.3	5.0	100.0
1997	17.7	62.8	14.3	5.2	100.0

Table 2A2: **Life Expectancy by Age and Gender, 1995**

	at birth	at 60	at 65
Males	65.3	14.8	12.1
Females	74.5	19.5	15.8

Table 2A3a: **Distribution of Pensioners by Household Size, in Percentages, 1987**

Household size	Pensioners	Others	Total
1	21.5	2.1	6.1
2	48.3	13.5	20.6
3	14.7	23.4	21.6
4	6.8	37.8	31.4
5	5.2	15.0	13.0
6+	3.6	8.3	7.3
Total	20.5	79.5	100
N=	11578	44861	56439

Table 2A3.b: Distribution of Pensioners by Household Size, in Percentages, 1992

Household size	Pensioner	Other	Total
1	22.4	2.2	6.9
2	49.2	12.4	20.9
3	16.0	23.3	21.6
4	5.3	36.0	28.9
5	3.9	16.5	13.6
6+	3.3	9.5	8.1
Total	100	100	100
N=	1325	4419	5744

Table 2A3c: Distribution of Pensioners by Household Size, in Percentages, 1996

Household size	Pensioner	Other	Total
1	21.2	2.0	6.7
2	45.6	21.2	19.3
3	17.6	45.6	20.9
4	6.9	17.6	28.3
5	4.2	6.9	14.3
6+	4.6	12.4	10.4
Total	100	100	100
N=	1305	3982	5287

Table 2A4a: **Distribution of Different Types of Households in Each Household Income Decile, in 1987 (horizontal distribution)**

Decile	Single male pensioner household	Single female pensioner household	Pensioner couple household	Other pensioner household	Non-pensioner household
Lowest	4.2	34.3	14.9	4.1	42.5
2	5.0	22.2	15.8	4.6	52.5
3	3.4	14.9	13.2	3.8	64.7
4	2.7	10.8	12.0	2.3	72.1
5	2.4	6.3	10.9	1.5	78.8
6	1.7	4.2	8.0	1.5	84.6
7	1.6	2.7	7.3	1.2	87.2
8	1.4	2.5	5.6	0.7	89.8
9	1.2	1.8	5.1	0.5	91.4
Highest	1.4	1.9	3.1	0.4	93.3
All	2.5	10.2	9.6	2.1	75.7

Table 2A4b: **Distribution of Different Types of Households in Each Household Income Decile, in 1992 (horizontal distribution)**

Decile	Single male pensioner household	Single female pensioner household	Pensioner couple household	Other pensioner household	Non-pensioner household
Lowest	2.1	26.4	1.5	22.0	47.9
2	6.7	30.5	11.0	11.0	40.7
3	3.5	27.2	17.8	9.4	42.1
4	5.1	9.9	22.1	6.5	56.4
5	2.9	7.7	20.9	6.8	61.7
6	2.6	6.3	17.4	4.1	69.5
7	1.8	2.0	10.4	2.2	83.6
8	2.1	2.8	9.0	2.4	83.7
9	2.8	1.1	6.8	2.6	86.6
Highest	1.9	2.4	1.8	2.8	91.0
All	3.2	11.6	11.9	7.0	66.3

Table 2A4c: **Distribution of Different Types of Households in Each Household Income Decile, in 1996 (horizontal distribution)**

Decile	Single male pensioner household	Single female pensioner household	Pensioner couple household	Other pensioner household	Non-pensioner household
Lowest	0	10.0	0.7	12.3	77.0
2	1.2	24.6	5.8	15.2	53.2
3	2.1	23.9	13.3	10.0	50.6
4	6.0	28.2	18.3	4.9	42.7
5	4.4	14.9	24.9	5.2	50.6
6	4.7	9.1	25.5	5.0	55.8
7	3.6	8.1	18.0	3.9	66.4
8	1.8	3.1	12.6	2.5	79.9
9	4.0	3.0	11.1	0.6	81.3
Highest	3.0	2.3	7.1	2.8	84.9
All	3.1	12.7	13.7	6.2	64.2

Table 2A5: **The Development of the Real Value of Wages and Different Kind of Social Assistance, Hungary, 1990-1996**

	1990	1991	1992	1993	1994	1995	1996	96/90
Child care allowance	-0.9	-8.0	-10.8	-5.9	-15.8	-22.0	-19.1	40.6
Minimum wage	0.6	8.0	-7.1	-8.2	-1.8	-9.4	-3.8	79.4
Net mean earnings	-4.0	-5.1	-1.9	-3.9	7.2	-13.8	-4.6	75.8
Unemployment benefit	-	-	4.0	-9.8	-4.3	-13.5	-14.0	66.8
Minimum pension	-0.1	-10.4	-10.9	-8.3	-1.6	-12.4	-7.5	58.2
Old-age pension	-3.3	-4.8	-6.8	-9.3	0.6	-7.3	-6.6	67.9

Source: TÁRKI, 1998: 60.

CHAPTER 3

Poland: Transition Gainers with an Uncertain Future

Adam Szulc

3.1 Introduction

Care for the elderly is one of the major challenges for many economies. Population ageing started two to three decades ago in most developed countries, and one of its consequences was a sizeable increase in the number of pensioners. Nowadays, even nations with relatively young populations in previous decades are expected to face the same problems in the near future. Poland is one of them, and its position is even more difficult because the unfavourable demographic trends are coupled with the public finance crisis that originated in the late 1980s and some negative consequences of the economic changes that started in 1990.

 In 1999, a new pension system was introduced in Poland, which will not have any major effects in the near future. The former system, whose effects will probably be felt for years to come, was criticized as ineffective, obscure and unjust by economists, politicians, journalists, and by the pensioners themselves. On the one hand, trying to maintain the benefits resulted in a growing fiscal burden. On the other hand, pensioners are widely recognized as one of the least-privileged socioeconomic groups. The reform of the pension system became necessary in order to avoid a collapse of the public finance system in the near future and the pauperization of a massive part of society. In 1995, the government launched the project of gradual replacement of the current system by the new one (see Office of the Government Plenipotentiary for Social Security Reform, 1997). It was modelled after those developed in most of the European Union countries, combining state guarantees with market elements. However, the pension systems in the EU are also at a turning point, so strictly following them would not ensure success.

The present study recapitulates a prospective monitoring system that would allow for a statistical control of the social effects of the reform by means of a household budget survey. This system might be employed as part of an 'early warning' system. Unacceptable changes in income distribution would be a premise for (any) modifications. The second goal of the present study is to illustrate changes in well-being of the elderly and pensioners, as an effect of economic transition.

After starting reforms in 1989, Poland experienced the scenario which became more or less common for many of the post-communist countries in Central and Eastern Europe: a severe drop in GDP at the beginning of the decade, followed by recovery. High inflation and increased unemployment are also inevitable elements of this path. In the late 1990s, however, considerable differences became apparent among the post-communist economies. Some of these countries, such as Russia or Romania, have not yet reversed negative trends. Others, especially the Visegrad countries[1] and Slovenia have been more successful. While Slovenia and the Czech Republic enjoy the highest levels of GDP per capita, Poland is the leader in terms of GDP growth, with high, stable rates (on average about 5.5% per year between 1994 and 1999, but recovery started as early as in 1992). Unemployment and inflation rates are still relatively high in Poland (the unemployment rate was around 13% in December 1999 and inflation was 7.3% in 1999).

Radical economic and institutional reorganization also affected income distributions and the standard of living of most of the socioeconomic groups in Poland. The focus of this study is on pensioners and the elderly, which are the groups expected to be most vulnerable, especially during rapid economic changes. Their incomes depend not only on the state of the economy, but are also very sensitive to political decisions. One of the questions raised in the present study is: are pensioners well protected, given the economic capacity of the country, and how has that changed over time. To answer this question, a statistical analysis of three household budget surveys was conducted. The surveys cover one pre-transition year (1987) and two transition years (1993 and 1996). The analysis focuses mainly on the relative position of pensioners and on trends, rather than on absolute measures.

The study is organized as follows. Section 3.2 briefly describes the former pension system in Poland and outlines the basic principles of the new system launched in 1999. Section 3.3 depicts the demographic situation of Poland. In Section 3.4 the database is introduced. The next three sections are devoted to an analysis of well-being, especially of income distribution, inequality, poverty and ownership of real assets. Section 3.8 presents conclusions.

3.2 General Description of the Pension System in Poland

3.2.1 The Former and the Current Systems: Basic Principles

The pension system prevailing in Poland until 1999 was founded on regulations that originated under the communist system. Eight years after starting the radical economic reforms (in 1990), the public social insurance system was still practically unchanged. The pension system was a 'pay as you go' one established on mandatory contributions with benefits based on imprecise and unstable criteria.[2] In 1989 the most serious post-war crisis in Poland hit the whole social insurance system. It was caused by demographic factors, early retirements and also by a general crisis in public finances. Although the authorities reacted by raising contribution rates, nonetheless the financial sustainability of the pension system could only be assured by subsidies from the state budget. It seems that this crisis accelerated the process of transformation. However, the first consequential decision on the reform was not reached until the end of 1995. The Office of the Government Plenipotentiary for Social Security Reform commenced a comprehensive reform project aimed at the creation of a system based on stable principles, long-term valuation and ensuring the security of assets. The initial stage of that project was inaugurated in 1999.

The new system is intended to gradually replace the present one, but one should not expect the first effects very soon. As an illustration, reducing contribution rates could not begin any earlier than ten years from the start of the reforms. The new system will be based on three interacting pillars: (1) 'pay as you go' mandatory system, (2) the mandatory funded system, and (3) voluntary insurance in private funds. The first pillar, in principle, maintains the current regulations, however a strict relationship between contributions and benefits will be respected. Benefits received will depend

101

on accumulated contributions and average life expectancy at the age of retirement (this age may be agreed by the employee individually, after passing a certain minimum age). These resources will be managed by the state Social Insurance Institute (Zaklad Ubezpieczeń Spolecznych – ZUS). The second pillar is founded on licensed, private pension funds. Participation in these funds is mandatory for all persons under 30 years of age in 1999 and optional for those between 30 and 50 years of age. Persons aged 50 and over are not allowed to participate in the second pillar. Participants will contribute to one of 16 funds, which were created during the initial period.[3] The third pillar is optional. Prospective participants may save with investment funds or insurance companies. They may also participate in pension programmes organized by employers.

The present analysis of the well-being of the elderly captures the pre-reform period only. Therefore, the old system is also presented.

3.2.2 The Social Insurance Crisis

The recent crisis was not a surprise. It resulted from the very nature of the Polish pension system and could not have been avoided without a fundamental change. The advantageous demographic structure of post-war Poland allowed for the continuation of an ineffective (and also unjust) system for several decades. The surplus generated, however, was not accumulated in the pension (state) fund, but was being used by the government to cover current expenditure. Nevertheless, natural demographic changes were not solely responsible for the sudden deterioration of the system. The crisis, and especially its intensity, had a strong social and economic rationale. At least two factors should be mentioned: (1) a rapid increase in the number of new pensioners, (2) an increase in unemployment, resulting in a decrease in the number of contributors. Moreover, for some years pensions had grown faster than wages (the replacement rates are shown in Table 3.1).

The demographic trends in Poland since the1980s leave no doubt about the worsening age structure. Like in most of Western Europe, the proportion of the elderly is increasing. The decrease in the fertility rate and also, although to a much lower extent, an increase in average life expectancy (see Tables 3.2 and 3.3) are the main reasons for this phenomenon. In the near future, the dependency ratio (i.e. ratio of the old-age population to the working-age population) will not change substantially, however, it may start to rapidly increase after 2010 (see Table 3.3). A brighter scenario may be derived from the prospective decrease in unemployment[4] that should have a positive impact on the number of contributors. The succeeding sections briefly present the demographic and economic situation.

Table 3.1: Average Replacement Rate

Year	Pension/net wage
1989	0.503
1990	0.588
1991	0.654
1992	0.629
1993	0.621
1994	0.641
1995	0.641
1996	0.613

Note: Early retirement pensions included.
Source: GUS, Rocznik Statystyczny.

Table 3.2: Fertility and Reproduction Rates

Year	Fertility rate[1]	Reproduction rate[2]
1970	64	2.200
1975	71	2.270
1980	76	2.276
1985	74	2.329
1990	58	2.039
1995	43	1.611
1996	42	1.580

Notes: [1] Live births per 1000 women aged 15 to 49 years.

[2] Number of births per woman.

Source: GUS, Rocznik Demograficzny.

Table 3.3: Proportion of the Elderly in the Total Population
(actual and projected values)

Year	Elderly (%)
1994	21.3
1996	21.7
1998	22.0*
2000	22.1*
2005	21.6*
2010	22.6*
2015	26.3*
2020	31.1*

Note: * Projected values.

Source: Office of the Government Plenipotentiary ... (1997).

3.2.3 Contributors

The former 'pay as you go' system was based on mandatory, universal contributions. The prevailing part came from employers (both state and private) who were paying most recently 45% on the before-tax wages[5] to the ZUS. There were several groups paying lower contributions (self-employed, prisoners, artists). The contributions from individual farmers and persons in military service were partly (the former) or fully (the latter ones) paid from the state budget. It should be mentioned here that some employers (mainly large, state-owned enterprises) still fail to pay their contributions. The expenditures of the social insurance system (for which the second part is constituted by the Farmers Social Insurance Fund – KRUS) cover retirement pensions, disability pensions and survivor pensions. Table 3.4 displays revenues and expenditures of the social insurance funds in Poland.

Under the new system, a number of privileged sectors will be severely restricted. The government is currently negotiating with trade unions on so-called 'bridge-type pensions', which allow for the gradual transition into retirement of employees in selected sectors (e.g. coal miners, railway workers).

In the new system a universal and mandatory pillar will be based on contributions, which may be equal to 45% or 30.4% of before-tax wages. The first rate is applied to those who did not decide or cannot (see section 3.2.1) participate in the second pillar. Those who decided or were obliged to join one of the private funds will pay 14.6% of before-tax wages (or 32.5% of the mandatory contribution).

Table 3.4: Revenues and Expenditures of Social Insurance Funds (as % of GDP)

Year	Revenues[1]	State subsidies	Expenditures	Public pensions[2]
1991	15.7	4.4	16.1	12.6
1992	18.1	6.3	17.8	14.6
1993	18.1	6.2	17.8	14.6
1994	18.6	6.2	18.5	15.4
1995	16.9	4.2	16.4	14.6
1996	16.9	4.2	17.2	15.2

Notes: [1] State subsidies included. [2] Disability and survivor pensions included.

Source: Office of the Government Plenipotentiary ... (1997).

3.2.4 *Benefits in the Current and in the Previous Systems*

3.2.4.1 Retirement Age

Receiving retirement benefits under the former system required passing an age criterion and a minimum participation period. The most typical age was 65 for men and 60 for women. The respective minimum contribution periods were 20 and 25 years. Nonetheless, numerous economic groups were entitled to retirement benefits at a lower age: miners, railway workers, and military personnel. Moreover, early retirement with lower benefits was possible for other persons. Table 3.5 displays trends in the average retirement age. It was stable between 1992 and 1996 and relatively low. In 1997 a slight drop occurred.

In the new system very few groups will be eligible for early retirement, however, they have not yet been decided upon. For most people, the age limit of 60/65 will be strictly enforced. There will be no minimum contribution period, but the minimum pension statutory guarantee will not apply to those with a contribution period less than 25 years.

Table 3.5: Average Retirement Age

Year	Men	Women
1992	59.0	55.0
1993	59.0	55.0
1994	59.1	55.2
1995	59.0	55.1
1996	59.0	54.9
1997	58.3	54.1

Source: Social Insurance Institute (ZUS), unpublished data.

3.2.4.2 Benefit Levels: Regulations and Trends

106

Retirement benefits under the former system depended on a person's wage during the five-year period prior to retirement and on the multiplier, which was prescribed arbitrarily by the government. The latter varied from industry to industry: it was advantageous for, among others, miners and military personnel. Eligibility for retirement benefits was suspended if a pensioner earned labour income exceeding a certain threshold (around the average wage). The indexation of benefits was based on average nominal net wage growth, and was applied whenever that growth exceeded a certain limit.

Table 3.1 shows the average replacement rate (i.e. ratio between mean retirement pension and mean net wage). Like most individual incomes, the average retirement pension also experienced a sharp drop in 1990. It amounted to 85% of the 1989 level, although that drop was much lower than that of real wages (25%). The replacement rate varied significantly between years. It reached its lowest level in 1989 (0.503) and its highest two years later (0.654). After 1992 the rate became more stable, although an important decrease (by approximately 3 percentage points) occurred in 1996. As the pensioner definition captures also the early retirement population, the ratios are relatively low.

3.2.5   Demographic Formations

3.2.5.1 Dependency Ratio

The increasing share of the elderly population, as experienced by Poland, is also typical for European countries, although relatively high birth rates were maintained until the late 1980s, which made the demographic structure more favourable than in most West European countries. Nevertheless, serious drops in fertility rates in the 1990s (see Table 3.2) together with the forthcoming retirement of people born after the Second World War will increase the proportion of the non-working population significantly in the coming decades (see Table 3.3). Table 3.6 presents the dependency ratio defined as the ratio of beneficiaries to active, insured persons during the 1990s. The results claim pessimistic trends in population activity, although the ratios after 1993 have been much more stable. The demographic process alone did not cause the increase in the dependency ratio at the beginning of the 1990s. A strong rise in early retirements between 1989 and 1992 was another reason for the rise in the relative number of beneficiaries. The total number of retirements was almost two times higher during this period than the average both before 1989 and after 1992. The main impulses behind these trends were unemployment fears (affecting both the government retirement programmes and individual decisions) and earnings uncertainty.

Table 3.6: Dependency Ratio

Year	Beneficiaries/insured
1989	0.372
1990	0.416
1991	0.476
1992	0.517
1993	0.553
1994	0.570
1995	0.575
1996	0.581

Source: ZUS, unpublished data.

3.2.5.2 Population Structure by Age and Life Expectancy

Table 3.7 displays the Polish population structure by age. The youngest cohort (0-14 years) was continuously decreasing, from 24.9% in 1990 to 21.9% in 1996. Out of all age groups, this was the largest decrease. The oldest age group (persons aged 75 and over) experienced a decrease from 4.1% to 3.8%, however, the proportion of persons in that age group stabilized after 1991. The two remaining age groups expanded their shares. A bigger increase was observed for people aged 61 to 74 (from 9.9% to 11.3%). All results are consistent with the decrease in fertility rates (see Table 3.2) and with the slight increase in life expectancy.

Table 3.7: Population by Age Groups

Year	Percentage of population at age:			
	0-14	15-60	61-74	75+
1990	24.9	61.1	9.9	4.1
1991	24.6	61.3	10.3	3.9
1992	24.1	61.5	10.6	3.8
1993	23.7	61.7	10.9	3.7
1994	23.1	62.1	11.1	3.7
1995	22.5	62.6	11.2	3.8
1996	21.9	63.0	11.3	3.8

Source: GUS, Rocznik Demograficzny.

Life expectancy in Poland for both men and women is relatively low (see Table 3.8), as compared to West European countries or Slovenia. However, a slight increase has been observed since 1993. Given the legal retirement ages, the average man is expected to receive retirement benefits for 12.9 years. For the average woman that period is much longer due to the lower retirement age, as well as to a longer life expectancy. It amounts to 20.5 years.

Table 3.8: Life Expectancy

Year	At age	Men	Women
1990	0	66.3	75.5
	60	15.3	20.0
	65	12.4	16.1
1993	0	67.2	75.8
	60	15.5	20.1
	65	12.5	16.2
1995	0	67.6	76.4
	60	15.8	20.5
	65	12.9	16.5
1996	0	68.1	76.6
	60	15.9	20.5
	65	12.9	16.5

Source: Rocznik Statystyczny, Polskie Tablice Trwania Zycia 1995-1996.

3.3 Household Data

3.3.1 Household Budget Survey, Choice of Time Period and Quality of Data

The core of the database used for measuring well-being came from the annual household budget survey undertaken by the Central Statistical Office of Poland (CSO). This survey was launched in the 1950s, with numerous important changes, both in sample size and sampling methods, introduced since then.

The data selected for this study are from the 1987, 1993 and 1996 surveys. They are intended to capture both pre-transition and transition years. The year 1987 was selected to represent the pre-transition period, because 1987 was the last year before any serious economic changes and reforms started (in 1990). The years 1988 and, especially, 1989 were characterized by high inflation rates and extensive market shortages making all monetary indicators completely inadequate for the measurement of well-being (this attribute was true for all centrally-planned economies, however, its extent varied between countries and time periods). The choice of 1993 has two rationales. First, the 1990-1992 period was characterized by rapid changes in income distributions, which eventually stabilized after 1993. Second, the CSO introduced important methodological changes in data collection during that year (see Szulc, 1998). The most seminal innovation consisted of introducing the monthly rotation of households instead of the quarterly rotation. Therefore, all comparisons between years before and after 1993 are biased. Unfortunately, it also affects the present study, which includes 1987 data. The third year, 1996, was the last one for which household information was available at the time this study was undertaken.

Until 1992, the CSO applied a type of statistical control of household income data. For some of the randomly selected households the income declarations were checked against information obtained at the source of income (usually state employers or pension and social benefit payers). Starting in 1990, this type of control was limited and eventually discontinued in 1992. Therefore, one may assume a lower degree of accuracy of the income data after that year. On the other hand, there was some evidence that income declarations of pensioners were relatively accurate, as compared to other socioeconomic groups.

3.3.2 Size and Structure of the Sample

Due to the methodological changes in the data collection method introduced in 1993 (see section 3.3.1), the samples from 1987 and the other years are not entirely comparable. Apart from modifying the rotation, two important socioeconomic groups were added in 1993: the self-employed and the recipients of state welfare benefits. This improved coverage of the general population (from 85% to almost 100%, as estimated by the CSO), however, this also changed the proportions in the sample. Table 3.9 displays the sample sizes, as well as the proportions of pensioners in the sample and those calculated at the national levels. The two latter figures (displayed in the two last columns) should not be directly compared. For the purpose of this study, an age limit was applied and therefore the proportions of pensioners in the sample differ from those estimated at the national level. Paradoxically, in 1987 the proportion of pensioners calculated from micro-data is higher than the national one due to an overrepresentation of pensioners in the sample.

Due to changes in the method of data collection as mentioned above, the structure of the sample after 1992 reflects the structure of the population more accurately.

Table 3.9: Structure of Persons and Households

	Persons	Households	Share of pensioners in the sample[1]	national[2]
		1987		
Pensioners	12,737	6,112	15.2%	13.7%
All	83,654	26,434		
		1993		
Pensioners	16,954	7,112	16.2%	18.3%
All	104,578	32,108		
		1996		
Pensioners	19,556	7,351	19.2%	19.2%
All	101,801	31,907		

Notes: [1] In accordance with the definition of a pensioner in section 1.4.1. [2] No age restrictions.

Source: Rocznik Statystyczny (last column), other numbers based on own calculations from individual data.

3.4 General Information about Pensioner Households

3.4.1 *Pensioners by Household Size*

Pensioners constitute a specific socioeconomic group, distinct not only by their particular source of income and age, but also by family composition and consumption patterns. This obviously influences their income levels and distributions. It is well known, for example, that small families without children can on average achieve higher standards of living than large families with children. Table 3.10 displays the household composition of pensioners as compared to the whole population. As expected, the average household size for pensioners is much smaller than that calculated for the general population. For all years considered, the largest proportion of pensioners lived in two-person households. Also, the share of pensioners liv-

111

ing alone was relatively high, much higher than the national level. The average household structure was different. Most people live in the two largest categories of households which constitute about 60% of the entire population.

Table 3.10: Population by Household Size (% of persons)

Category	Household size				
of person	1	2	3	4	5+
			1987		
Pensioners	19.4	36.8	18.9	9.6	15.3
All persons	5.1	13.8	20.8	28.6	31.8
			1993		
Pensioners	17.2	44.8	16.0	7.5	14.5
All persons	4.0	14.6	18.9	28.8	33.7
			1996		
Pensioners	16.8	43.9	16.7	7.6	15.1
All persons	4.3	15.5	19.9	27.7	32.7

Source: Own calculations from individual household data.

3.4.2 Income Sources of Pensioners

Table 3.11 displays the structure of pensioner incomes. The main source is, of course, retirement pension. Its contribution, however, decreased significantly after 1987. This happened due to an increased number of 'new pensioners' (see sections 3.2.2 and 3.2.5.1) in 1989 and 1990 with relatively low benefits. Many of them were disability pension recipients, which resulted in a massive increase in the share of disability pensions in 1993. A rather significant part of these incomes had come from other sources. The role of social assistance in pensioners' incomes was relatively low in 1993 and 1996, but much higher in 1987 (the share of social benefits was close to that observed for all households). Also, the share of labour income decreased substantially in the 1990s. This may be explained by the part-time jobs taken on by pensioners much more frequently in the 1980s. By contrast, the significance of 'other sources' increased considerably in the 1990s as compared to 1987. This income source captures mainly income from self-employment and, to a lesser extent, capital revenues.

Table 3.11:   Pensioner Households by Income Source (% of total income)

Type of household	Share of total income from the source:				
	Retirement pension	Disability pension	Labour income	Social benefits	Other sources
			1987		
Pensioner	75.1	6.6	8.9	6.9	2.4
All	18.1	12.0	61.0	7.7	1.2
			1993		
Pensioner	55.8	26.5	0.1	2.6	14.8
All	15.2	8.4	40.4	9.5	26.1
			1996		
Pensioner	56.3	25.7	0.0	3.2	14.8
All	17.5	12.1	45.8	7.7	16.8

Source: Own calculations from individual household data.

3.4.3 Trends in Real Income

Table 3.12 illustrates changes in real income over the investigated decade. However, the relative income position of pensioner households did not change significantly. The average income of all pensioner households ranged from 91% of the national average in 1987 to 98% in 1993. The highest real income of pensioners was observed in 1996, the lowest in 1993. Moreover, the mean equivalent income of pensioners was higher than the national mean for both 1993 and 1996. The latter year was characterized by the highest incomes of the whole period investigated for both pensioners in general and 'all' households. When considering the various types of pensioner household, the 'other' type was the only exception to that rule. Of course, this also means the deterioration of the relative incomes in that household type, as compared to the remaining ones. This change was the most significant as far as relations between types of households are considered. In 1987, the households of that type had the highest mean income, while in 1993 and 1996 it was the lowest. The highest incomes in 1993 were observed for single males and in 1996 for pensioner couples. Single females represented the least privileged group in both 1993 and 1996.

Table 3.12:   Trends in Household Equivalent Incomes, 1987-1996

Year	Income	Pensioner households					All households
		Single male	Single female	Couple	Other	All	
1987	Nominal[1]	1.9094	1.5973	1.9325	2.0423	1.9007	2.0661
	Real[2]	494.0	413.2	499.9	528.4	491.7	534.5
1993	Nominal[1]	265.8	224.0	261.4	199.4	234.9	240.6
	Real[2]	539.8	454.9	530.8	404.9	477.0	488.6
1996	Nominal[1]	553.0	491.2	573.3	426.3	512.1	541.6
	Real[2]	553.0	491.2	573.3	426.3	512.1	541.6

Notes: [1] For 1987 and 1993 recalculated to the new zloty (nominal values divided by 10,000).

[2] In 1996 prices.

[3] 1993: 1 ECU = 2.13 (new) zloty, 1996: 1 ECU=3.50 zloty (Central Bank of Poland, unp. data).

Source: Own calculations from individual household data.

3.5 Income Distribution: Decile Analysis

3.5.1 Households

Pensioners' income distribution is presented in this part of the study by means of a decile analysis. Income deciles are defined for all households, therefore each decile group contains 10% of them. For each decile group, percentages of various types of pensioner households are calculated. This simple technique allows for a general evaluation of the income position of pensioner households against the whole population and also illustrates within-group income distribution(s). If the pensioner percentage reaches the highest values in the lower deciles, this may be interpreted as a relatively high proportion of poor among them and, consequently, usually a low average income position for these types of households. And vice versa, lower percentages in the low decile groups imply a relatively good income position. An analogous inference may be applied to the highest decile groups. One reservation, however, should be added to the above interpretation. If pensioner shares are relatively low both in the lowest and in the highest deciles, it means a relatively equal income distribution, but hardly translates into average income (due to the trade-off between lowest and highest deciles). Empirical results for 1987, 1993, and 1996 are displayed in Tables 3.13a–c.

Table 3.13a: Percentage of Households by Equivalent Income Deciles, 1987

Decile	Pensioner households					Non-pensioner
	Single male	Single female	Couple	Other	All	households
1	1.0	8.1	3.6	11.1	23.8	76.2
2	1.0	15.1	3.0	15.4	34.5	65.5
3	1.7	18.2	4.4	14.0	38.3	61.7
4	1.4	13.7	6.8	10.4	32.3	67.7
5	1.7	9.5	7.7	8.3	27.2	72.8
6	1.2	5.5	7.1	8.6	22.4	77.6
7	0.9	2.5	5.0	6.9	15.3	84.7
8	1.1	3.3	4.9	4.9	14.2	85.8
9	0.7	2.9	2.8	5.1	11.5	88.5
10	0.8	3.1	2.3	5.7	11.9	88.1
All	1.2	8.2	4.8	8.9	23.1	76.9

Source: Own calculations from individual household data.

In 1993, and especially in 1996, the percentages of 'all' pensioners in the lowest deciles were small, as compared to the middle deciles. This may be translated into low numbers of pensioners among the poorest households. In 1987, the relative position of pensioners was worse: their shares in the lowest deciles were higher than on average. By looking at the highest deciles, one may derive similar conclusions. In 1993 and 1996, there was a greater-than-average chance of the pensioners appearing in the highest deciles, although the tenth decile was an exception to that rule. In 1987, one could make this statement only up to the fifth decile.

Table 3.13b: Percentage of Households by Equivalent Income Deciles, 1993

Decile	Pensioner households					Non-pensioner
	Single male	Single female	Couple	Other	All	households
1	0.5	2.8	0.9	6.3	10.5	89.5
2	0.8	8.9	3.4	7.7	20.8	79.2
3	1.3	11.4	5.2	5.8	23.7	76.3
4	1.1	10.9	8.2	6.0	26.2	73.8
5	1.1	9.4	8.6	6.4	25.5	74.5
6	1.6	9.6	10.2	5.4	26.8	73.2
7	1.3	7.4	12.9	4.6	26.2	73.8
8	1.6	7.3	12.6	3.4	24.9	75.1
9	2.1	5.7	11.0	3.4	22.2	77.8
10	1.6	4.6	7.1	2.0	15.3	84.7
All	1.3	7.8	8.0	5.1	22.1	87.9

Table 3.13c: Percentage of Households by Equivalent Income Deciles, 1996

Decile	Pensioner households					Non-pensioner
	Single male	Single female	Couple	Other	All	households
1	0.4	1.7	0.3	6.3	8.7	91.4
2	1.0	7.1	2.1	7.3	17.3	82.7
3	1.6	11.3	5.1	6.4	24.6	75.4
4	1.8	12.0	8.5	6.7	28.7	71.3
5	1.6	11.1	10.7	6.0	29.4	70.7
6	1.7	10.5	12.8	4.4	29.4	70.7
7	1.6	9.3	13.2	5.0	29.2	70.8
8	1.7	7.5	13.7	3.3	26.3	73.7
9	2.2	6.6	12.7	2.2	23.7	76.3
10	1.4	3.8	6.7	1.4	13.3	86.7
All	1.5	8.1	8.6	4.7	23.0	77.0

In 1993 and 1996, distributions were more equal than in 1987, as reflected by the differences among deciles. In other words, in the 1990s the pensioner households moved on average to higher deciles. The most privileged types of pensioner households, in terms of income, were single male and pensioner couples. This was also true in 1987, in spite of the better average income of 'other' pensioner households.

In general, income distribution among pensioner households was relatively egalitarian. Such findings are not surprising, given the empirical results obtained for both the 1980s (Panek and Szulc, 1991) and the 1990s (Szulc, 1994; Perek-Bialas and Topińska, 1998) for Poland, although the definitions of pensioner households applied in those studies were different from the present definition.

3.5.2 Persons

A similar decile analysis was applied using persons as units (i.e. each decile contains 10% of the persons). The results are presented in Tables 3.14a-c. In general, the results are close to those obtained for households. Pensioners are less likely to appear in the lowest deciles, especially in 1996. Moreover, their shares in the highest deciles increased after 1987. In 1996, the proportion of pensioners was higher than on average in the tenth decile as well. The income position of pensioners living in pensioner households is slightly worse than that of pensioners as a whole for all years, as they less frequently appear in the highest deciles (on the other hand, in 1996 pensioners living in pensioner households were less likely to appear in the lowest deciles). This may mean that pensioners cohabitating with non-pensioners also share their incomes. Persons aged 60 and over also achieved relatively good positions. This is especially true for 1996 and, to lesser extent, for 1993.

Table 3.14a: Percentage of Pensioners by Equivalent Income Deciles, 1987

Decile	Pensioners in pensioner households	All pensioners	Persons aged 60 and over
1	8.6	11.6	11.5
2	11.5	14.2	14.1
3	14.5	17.7	16.2
4	13.8	17.7	16.2
5	12.2	17.2	15.2
6	10.1	17.1	14.0
7	7.3	14.8	12.8
8	6.6	15.4	12.3
9	5.9	13.9	10.9
10	5.8	12.7	10.7
All	9.6	15.2	13.4

Source: Own calculations from individual household data.

Table 3.14b: Percentage of Pensioners by Equivalent Income Deciles, 1993

Decile	Pensioners in pensioner households	All pensioners	Persons aged 60 and over
1	4.6	11.2	7.7
2	7.1	12.9	9.3
3	8.9	14.6	12.4
4	9.9	15.0	14.1
5	11.3	18.7	15.7
6	13.5	20.2	17.4
7	13.3	22.1	17.9
8	11.1	20.3	18.3
9	10.1	16.1	18.1
10	8.2	10.9	14.5
All	9.8	16.2	14.5

Table 3.14c: Percentage of Pensioners by Equivalent Income Deciles, 1996

Decile	Pensioners in pensioner households	All pensioners	Persons aged 60 and over
1	1.5	6.6	6.3
2	4.3	10.5	9.6
3	7.5	14.9	13.1
4	10.1	18.4	16.7
5	13.3	22.9	17.8
6	13.9	23.8	19.0
7	14.9	24.6	19.9
8	14.7	25.1	20.1
9	13.4	25.3	19.5
10	8.5	20.1	15.4
All	10.2	19.2	15.1

The analysis for age groups is illustrated in Tables 3.15a-c. As in the previous case, income distribution changed considerably between 1987 and the 1990s. For all age cohorts, left skewness was milder in the 1990s. Also in 1996, the percentages in the tenth decile are higher than average. The least privileged group are persons aged 80 and over, the best position is held by the youngest age cohort (from 50 to 59 years).

Table 13.5a: Percentage of Persons by Equivalent Income Deciles, by Age, 1987

Decile	Age cohort			
	50-59	60-69	70-79	80+
1	8.2	7.1	4.2	1.0
2	7.9	8.3	5.2	1.5
3	9.1	9.3	5.9	1.9
4	9.3	9.7	5.5	2.0
5	9.9	9.6	5.3	1.5
6	11.0	9.3	4.2	1.6
7	12.4	8.9	3.5	1.5
8	14.5	8.6	3.4	1.4
9	18.1	8.7	2.6	1.1
10	22.9	8.7	2.5	1.1
All	12.3	8.8	4.2	1.5

Source: Own calculations from individual household data.

Table 3.15b: Percentage of Persons by Equivalent Income Deciles, by Age, 1993

Decile	Age cohort			
	50-59	60-69	70-79	80+
1	7.6	4.9	1.6	0.8
2	6.7	5.5	2.4	1.4
3	7.8	7.5	3.7	1.2
4	8.7	8.6	3.7	1.7
5	9.7	9.5	4.3	1.6
6	10.4	10.4	5.0	2.1
7	12.1	11.4	4.5	1.8
8	12.4	12.2	4.4	1.6
9	13.5	12.0	4.3	1.7
10	14.8	9.5	3.6	1.7
All	10.4	9.1	3.7	1.5

Table 3.15c: Percentage of Persons by Equivalent Income Deciles, by Age, 1996

Decile	Age cohort			
	50-59	60-69	70-79	80+
1	6.0	3.8	1.3	0.5
2	7.3	5.8	1.8	0.6
3	8.7	7.6	2.9	0.8
4	9.4	10.1	3.3	1.1
5	10.7	10.6	3.9	1.3
6	11.3	12.0	4.0	1.4
7	11.5	12.5	4.1	1.1
8	12.9	13.0	3.8	1.3
9	13.5	12.4	4.0	1.3
10	14.3	9.9	3.0	1.1
All	10.2	9.3	3.2	1.0

It should be mentioned here that impressive improvement in the relative income position of pensioners and the elderly is only partly caused by the increase in their real incomes between 1987 and 1996. As shown in Table 3.12 that increase was quite modest (about 4%). This is because the increases in real income of the pensioners allocated to the 'single' and 'couple' categories were mitigated by substantial decreases among 'other' pensioner households. The 'other' pensioner households usually capture relatively large numbers of non-pensioners (who did not benefit from the pension increases). As they are omitted in the decile analyses of persons (Tables 3.14a-c), the 'paradoxical' disproportion between real income growth and spectacular improvement in the relative income position of pensioners, may find a rationale. A similar phenomenon may be observed for household deciles (Tables 3.13a-c), possibly justified by not weighting households. As 'other' pensioner households are on average larger than the remaining ones, the impact of households of that type on the average income level is milder. However, weights are applied in calculating the mean incomes reported in Table 3.12.

3.5.3 Gender Disparities

In Tables 3.16a-c the decile analysis of pensioners aged 60 and over is broken down by gender. Contrary to the other decile tables, the distribution here is vertical rather than horizontal. It provides, together with Tables 3.13a-c, information on the income disparities between men and women. The general results are hardly surprising. Males more frequently appear in the top deciles and less frequently in the bottom ones. The absolute magnitude of disparities is not large and is diminishing over time.

Table 3.16a: Percentage of Pensioners and Elderly by Equivalent Income Decile, by Gender (vertical distribution), 1987

Decile	Pensioners		Persons aged 60 and over	
	Male	Female	Male	Female
1	5.1	6.9	7.8	9.0
2	6.2	7.3	9.0	11.2
3	9.6	10.1	10.0	13.3
4	12.1	12.3	10.5	12.8
5	13.9	15.7	11.2	11.4
6	13.6	12.4	10.8	10.1
7	13.0	10.8	10.5	9.0
8	11.7	9.6	10.0	8.7
9	8.2	9.1	9.7	7.8
10	6.6	5.8	10.2	7.3
All	100	100	100	100

Source: Own calculations from individual household data.

Table 3.16b: Percentage of Pensioners and Elderly by Equivalent Income Decile, by Gender (vertical distribution), 1993

Decile	Pensioners		Persons aged 60 and over	
	Male	Female	Male	Female
1	6.1	7.5	5.7	5.7
2	6.3	8.1	5.8	7.8
3	8.1	10.6	7.3	10.1
4	9.9	11.1	9.0	10.7
5	11.0	11.4	9.8	11.7
6	12.2	11.9	11.7	12.1
7	13.0	11.9	12.3	11.7
8	13.3	11.2	13.4	10.9
9	11.6	9.6	13.6	11.1
10	8.5	7.0	11.1	8.4
All	100	100	100	100

Table 3.16c: Percentage of Pensioners and Elderly by Equivalent Income Decile, by Gender (vertical distribution), 1996

Decile	Pensioners		Persons aged 60 and over	
	Male	Female	Male	Female
1	3.1	3.6	5.1	4.6
2	5.1	5.7	5.8	6.1
3	7.6	7.9	7.5	7.9
4	8.9	10.0	8.5	9.7
5	11.5	12.2	10.3	11.5
6	12.2	12.5	11.2	11.7
7	12.8	12.8	12.1	12.2
8	13.8	12.6	13.0	12.3
9	13.9	12.6	13.7	12.7
10	11.1	10.0	12.8	11.3
All	100	100	100	100

3.6 Poverty and Inequality among Pensioners

3.6.1 *Poverty Incidence*

Poverty measurement is extremely important in order to evaluate standards of living. Although it focuses on the low-income population, poverty indicators also provide meaningful information about the general economic efficiency and effectiveness of social policy. Even a high performance economy cannot be considered entirely successful if economic growth is not accompanied by a decrease in the incidence of poverty.

For the purpose of this study, poverty is defined in relative terms. This approach allows us to disregard the problem of calculating an absolute poverty line. The latter is usually interpreted as the cost of a bundle of basic commodities considered obvious choices for the poverty threshold. However, in practice it is impossible to calculate a value that is widely accepted. Therefore, this concept has not been implemented here. The relative poverty line is defined as a certain proportion of the mean or median equivalent income. Since there are no grounds on which to decide which proportion is 'appropriate', four poverty lines have been selected for this study: 40%, 50%, 60% and 70% of median equivalent income. The first one may be informally regarded as 'subsistence minimum' (an amount necessary for biological survival), the last one as a 'social minimum' (an amount allowing one to purchase goods necessary to participate in 'social life').

Indicators of the incidence of poverty (shares of persons below the poverty lines, also referred to as 'head count ratios') are presented in Tables 3.17a-c. As poverty indices based on relative lines are conceptually close to the inequality measures,[6] the general conclusions are not very different from those derived from the decile analysis presented in section 3.5. For each year, almost all poverty indices are much lower for pensioners and elderly than the national average. The only exception is the 1987 head count ratio for pensioners in pensioner households, based on the 70% poverty line.[7] Discrepancies between the pensioners' and the national poverty indices are much higher for 1993 and especially high for 1996 if compared to 1987. On the other hand, for all years the differences between the pensioners' and the national poverty indices decrease with respect to the increase in poverty lines.

Table 3.17a: Poverty Rate (% of persons below poverty line), 1987

| Category | | Poverty line (% of median equivalent income) | | | |
of person		40%	50%	60%	70%
Pensioners	M	5.4	8.1	13.3	20.7
	F	5.6	8.9	13.8	22.1
	All	5.5	8.7	13.6	21.5
Pensioners	M	6.3	10.2	16.3	25.6
in pensioner	F	6.4	10.4	16.4	27.6
households	All	6.3	10.3	16.4	26.8
Aged 60	M	5.6	8.9	13.7	20.8
and over	F	6.5	10.1	16.0	25.3
	All	6.1	9.7	15.1	23.5
All persons	M	7.6	11.5	17.0	24.5
	F	7.4	11.2	16.7	24.0
	All	7.5	11.4	16.9	24.2

Note: M = male, F = female.

Source: Own calculations from individual household data.

Table 3.17b: Poverty Rate (% of persons below poverty line), 1993

Category		*Poverty line (% of median equivalent income)*			
of person		40%	50%	60%	70%
Pensioners	M	1.9	3.8	7.0	12.5
	F	2.2	4.1	7.7	13.9
	All	2.1	4.0	7.4	13.3
Pensioners	M	0.7	1.9	4.2	8.9
in pensioner	F	0.7	2.0	4.6	10.1
households	All	2.8	5.0	8.5	14.7
Aged 60	M	2.9	5.0	7.9	13.3
and over	F	2.7	5.0	9.0	15.6
	All	2.8	5.0	8.5	14.7
All persons	M	4.8	9.1	15.3	23.3
	F	4.2	8.2	14.2	22.1
	All	4.5	8.6	14.7	22.7

Table 3.17c: Poverty Rate (% of persons below poverty line), 1996

Category		*Poverty line (% of median equivalent income)*			
of person		40%	50%	60%	70%
Pensioners	M	1.1	2.4	5.6	10.3
	F	1.3	2.9	6.2	11.1
	All	1.2	2.7	6.0	10.6
Pensioners	M	0.3	1.0	3.4	6.9
in pensioner	F	0.4	1.2	3.7	7.9
households	All	0.4	1.1	3.6	7.5
Aged 60	M	1.6	2.85	5.6	9.4
and over	F	1.5	3.31	6.6	11.6
	All	1.5	3.1	6.2	10.7
All persons	M	4.4	8.7	14.8	22.3
	F	4.0	8.0	13.8	21.3
	All	4.2	8.4	14.3	21.8

It seems that some reservations should apply to the preceding figures. Poverty indices based on relative thresholds provide information about income distribution rather than about poverty itself, i.e. the inability to acquire a certain bundle of goods. Due to the small proportions of persons/households below the poverty line, minor shifts in the overall income distribution may change their position dramatically. In other words, relatively small transfers addressed to a small group may be very effective, so the impressive decreases in the number of poor pensioners should not be misinterpreted.

The analysis by gender does not show large differences in poverty rates. In general, men are better off than women, however, some exceptions occur at the lowest poverty line. The gender disparities are higher for pensioners than for the general population.

3.6.2 Income Inequality

Inequality indices are usually calculated complementary to poverty measures. Unlike a decile analysis, inequality indices are able to gather information on inequality in a single indicator. The most popular formula for measuring inequality is the Gini coefficient. In this study it is supplemented by two percentile ratios: 90/10 and 75/25. Viewed together, all these indicators should provide comprehensive information on inequality. The Gini coefficient, contrary to the decile ratios, captures the whole range of incomes. In other words, it is sensitive to changes in all ranges of income. Therefore, an increase in inequality among the 'poor' contributes to overall inequality to a similar extent as an increase among the 'rich'. The 90/10-ratio focuses on the relative disparities between extreme incomes, while the 75/25-ratio captures the ones closer to the middle. It is justified to expect large disparities between countries with high (Sweden) and low (the USA) degrees of income redistribution. In countries of the first type, both income extremes are tempered by state policy. On the other hand, cross-national disparities between the 75/25-ratios should not be as pronounced, as the middle income groups do not participate as much in income redistribution. The study by Atkinson et al. (1995) confirms the above hypotheses. The 90/10-ratios amount to 5.94 and 2.72 for the USA (1986) and for Sweden (1987), respectively, while the 75/25-ratios amount to 2.42 and 1.65.

The Gini coefficient, informally speaking, combines information incorporated in the whole range of deciles. Nevertheless, like any single indicator it is unable to provide detailed information about all aspects of distribution.

The most important conclusions derived from the results displayed in Tables 3.18a-c are more or less consistent with those based on the decile analysis. Income distribution among pensioners is much more equal than the distribution among all persons. By contrast to the decile analysis, there are no significant changes in the overall equivalent income inequality between the years reviewed. The 90/10-ratio decreased slightly for pensioners after 1987 (due to increases in the lowest incomes, see Tables 3.17a-c), however, most of the others remained at approximately the same level. Both minor increases and decreases have been observed. There were no large discrepancies between changes in the Gini coefficients and the decile ratios, although some exceptions did occur. For example, a decrease in the Gini coefficient between 1987 and 1996 for pensioners in pensioner households was accompanied by an increase in the 75/25-ratio.

Table 3.18a: Income Inequality (persons), 1987

Type of person	Pension			Income per head			Equivalent income		
	Gini	90/10	75/25	Gini	90/10	75/25	Gini	90/10	75/25
Pensioners	0.205	2.44	1.57	0.255	3.21	1.70	0.255	3.12	1.76
male	0.209	2.24	1.61	0.258	3.26	1.77	0.252	3.11	1.74
female	0.164	2.03	1.43	0.253	3.18	1.66	0.257	3.15	1.75
Pensioners in pensioner households	0.211	2.59	1.62	0.241	3.12	1.61	0.230	2.99	1.56
male	0.219	2.67	1.67	0.242	3.10	1.60	0.229	2.96	1.57
female	0.203	2.43	1.58	0.246	3.19	1.66	0.233	2.99	1.56
Persons 60+	-	-	-	0.260	3.20	1.75	0.251	3.02	1.69
male	-	-	-	0.261	3.19	1.72	0.259	3.07	1.72
female	-	-	-	0.256	3.22	1.76	0.252	3.01	1.63
All persons	-	-	-	0.299	4.14	2.00	0.278	3.72	1.88
male	-	-	-	0.301	4.12	1.97	0.289	3.90	1.90
female	-	-	-	0.306	4.19	2.03	0.273	3.69	1.87

Source: Own calculations from individual household data.

Table 3.18b: Income Inequality (persons), 1993

Type of person	Pension			Income per head			Equivalent income		
	Gini	90/10	75/25	Gini	90/10	75/25	Gini	90/10	75/25
Pensioners	0.357	4.27	2.12	0.256	3.01	1.71	0.245	2.79	1.68
male	0.359	4.42	2.21	0.263	3.05	1.76	0.250	2.84	1.68
female	0.260	4.09	1.99	0.257	3.00	1.73	0.246	2.73	1.67
Pensioners in pensioner households	0.371	4.24	2.10	0.238	2.83	1.65	0.230	2.69	1.65
male	0.350	4.39	2.16	0.255	2.98	1.69	0.241	2.76	1.66
female	0.352	4.06	1.85	0.227	2.74	1.64	0.221	2.63	1.64
Persons 60+	-	-	-	0.282	3.29	1.77	0.270	3.01	1.73
male	-	-	-	0.290	3.36	1.80	0.271	3.09	1.76
female	-	-	-	0.281	2.27	1.74	0.265	3.00	1.70
All persons	-	-	-	0.331	4.12	2.05	0.308	3.69	1.91
male	-	-	-	0.336	4.23	2.07	0.313	3.77	1.93
female	-	-	-	0.326	4.14	2.04	0.303	3.63	1.90

Pension inequality (for both pensioners and pensioners living in pensioner households) is another story. It changed enormously after 1987. In that year pension inequality was significantly below equivalent income inequality of both pensioners and the general population. In 1993 and, to a slightly lesser extent, in 1996, pension inequality exceeded not only income inequality among pensioners, but also the equivalent income inequality of the whole population. There are at least two independent rationales behind these surprisingly high increases. The first one is a consequence of the political changes allowing a much higher variation of pensions. Next, the large numbers of 'new pensioners' (see sections 3.2.2 and 3.2.5.1) in 1990 and 1991 with relatively low benefits increased the disparities between the lowest and the highest pensions. It seems that disability pensioners (whose share increased considerably in the 1990s, see Table 3.11) contributed the most significant part to those changes. As many of them share their incomes with other household members, this did not substantially increase pensioner inequality. Taking into account only retirement benefits (see Szulc, 1999) pension inequality is much lower. This did not differ substantially from pensioners' income inequality.

Table 3.18c: Income Inequality (persons), 1996

Type of person	Pension			Income per head			Equivalent income		
	Gini	90/10	75/25	Gini	90/10	75/25	Gini	90/10	75/25
Pensioners	0.328	3.94	1.86	0.260	3.08	1.72	0.249	2.79	1.72
male	0.329	4.03	1.90	0.257	3.10	1.72	0.261	2.85	1.74
female	0.298	3.89	1.81	0.253	2.99	1.70	0.232	2.74	1.69
Pensioners in pensioner households	0.344	4.16	1.88	0.227	2.76	1.63	0.218	2.60	1.60
male	0.340	4.25	2.02	0.233	2.86	1.66	0.222	2.68	1.62
female	0.316	4.01	1.72	0.223	2.70	1.61	0.214	2.55	1.60
Persons 60+	-	-	-	0.272	3.12	1.74	0.260	2.85	1.68
male	-	-	-	0.258	3.11	1.72	0.247	2.81	1.67
female	-	-	-	0.264	3.13	1.73	0.254	2.83	1.68
All persons	-	-	-	0.331	4.16	2.00	0.309	3.62	1.88
male	-	-	-	0.336	4.16	2.05	0.316	3.69	1.91
female	-	-	-	0.332	4.16	2.04	0.310	3.67	1.87

It is interesting to note that pension inequality in 1993 was much higher than the earnings' inequality reported by Rutkowski (1996), both in terms of the 90/10 and the 75/25-ratios and Gini coefficients, calculated for that same year. On the contrary, in 1987 pension inequality was much lower than earnings' inequality.

3.7 Resources in Pensioner Households

The preceding analysis focused on the current incomes of pensioners and the elderly. These incomes are very sensitive to temporal changes in economic and political circumstances. This is especially true for the countries undergoing transition, for which substantial economic and political alterations are not uncommon. Hence, indicators based on current incomes and calculated for particular years may poorly reflect actual well-being. To provide a more complete picture of standards of living, indicators based on resources rather than on cash flows are inspected in this section. They comprise dwelling conditions and selected household durables.

The results are displayed in Table 3.19. It is not surprising that dwelling conditions of pensioners, measured by the number of persons per room are better than the national average. The average number of persons per room was by 33% (in 1987) or 38% (in 1996) lower for pensioners than for the whole population, whilst the average apartment size for pensioners was smaller by approximately 4 m^2 in 1987 (or 7%) and by 10 m^2 (15%) in 1993 and 1996. These results are mainly due to the lower number of persons per family and to their positions in the life cycle. Other durables and installations such as central heating, a running water supply, a bathroom in the household, telephone, car and a colour TV set are less likely to appear in pensioner households. The differences, however, are not very large. With a car being the only exception, in the 1990s, it was more than twice as unlikely to appear in pensioner households. To conclude, pensioners are living in relatively larger households that are typically less equipped with durables and installations.

130   **Table 3.19:   Housing Conditions and Household Equipment**

	Persons per room	Apt. size (m^2)	Central heating	Bath-room	Running water	Phone	Car	Colour TV
				1987				
Pensioners	0.92	54.6	49.9%	71.5%	83.0%	n.a.	16.7%	16.7%
All persons	1.38	58.5	59.2%	75.8%	85.2%	n.a.	26.8%	24.6%
				1993				
Pensioners	0.72	54.5	59.6%	74.1%	87.0%	24.2%	15.8%	59.7%
All persons	1.18	64.6	66.7%	81.2%	91.0%	28.7%	43.2%	81.1%
				1996				
Pensioners	0.71	56.8	57.9%	81.6%	90.6%	37.8%	16.1%	80.7%
All persons	1.15	66.7	68.0%	84.6%	93.5%	41.0%	48.0%	91.7%

Source: Own calculations from individual household data.

3.8 Some Concluding Remarks

3.8.1 Well-Being of the Elderly on the Eve of the New Pension System

The general results on the well-being of the elderly in Poland may be found to be somewhat surprising. Their material status in 1993 and especially in 1996, was relatively good. Moreover, it has improved between 1987 and 1996 (in some cases, opposite to national trends). Pensioners experienced significant shifts towards higher deciles in income distribution both in 1993 and 1996. Moreover, their poverty rates were much lower in the 1990s, while inequality measures did not differ significantly from those calculated for 1987 in spite of the large increase in pension inequality in 1993. A good material status may be attributed especially to those receiving retirement pension. Nonetheless, the results of comparing pensioners and the elderly against other types of persons or households should be interpreted very carefully. First of all, the favourable income position of pensioner households results, to some extent, from their size and composition. They are, on average, much smaller than most of the remaining types of households. It is well-known that large families with children usually attain lower standards of living than small, childless families. Moreover, there is some evidence from the past that the extent of income underreporting among pensioners is lower than observed among other types of households.

131

In spite of the reservations, which should apply to some of the statistical results on well-being, it is obvious that pensioners in Poland were not disadvantaged by the economic transformation.[8] Ironically, the widely criticized pension system protects them quite well. Nonetheless, the current system in Poland is at a turning point. In the coming years, demographic changes will raise the question of how to support an enlarging group of non-working elderly. It is obvious that the reforms launched in 1999 will not have instant effects, as the consequences of economic events that took place in the past are long-lasting. Maintaining an ineffective pension system for 50 years, together with early retirements and increasing benefits caused pension system expenditures to skyrocket and to exceed revenues in 1990. High unemployment rates also contributed significantly to this situation. Subsidies from the state budget became necessary to maintain the pension system.[9][10] The subsidization will continue even after the start of the reform process, which introduced free-market elements (voluntary capital funds) into the system and assured a strictly defined relation between individual contributions and benefits in the component to be under state control. It is expected that 'new pensioners' will gradually replace those benefiting from the old system, but this process may take several decades.

3.8.2 *On the Necessity of Monitoring the Well-Being of the Elderly*

The system capable of monitoring the consequences of both political decisions and people's individual choices seems to be an effective 'early warning' strategy. An already existing and relatively well-developed household budget survey conducted annually by the CSO establishes a sufficient database for that purpose. The present study displays the results of such an examination. Nonetheless, pension benefits and, consequently, the standards of living of a major part of the population in the third millennium are uncertain. In the coming decades, pensioners will cease to be a relatively consistent group.[11] Their incomes will depend on the state of the economy, the authorities' decisions, demographic processes, the performance of funds and, last but not least, people's individual choices. None of these factors are perfectly predictable. Nonetheless, it is possible to evaluate (by means of simulation methods) the impact of various strategies and processes on the well-being of the elderly. As they compose a significant and increasingly larger part of society, their well-being will have a considerable impact on the well-being of the nation as a whole.

Notes

1   Czech and Slovak Republics, Hungary and Poland.
2   The level of benefits might be changed by the parliament.
3   In January 2000, the second pillar programme covered about 12 million persons . A strong diversification of the numbers of customers among funds has been observed. The three largest ones covered more than 50% of persons participating in the second pillar programmes. It is estimated that the number of funds which may effectively exist on the Polish market, is between 8 and 10. Therefore, mergers are expected.
4   Although the recent figures and trends are less optimistic than those observed in 1996 and 1997.
5   25% after 1981, 38% after 1987, and 45% after 1989.
6   Although they cannot be considered as strict inequality measures as they lack some obvious properties. Namely, it is easy to demonstrate that the head count ratio decreases if the lowest incomes diminish (which results in a decline in the poverty line) but other incomes remain unchanged.
7   As stated in Szulc (1995), pensioner households were affected by the highest poverty over almost the entire 1980s if the absolute poverty line (the 'social minimum') is applied. It should be noted, however, that the pensioner household definition was based only on the main source of income of the head of the household.
8   This is claimed also for the Czech and Slovak Republics as well as for Hungary (see Schrooten et al., 1998).
9   It has been pointed out by Rutkowski (1998) that the pension system and unemployment allowances had contributed the most significant shares to the increase in relative and absolute social expenditures between 1987 and 1995.
10   The expansion of the social sector in order to maintain an ineffective system would also have long-term consequences for the economy as a whole. It is well-known that increasing the share of public expenditure retards economic growth (see, for example, Barro, 1997).
11   This process started in the early 1990s.

References

Atkinson, A./Rainwater, L./Smeeding, T. (1995) 'Income Distribution in European Countries', DAE Working Papers, MU 9506. Cambridge: The Microsimulation Unit, Department of Applied Economics, University of Cambridge.

Barro, R. J. (1997) *Determinants of Economics Growth; A Cross-Country Empirical Study*. Cambridge, Massachusetts: The MIT Press.

Office of the Government Plenipotentiary for Social Security Reform (1997) *Security through Diversity – Reform of the Pension System in Poland*. Warsaw.

Panek, T./ Szulc, A. (1991) *Income Distribution and Poverty – Theory and a Case Study of Poland in the 1980s*. Warsaw: Research Centre for Economic and Statistical Studies.

Perek-Bialas, J./ Topińska, I. (1998) Ubóstwo wśród emerytów i rencistów w Polsce, *Wiadomości Statystyczne*, 10: 19-24.

Polskie Tablice Trwania Zycia 1995-1996 (1997) Warsaw: Główny Urzad Statystyczny.

Rocznik Demograficzny, annually. Warsaw: Główny Urzad Statystyczny.

Rocznik Statystyczny, annually. Warsaw: Główny Urzad Statystyczny.

Rutkowski, J. J. (1996) 'Changes in the Wage Structure during Economic Transition in Central and Eastern Europe', World Bank Technical Paper no. 340, Washington, D. C.

Rutkowski, J. J. (1998) 'Welfare and the Labor Market in Poland', World Bank Technical Paper no. 417, Washington, D. C.

Schrooten, M./Smeeding, T./ Wagner, G. G. (1998) 'Old-Age Security Reforms in Central-Eastern Europe: The Cases of Czech Republic, Slovak, Hungary and Poland', Luxembourg Income Study Working Paper No. 189, Differdange.

Szulc, A. (1994) 'Poverty in Poland during the Transition Period: 1990-1992 Evidence', *Statistics in Transition*, 5: 669-682.

Szulc, A. (1995) 'Measurement of Poverty: Poland in the 1980s', *Review of Income and Wealth*, 2: 191-205.

Szulc, A. (1998) 'Poverty and Inequality in Poland in the 1990s', *RECESS Research Bulletin*, 3: 27-49.

Szulc, A. (1999) 'Trends in Economic Well-Being of the Elderly in Poland: 1987-1996', *Statistics in Transition*, 1: 79-101.

CHAPTER 4

Slovenia: Income Stability in a Turbulent Period of Economic Transition

Tine Stanovnik
Nada Stropnik

135

4.1 Introduction

All Central and East European countries have experienced major political, economic and social changes in the recent past, though the extent and depth of these changes vary considerably from country to country. Due to the fact that Slovenia had a fairly well-developed market economy even prior to the transition, the initial transition phase was perhaps less traumatic for Slovenia than for most other countries, which abruptly changed their political and economic system. Although it did experience a "transformation depression" (to use a Kornai expression), this was caused more by the independence proclaimed in 1991 and the dramatic changes in trade patterns which ensued, than by fundamental changes in the economic system. After the initial slump between 1990 and 1992, output has been increasing steadily, albeit at a modest rate. Slovenia now has a relatively high GDP per capita (actually the highest among all Central and East European countries in transition), a low inflation rate, a low level of public debt and an almost balanced general government budget. On the less bright side, Slovenia experienced a sharp drop in employment and a large increase in unemployed persons and pensioners. These developments can actually be traced back to the pre-transition period, since output and employment started decreasing already in 1989.

The initial drop in output and the more persistent decrease in employment are the two elements that form part of the underlying transition 'scenario' for almost all Central and East European countries. The decrease in output occurred at a time of rising social needs caused by the large increase in the potentially vulnerable population – mostly the unemployed and pensioners – and it presented very serious challenges to the public authorities in these countries. The initial response was in quite a number of cases, but by no means all, the desire to retain the existing level of social benefits. The consequence was predictable: a large increase in the overall costs of social insurance. Taking a long-term view, it seems obvious that this continuous rise (measured, say, as a percentage of GDP) is untenable and unsustainable. It is thus not surprising that the reform of social insurance systems, and pension reform in particular, enjoy high priority on the agenda in all transition countries. True, the need for pension reform is also evident in the member states of the European Union, but this reform is driven more by unfavourable long-term demographic trends. It is not the result of a sudden and rapid increase in the cost of social insurance systems, caused mostly by structural shifts and large increases in potentially vulnerable segments of the population.

All three countries in transition represented in this book have undergone reforms in their pension systems. In the case of Hungary and Poland these may be labelled as fundamental, since part of the pension system has – in effect – been privatized through the introduction of privately-managed pension saving schemes. Slovenia has opted for a less radical, but nevertheless quite comprehensive pension reform, introduced in January 2000. This includes not only changes in the first pillar, but also provides the legal framework for the introduction of occupational pension schemes, i.e. the 'classic' second pillar.

This study will not concentrate on the description of the pension system (and pension reforms) in Slovenia, but rather on the most important outcomes. In other words, it will present a detailed analysis of the socio-economic position of pensioners and the elderly in Slovenia. While such an analysis is important *per se*, it also provides a basis for the evaluation and monitoring of the pension reform. Though considerable research on the socio-economic position of pensioners and the elderly in Slovenia has already been performed (see Stanovnik, 1997), this paper differs from previous research in that it is conducted under a unified framework and methodology, which enables important and vital cross-country comparisons.

The structure of our study is as follows. Section 4.2 briefly describes the basic elements and features of the Slovenian pension system as well as the most recent developments. Section 4.3 provides information on data sources, whereas section 4.4 presents some general information on the socio-economic characteristics of pensioners and pensioner households in Slovenia. Section 4.5 provides a detailed assessment of the income dynamics and income sources of pensioner households. Section 4.6, by means of a decile analysis, probes into the income distribution of various types of pensioner households. This section also provides results on poverty incidence and income inequality. In section 4.7 home ownership, quality of housing and ownership of consumer durables are analysed, whereas section 4.8 offers some concluding remarks.

4.2 Institutional Framework and Demographic and Economic Changes

137

The Slovenian social security system is a social insurance system and is organized as follows: mandatory health insurance falls under the responsibility of the National Health Administration (NHA), while mandatory pension and invalidity insurance is under the responsibility of the National Pension Administration (NPA). These two institutions are semi-autonomous and separate entities of public finance. They are financed mostly through contributions, although transfers from the central government budget are becoming an increasingly important source of revenue of the NPA, as is shown in Table 4.7. Other forms of coverage of social risks (unemployment benefits, maternity leave) are also partly financed by contributions, but these social benefits are financed by institutions of the central government. For example, unemployment benefits are financed by the National Employment Office. Of the total consolidated public finance expenditures, the share of the central government accounts for about 45%, the NPA for 30%, the NHA for c. 15% and local public budgets for c.10%.

Like most public pension systems in Europe, the Slovenian pension system has been under considerable strain since the beginning of the 1990s. Unfortunately, there was no early consensus on the necessary reform measures, in spite of the fact that the awareness of the need for reforms was widespread.[1] Consequently, the system did not undergo any noteworthy changes in the period 1992-1999 and it took until the end of 1999 for the new Pension Act to be enacted by parliament. This long period of inactivity may appear surprising, not only in view of the large changes in labour force participation and the restructuring of the Slovenian economy, but also in the light of the pace of pension reform in some of the other Central European countries in transition.

Obviously, the pension system cannot be presented without looking more closely at the underlying changes in economic and demographic conditions, labour force participation, GDP growth, etc. This positive description will be interspersed with a more normative description of some of the salient features of the pension system and the relevant changes introduced by the new 1999 Pension Act.

4.2.1 Legal Retirement Age

Eligibility for retirement depends not only on age, but also on the contribution period of the insured. As a rule, the longer the contribution period, the earlier one may enter the pension system. Thus, for an insured person having a full contribution period, which was 40 years for men and 35 for women, the legal retirement age in Slovenia was 58 years for men and 53 for women. Both criteria (age and contribution period) must be met in order to qualify for a full old-age pension. According to the 1999 Pension Act, the retirement age for women will be gradually increased to 58 years, and the qualifying contribution period to 38 years.

A partial old-age pension is granted to persons aged 63 (men) and 58 (women) who have contributed for at least 20 years. The age criterion for women will gradually increase to 61. Alternately, the partial old-age pension is granted to persons aged 65 (men) and 60 (women) who have a contribution period of at least 15 years. Also, according to the new Pension Act, the age criterion for women will gradually increase to 63.

4.2.2 Average Retirement Age and Life Expectancy

The average retirement age is shown in Table 4.1. Severe macroeconomic conditions and profligate early retirement schemes caused a decrease in the average retirement age in 1990, bottoming out in 1991. Since then, the average retirement age has somewhat increased: in 1997, it was 57.5 for men and 54.0 for women.

Table 4.1: Average Retirement Age (old-age retirement), Slovenia

Year	Men	Women
1989	58.3	55.2
1990	57.7	53.6
1991	56.1	52.3
1992	56.2	52.5
1993	56.2	53.3
1994	57.6	53.2
1995	57.5	53.1
1996	57.5	54.0
1997	57.5	54.0

Sources: National Pension Administration, statistical reports.

Assuming the current average retirement age as well as the current life expectancy to be as shown in Tables 4.1 and 4.2, a male pensioner in Slovenia would receive a pension for an average of about 18 years, and a female pensioner for about 26 years. Of course, the actual figures are lower. Thus, in 1997, a male old-age pensioner received – on average – a pension for 12.3 years, and the comparable figure for a female old-age pensioner was 15.4 years.[2]

Table 4.2: Life Expectancy, Slovenia, 1970-1972, 1980-1982 and 1995-1996

Life expectancy	Men			Women		
	1970-72	1980-82	1995-96	1970-72	1980-82	1995-96
At birth	65.4	67.5	70.8	72.9	75.1	78.3
At age 60	14.7	15.8	16.8	18.4	19.7	21.5

Source: Statistical Yearbook (1997), Statistical Office of the Republic of Slovenia, statistical reports (for life expectancy at 60 in 1970-1972 and 1980-1982).

4.2.3 Population, Activity Rates, and the Ratio between Contributors and Pensioners

Due to the very low fertility rate in Slovenia, the share of the population under the age of 15 has been decreasing, while the share of the population aged 60 and over has been increasing steadily (Table 4.3). Although fertility in Slovenia has been decreasing for the past 100 years, the pace has accelerated in the recent past: in the period 1980-1997 the number of live births per year decreased by 39%. By 1980 the total fertility rate per woman had fallen below 2.15 – the number of children, which a generation needs to ensure its replacement – and by 1997 it was merely 1.25.

Table 4.3: Population of Slovenia, by Age Group (percentage)

Year	Shares of population (%)			
	0-14 years	15-59	60-74	75 and over
1971	24.1	60.9	12.1	2.9
1981	23.0	63.5	9.8	3.7
1991	20.0	63.6	11.9	4.5
1992	19.6	63.6	12.5	4.3
1993	19.1	63.8	13.0	4.1
1994	18.5	64.0	13.3	4.2
1995	18.0	64.1	13.6	4.3
1996	17.5	64.4	13.7	4.4
1997	17.0	64.5	13.9	4.6

Source: Statistical Yearbook (1990-1998).

According to the 1991 data on the activity of the Slovenian population, which are shown in Table 4.4, 61.5% of the population aged 50-54 were employed. For the age cohort 55-59, this share was 33.3%, whereas it was 22.5% for the age cohort 60-64. As compared to 1981, the share of employed persons considerably decreased for the age cohorts 50-54 and 55-59. It has, however, increased for the age cohort 65-69 in which, in 1991, it amounted to a full 19.5%. It looks as though early retirement was more attractive to those up to 64 years of age. Also, it is interesting to note that one in twenty persons aged 70 and over remained employed in 1991, which was still much less than one in nine persons in 1981.

Table 4.4: Activity of Population Aged 50 and Over, Slovenia

					1981			
Age group	*Population* (000)	*Active* (000)	%	*Employed* (000)	%	*Inactive* (000)	%
50-54	115	78	67.6	78	67.4	37	32.4
55-59	96	38	39.5	38	39.4	58	60.5
60-64	56	13	23.9	13	23.9	43	76.1
65-69	70	12	17.0	12	17.0	58	82.9
70+	138	15	11.2	15	11.2	123	88.8
Total	476	157	32.9	156	32.8	320	67.1
					1991			
Age group	*Population* (000)	*Active* (000)	%	*Employed* (000)	%	*Inactive* (000)	%
50-54	110	70	63.3	68	61.5	40	36.7
55-59	109	37	33.9	36	33.3	72	66.1
60-64	102	23	22.7	23	22.5	79	77.3
65-69	81	16	19.6	16	19.5	65	80.4
70+	133	7	5.2	7	5.1	126	94.8
Total	535	153	28.5	150	28.0	382	71.5

Note: Errors are due to rounding. Percentages are based on non-rounded figures.
Source: Statistical Office of the Republic of Slovenia.

Table 4.5: Contributors/pensioners Ratio, Slovenia

Year	Contributors/Pensioners
1983	3.64
1989	2.75
1990	2.48
1991	2.08
1992	1.80
1993	1.79
1994	1.76
1995	1.74
1996	1.71
1997	1.73

Note: Pensioners refer to old-age, disability and survivor pensioners.
Source: National Pension Administration, 1997: 10, 19.

Due to the decrease in activity rates, the ratio between pension contributors
– i.e. the employed and self-employed – and pensioners deteriorated significantly, as is shown in Table 4.5.

Table 4.6 offers a glimpse of the absolute magnitude of the increase in
the number of pensioners, occurring in a period of stagnating population
growth and negative or modestly positive GDP growth rates.

Table 4.6: GDP, Population and Pensioners in Slovenia

Year	GDP (billion US$)	Population (000)	Pensioners (000)
1983	6.6	1,933	288
1985	7.4	1,933	311
1990	17.4	1,998	384
1991	12.7	2,002	419
1992	12.5	1,996	449
1993	12.7	1,991	458
1994	14.4	1,989	458
1995	18.7	1,988	460
1996	18.9	1,991	463
1997	-	1,985	468

Note: Pensioners refer to old-age, disability and survivor pensioners.

Source: Statistical Yearbook (1990-1998), National Pension Administration, statistical reports.

4.2.4 Early Retirement

The increasing number of pensioners in Slovenia was very much caused by
the increase in early retirement that resulted from the economic transition
which started in 1990. Early retirement seemed at the time to be the least
painful solution for alleviating tensions on the labour market and an effective measure for preventing an even larger increase in unemployment. In
retrospect, it entailed quite large social costs without commensurate benefits. This measure prevented massive unemployment among the elderly,
but it did not open up employment opportunities for the young: their labour force participation rate is low and their unemployment rate quite high.

In order to appreciate the magnitude of the increase in the number of
pensioners in the first years of transition, Table 4.7 shows (for the 1990s) the
annual inflow of new pensioners into the pension system.

Table 4.7: Annual Inflow of Pensioners, Slovenia

Year	Total inflow (000)	Inflow of old-age pensioners (000)
1990	75.3	49.2
1991	76.1	48.8
1992	67.4	43.2
1993	53.0	25.9
1994	45.2	21.2
1995	46.6	22.8
1996	53.6	26.4
1997	47.8	22.8

Note: Early retirement is included in the category of old-age pensioners.

Source: National Pension Administration, statistical reports.

4.2.5 The Level of Pensions

Pensions are calculated on the basis of the best 10-year average of (net) wages; the 1999 Pension Act gradually extends this period to the best 18-year average. The monthly amount of this calculated average is the so-called pension base. Employees do not have the option to choose their base for pension contribution payments, which is simply their gross wage. Farmers, self-employed and employers in the private sector have a certain latitude in their choice of the base for paying pension contributions, however, this amount cannot be less than 64% of the average gross wage; the new Pension Act sets the floor at the level of the minimum wage, which is currently 43% of the average gross wage.

For the minimum contribution period, i.e. 15 years, pensions currently amount to 35% for men and 40% for women of the computed pension base. According to the new Pension Act, these values will be 35% for men and 38% for women. The present accrual rate, which is the increase in pension for each additional year of contribution (above the minimum contribution period), is 2 percentage points for men and 2.25 percentage points for women. In other words, the replacement rate for men with a full 40-year contribution record reached 85% of their best 10-year average wage. The new Pension Act stipulates a considerable decrease and gender equalization of accrual rates, i.e. the accrual rate is to be 1.5 percentage points for both sexes. This means that the replacement rate for men with a 40-year contribution record will reach 72.5% of their best 18-year average wage. Bearing in mind that the average in the former case is based on the best 10-year period, whereas in the latter case it is based on the best 18-year period, the real decrease in pensions is actually greater than can be surmised by these percentages.

The Pension Act will not change pension indexation, which will still be based on the rise in the average net wage, though pension up-rating is to be less frequent than in the past. This up-rating will not be automatic, as it was in the past, but will be contingent on the signing of new national wage contracts; thus, quite possibly, pension up-rating could occur only once per year. The indexation rules which were applied in the period following the 1992 Pension Act explain why, in spite of very unfavourable macroeconomic conditions and demographic trends, the ratio between the average net old-age pension and average net wage in Slovenia has remained fairly stable and very high (Table 4.8).

144

Table 4.8: Average Net Old-age Pension and Net Wage, Slovenia

Year	Average net old-age pension / net wage
1983	71.9
1989	80.0
1990	89.2
1991	73.8
1992	78.4
1993	74.5
1994	77.2
1995	77.9
1996	75.8
1997	75.4

Note: The high replacement rate in 1990 was due to the indexation rule valid at that time. Because of this rule, the high inflation rate in 1989 caused a pension 'spill-over' effect in 1990.

Source: National Pension Administration, 1997: 24.

There are a floor and a ceiling on the pension base in the new Pension Act. The minimum pension base is set at 64% of the net average wage, whereas the maximum pension base is set at four times the minimum pension base. The ratio between the maximum and minimum pension base has actually decreased, since according to the 1992 Pension Act it was 4.8. In other words, pensions for persons with the same contribution period will not exceed the 4:1 ratio. Of course, people do not have the same contribution period and pension differences will be larger than 4:1. The lowest possible old-age pension is equal to 35% of the minimum pension base, which amounts to 22% of average net wage (0.35 x 0.64). Farmers are virtually the sole beneficiaries of this provision.

A supplementary allowance is paid by the National Pension Administration to all pensioners whose pension is lower than the lowest pension for the full contribution period, and whose total income is below the minimum cost of living of a pensioner or a pensioner household. It is aimed at ensuring a social minimum for pensioners. In 1997, supplementary allowances amounted to 1.4% of all outlays of the National Pension Administration.

145

The level of supplementary allowance depends on the contribution period for all types of pensions except for survivor pensions, where it depends on the number of family members as well. The basis for determining the supplementary allowance level is the difference between the individual's pension and the lowest pension for the full contribution period. Supplementary allowance amounts to 60% (for male pensioners) and 70% (for female pensioners) of the basis for the contribution period of 15 years or less. For each additional year, supplementary allowance increases by 2%, but cannot be higher than 100% of the basis. The average amount of supplementary allowance increased from 15.3% of the average pension in 1991 to 16.7% in 1997.

On the other hand, the number of supplementary allowance recipients has been decreasing relative to the total number of pensioners: in 1991, the share of supplementary allowance recipients among pensioners was 15.5%, and 9.9% in 1997. The highest share of the supplementary allowance recipients was among pensioners receiving survivor pensions; this sub-group also received the highest average level of supplementary allowance.

4.2.6 Financing of Pensions

In spite of the decreasing contributor/pensioner ratio, the average replacement rate has not changed much since 1991. This, of course, means that the ratio between pension expenditures and GDP has been increasing since 1991, as shown in Table 4.9.

Table 4.9: Revenues and Expenditures of the NPA, as a Percentage of GDP

Year	Revenues without state subsidies	State subsidies	All expenditures[3]
1991	12.72	0.15	10.92
1992	13.44	0.01	13.46
1993	13.97	0.45	14.05
1994	13.50	0.87	14.42
1995	12.98	1.12	14.67
1996	11.18	3.27	14.48

Note: In the years 1991 and 1993, the balance of the NPA was in surplus, while in other years the NPA incurred a deficit.

Source: National Pension Administration (1991-1997).

As mentioned earlier, pensions are mostly financed through contributions. In 1997, the total contribution rate was 24.35% of the employee's gross wage (Table 4.10); the employers' share was 8.85%, and the employees' share was 15.50%. The somewhat surprising decrease in contribution rates in 1996 and 1997, which also continued in 1998, was a result of macroeconomic policy considerations; it was hoped that this measure would improve the competitiveness of the Slovenian economy. In fact, this hope did not materialize. Wages increased in real terms, the net result being that labour costs did not decrease by much.

Since 1996, the gap between the NPA's own revenues and expenditures has been widening and is being covered by transfers from the central government budget. Actually, budget transfers commenced at an earlier date, in 1993, when the central government started honouring its obligations toward the NPA. This means that it started paying for the pension benefits that were imposed on the NPA by parliament (favourable pensions for the military personnel and policemen, payment of the employer's part for farm-

146

ers, etc.). Since 1996, however, the major purpose of transfers from the central government budget has been to compensate the revenue loss which resulted from the decrease in the employers' contribution rate in 1996.

Table 4.10:   Pension Contribution Rates

Year	Contribution rate as a percentage of gross wages		
	Employer	Employee	Total
1989	3.45	19.10	22.55
1990	3.62	19.10	22.72
1991	14.40	14.40	28.80
1992	14.40	14.40	28.80
1993	15.41	15.41	30.82
1994	15.50	15.50	31.00
1995	15.50	15.50	31.00
1996	11.07	15.50	26.57
1997	8.85	15.50	24.35

Source: National Pension Administration, statistical reports.

4.2.7 Pension System Reform

As already observed in the preceding sections, the 1999 Pension Act introduced a number of parameter changes within the first pillar, the most important being more stringent entrance conditions and the reduction in the level of pension benefits. Of course, these changes are to be phased-in gradually and their full effect will be felt by the year 2019. The 1999 Pension Act introduced a number of innovations of the incentive-disincentive type. Additional contribution years above the maximum number (40 for men and 38 for women) will receive higher pension accrual rates; similarly, persons who enter the pension system in the age bracket of 58 to 63 and do not have the necessary maximum contribution period receive a negative accrual rate, which varies between 3.6% and 1.2% (depending on age).

The 1999 Pension Act introduced a national pension for those who do not receive any pension income (either in Slovenia or from abroad). Persons 65 years of age who have lived in Slovenia for at least 30 years and have low income from other sources are eligible for this benefit. In effect, it will be means-tested.

The 1999 Pension Act also provides the legal framework for occupational pension schemes, i.e. the second pillar of the pension system. For some occupations, participation in these schemes will be mandatory and the organization of these schemes will be the responsibility of the employer. In the previous system, the first pillar integrated all risks and certain occupations had very favourable treatment (for example, one contribution year was counted as 16 months). These occupational risks will now be relegated to the second pillar. For other firms, participation in the second pillar is voluntary, but employers must provide equal access to all employees. At present it is quite difficult to speculate how widespread these schemes might become, since much depends on the initiative of large employers and tax incentives, some of which have yet to materialize.

4.3 Data Sources

Our analysis is based on the Household Expenditure Survey (HES) data. These surveys contain a wealth of data not only on household income and expenditure, but also on the social and demographic characteristics of household members, housing and the ownership of consumer durables. The surveys have been undertaken by the Statistical Office of Slovenia since 1963 at regular 5-year intervals, with the last one undertaken in 1993. In 1997, the Statistical Office started a 'new' HES, based on a new methodology (more extensive use of diaries etc.), covering the same topic area (income, expenditure, assets and socio-economic characteristics of household members). The 1997, 1998 and 1999 surveys are to be suitably merged to produce a data set comparable in size to the 1993 HES.

Besides these large-scale surveys carried out on a large sample and in 5-year intervals, there were also smaller annual surveys carried out on a sample approximately one third of the size of the 'big' sample, meaning some 1,000 households. This sample size is too small for the purposes of our analysis. Though, it has to be stated that Milanovic (1998) has performed some analyses on the basis of these smaller surveys. His results, which extend to 1995, show that there are no noteworthy changes in the general trends discernible from the 1993 survey. Because of the small sample size, his analysis does not extend to population subgroups.

The HES is a two-stage stratified sample, with the primary sampling units being census districts and households being the secondary units (five households in each chosen primary unit). The stratification has been subject to various changes throughout the years. Also, in 1993, households were weighted according to the differing sampling probabilities of households of different size.

Generally speaking, the quality of the survey is satisfactory, although not without its ups and downs. The 1988 survey was at the lower end of the spectrum, due doubtlessly to the high inflation rate, the poor training of collectors and generally poor organization. Thus, our analysis is performed on two HES data sets, i.e. surveys conducted in the years 1983 and 1993. This enables the comparison between the pre-transition and transition point in time. The sample comprised 3,992 households in 1983, and 3,270 in 1993.

The survey questionnaire does not contain data on individual sources of income, but only household aggregates for each source. Thus, for example, if two household members are pensioners, one cannot deduce the pension of each member but only their joint (total) amount of pension received in a given year.

149

4.4 Some Socio-Economic Characteristics of Households, Pensioners and Pensioner Households

4.4.1 Pensioners and the Socio-Economic Structure of the Slovenian Population

For most Central and East European countries, the large increase in the number of pensioners has been one of the more important phenomena observed during the first years of transition (Stanovnik and Stropnik, 1996). As we have already noted, in Slovenia this increase was mostly due to generous early retirement schemes.

In the period 1983-1993, the share of pensioners in the total population increased from 15.5% to 19.7%. The increase was larger for female pensioners: in 1983 they represented 16.1%, whereas in 1993 they represented a full 22% of the total female population. The increase in the share of male pensioners was less pronounced: in 1983 they represented 14.7%, whereas in 1993 their share increased to 17.6% of the total male population.

Changes in the socio-economic status of the household members in Slovenia
are shown in Table 4.11. It is quite evident that in the 10-year time span, along
with a decrease in the average household size by 0.13 persons, the structure
of household members according to socio-economic status has changed
considerably.

Thus, the share of employees decreased significantly, followed by a
large increase in the share of unemployed persons and pensioners. Also, the
share of dependants decreased, due not only to the diminishing number of
children, but also to the decreasing number of elderly without any income
sources.[4]

Table 4.11: **The Structure of Household Members According to Their
Socio-economic Status; Slovenia 1983 and 1993**

Year	1983	1993
Status of household members (%)		
Employee	43.2	36.2
Active in agriculture*	0.0	2.6
Active in other occupations*	4.1	2.3
Unemployed	0.3	5.3
Pensioner	15.5	19.7
Dependent	36.3	30.9
Other	0.6	3.0
Total	100.0	100.0
Average size of household	3.17	3.04

Note: * In 1983 there was no distinction between these two categories; the figure 4.1 refers to persons
active in agriculture and other occupations.

Source: Household Expenditure Survey (1983, 1993), own calculations.

In Table 4.12, one can see that in 1983 the share of pensioners was decreasing – roughly speaking – when moving from the lowest to the highest income decile. In 1993, however, with the exception of the top income decile,
pensioners were fairly evenly distributed across all income deciles.[5] This indicates that in Slovenia, the presence of a pensioner does not necessarily increase the probability of a more unfavourable financial situation of the household. It also provides evidence on the micro level that the new pensioners
retired under favourable conditions.

Table 4.12:   Share of Pensioners, as a Percentage of All Persons in an Income
Decile, 1983 and 1993

	Income deciles										
1983	1	2	3	4	5	6	7	8	9	10	All
Share of pensioners	20.9	22.3	18.7	16.8	13.9	13.0	13.4	10.9	12.7	11.8	15.5
Average size of household	3.01	3.00	3.26	3.33	3.45	3.32	3.21	3.22	3.15	2.79	3.17
1993											
Share of pensioners	20.7	21.4	22.6	20.4	20.8	20.2	23.8	19.0	16.7	13.1	19.7
Average size of household	2.75	3.07	3.06	3.15	3.11	3.15	3.03	3.12	3.07	2.85	3.04

Note: Income deciles are appointed for the whole population of households, i.e. each decile contains
10% of all households.

Source: Household Expenditure Survey (1983, 1993), own calculations.

4.4.2 Pensioner Age

The average age of the pensioner population is not increasing, in spite of
the increase in life expectancy. In 1983, the average age of all pensioners was
65.4 years, and in 1993 it was 64.1 years (Table 4.13), i.e. a decrease of 1.3
years, in a decade in which life expectancy increased by 2.6 years for men
and 2.3 years for women! This decrease is mostly due to the large inflow of
new 'young' pensioners.

The average age of heads of pensioner households in 1983 and 1993, in
total and by four household types and income deciles, is also shown in Table 4.13. Pensioners living in single pensioner households are – on average
– older than the total pensioner population. The same can be said for heads
of couple pensioner households: their age is – on average – higher than the
average for all pensioners. In this case, the difference is not large; in 1993
the average age of head of couple pensioner household was 64.9 years,
whereas the average age of all pensioners was 64.1.

Table 4.13: Average Age of All Pensioners and of Heads of Pensioner Households, by Income Deciles, 1983 and 1993

Income deciles	1983						1993					
	All pens.	All	Average age of heads of pensioner households				All pens.	All	Average age of heads of pensioner households			
			Single male	Single female	Couple	Other			Single male	Single female	Couple	Other
1	68.4	69.8	(78.5)	71.9	71.0	63.0	66.0	66.6	(61.2)	69.0	66.0	65.6
2	66.6	67.4	(68.4)	68.4	68.5	62.3	67.1	69.4	(69.8)	71.6	69.2	59.1
3	67.4	68.8	(71.8)	71.3	67.6	62.7	63.9	64.9	(71.3)	66.7	64.7	57.4
4	65.5	67.6	(67.5)	69.8	67.7	63.5	64.4	64.9	(61.2)	67.3	63.1	65.4
5	65.9	67.1	(69.5)	69.6	64.5	68.0	62.5	62.9	(67.1)	65.0	60.9	56.4
6	62.6	65.5	(75.0)	65.3	65.6	60.2	63.5	66.7	(68.0)	68.6	65.4	66.0
7	62.9	64.9	(83.5)	66.3	64.0	60.3	63.3	66.4	(69.6)	70.6	64.0	61.5
8	64.7	66.2	(63.5)	64.8	67.4	64.5	62.9	66.2	(69.5)	70.0	65.1	59.9
9	64.0	65.6	(67.0)	64.2	65.0	67.7	64.1	67.1	(64.0)	70.1	64.7	72.6
10	62.3	63.5	(73.0)	63.6	63.9	58.0	62.7	66.5	(63.6)	68.7	66.6	61.2
Total	65.4	67.4	71.1	68.7	67.3	63.1	64.1	66.2	66.1	68.7	64.9	62.0

Note: 1. Income deciles are appointed for the whole population of households, i.e. each decile contains 10% of all households.

2. Brackets indicate small sample size.

Source: Household Expenditure Survey (1983, 1993), own calculations.

4.4.3 Pensioners and Household Size

Table 4.14 shows the distribution of all persons and pensioners according to household size. The quite high concentration of pensioners in small households is well evident. In 1993, 19.8% of all pensioners and only 5.4% of the total population lived in single households. Pensioners are particularly concentrated in two-person households; in 1983, 42.8% of all pensioners lived in this type of household, while the comparable figure for 1993 was 39.6%.

Table 4.14: **Distribution of All Persons and Pensioners by Household Size (percentage)**

Year	Household size				
	1 person	2 persons	3 persons	4 persons	≥ 5 persons
1983					
All persons (%)	4.1	14.6	20.4	34.0	26.9
Pensioners (%)	17.3	42.8	16.9	8.7	14.4
1993					
All persons (%)	5.4	14.6	22.8	33.5	23.6
Pensioners (%)	19.8	39.6	18.4	9.7	12.4

Source: Household Expenditure Survey (1983, 1993), own calculations.

Table 4.15 shows the shares of pensioners living in different types of pensioner households as a percentage of all pensioners. One can observe that the share of pensioners living in pensioner households has been steadily increasing. There is a gender difference, though it is not very pronounced, if we compare only the aggregates, i.e. all pensioner households. This shows that 59.3% of all female pensioners lived in pensioner households in 1993, whereas the comparable figure for male pensioners is 52.7%. However, a comparison of specific types of pensioner households reveals important differences: female pensioners are more likely to live in single households: a full 28.7% of all female pensioners in 1993 lived alone. On the other hand, male pensioners are more likely to live in couple pensioner households. In 1993, 35.8% of all male pensioners lived in couple pensioner households. This, of course, corresponds to our expectations, since women tend to live longer than men.

Table 4.15:   Pensioners Living in Pensioner Households, by Gender, in 1983 and 1993, as a Percentage of All Pensioners (within gender)

1983	Male	Female	All
Pensioners in single households	5.2	27.7	17.3
Pensioners in couple pensioner households	38.9	16.6	26.9
Pensioners in other pensioner households	9.1	10.7	10.0
Pensioners in pensioner households	53.2	55.0	54.2
Other pensioners	46.8	45.0	45.8
All pensioners	100.0	100.0	100.0
1993	*Male*	*Female*	*All*
Pensioners in single households	7.9	28.7	19.8
Pensioners in couple pensioner households	35.8	21.5	27.6
Pensioners in other pensioner households	9.0	9.0	9.0
Pensioners in pensioner households	52.7	59.3	56.4
Other pensioners	47.3	40.7	43.6
All pensioners	100.0	100.0	100.0

Source: Household Expenditure Survey (1983, 1993), own calculations.

4.5   Income and Income Sources of Pensioner Households

4.5.1 Pensions and Household Income

Table 4.11 shows us the large changes in the socio-economic structure of Slovenian households in the period 1983-1993. The number of employees decreased considerably, whereas the number of pensioners, self-employed and unemployed increased. From Table 4.12 we can see that the share of pensioners increased from 15.5% in 1983 to 19.7% in 1993. Although the proportion of pensioners increased in all income deciles, the increase was actually more pronounced in the higher income deciles, showing that pensioners have improved their relative income position.

In other words, the share of pensions, as a percentage of household income, increased in all income deciles, but was more pronounced in the higher deciles. Overall, the share of pensions in household current monetary income in Slovenia was 14.6% in 1983, and 20.7% in 1993, as shown in Table 4.16.

Table 4.16:   Income Sources of All Households, by Income Deciles (percentage)

Decile	\ Income sources, 1983							
	A	B	C	D	E	F	G	H	I
1	42.7	2.1	30.1	8.4	0.5	14.1	0.7	1.3	0.1
2	56.0	1.4	28.5	6.3	1.1	5.6	0.4	0.8	0.0
3	65.8	1.3	21.4	3.2	0.7	6.1	0.4	1.0	0.2
4	71.3	0.8	19.9	2.9	0.5	3.0	0.5	0.8	0.0
5	76.2	1.1	13.6	2.8	0.5	4.0	0.8	0.9	0.0
6	76.9	0.9	13.6	1.7	0.5	4.9	0.6	1.0	0.1
7	78.5	1.2	13.0	1.8	0.3	3.8	0.7	0.6	0.0
8	79.8	1.0	11.2	1.9	0.3	4.8	0.3	0.6	0.2
9	74.9	1.9	11.5	1.2	1.8	6.6	1.2	0.8	0.2
10	67.4	1.8	9.2	0.9	2.7	12.2	3.2	1.6	1.0
All	71.7	1.3	14.6	2.3	1.1	6.6	1.1	1.0	0.3

Decile	\ Income sources, 1993							
	A	B	C	D	E	F	G	H	I
1	32.7	2.4	37.9	16.0	0.6	8.7	0.3	1.4	0.0
2	44.6	1.9	31.9	11.1	0.2	9.0	0.2	0.9	0.1
3	55.6	1.5	29.9	6.4	0.9	4.5	0.2	0.8	0.0
4	57.9	2.3	23.8	6.1	0.7	7.5	0.8	0.9	0.0
5	63.1	2.0	21.9	5.1	0.9	5.7	0.3	0.9	0.0
6	58.8	3.0	24.6	5.2	1.3	5.7	0.6	0.8	0.0
7	60.3	2.5	23.3	3.6	1.6	6.6	1.3	0.8	0.0
8	62.4	2.5	21.7	2.4	1.0	7.0	1.0	2.0	0.0
9	61.9	3.3	15.8	2.0	2.7	11.3	2.1	0.8	0.0
10	54.7	4.3	10.8	0.9	3.8	16.4	5.6	2.9	0.6
All	57.4	2.9	20.7	4.1	1.9	9.5	2.0	1.4	0.2

Note: Deciles are appointed for the whole population of households, i.e. each decile contains 10% of all households.

Legend: A. Wages and salaries from primary employment; B. Income from secondary employment; C. Pensions (old-age, disability, survivor); D. Other social benefits (unemployment benefit, income supplement, child allowance, sick pay, maternity and parental leave, scholarships, etc.); E. Income from abroad; F. Self-employment income; G. Income from sales and rent of property; H. Gifts, lottery, etc.; I. Other.

Source: Household Expenditure Survey (1983, 1993), own calculations.

Although the share of pensions in the highest (10th) income decile increased modestly, from 9.2% to 10.8%, the increase in other higher income deciles has been considerable as well. Thus, for households in the 9th income decile pensions represented 15.8% of their current monetary income in 1993 whereas for households, which were situated in the 9th income decile in 1983, pensions represented only 11.5% of their current monetary income.

Table 4.16 shows that primary employment is still the most important income source for the category 'all households' but its share decreased from 71.7% (in 1983) to 57.4% of the household total current monetary income by 1993. Income from part-time employment ('secondary employment') and income from self-employment have increased their shares, as well as income received as social benefits (apart from pensions).[6]

4.5.2 Income Dynamics of Pensioner Households

156

In section 4.5.1, we concluded that the relative income position of pensioners has improved in the 10-year period 1983-1993. It is important to ascertain not only the relative income position, but also the dynamics of the absolute income levels. This is shown in Table 4.17, which presents the median equivalent household current monetary income for various household types for the two points in time, the years 1983 and 1993.

Table 4.17:   Median Equivalent Household Current Monetary Income in 1983 and 1993 (annual amounts, income in thousands of 1993 tolars)

Household type	1983	1993	Index (1983=100)
All households	490.5	422.3	86
All pensioner households	377.2	376.0	100
– single female	367.7	352.0	96
– single male	376.6	372.0	99
– couple	402.5	425.3	106
– other	338.8	324.7	96
Average net wage	651.8	561.9	86
Average net old-age pension	468.9	413.2	88

Source: Household Expenditure Survey (1983, 1993), own calculations; Statistical Yearbook (1997) (for average wage); NPA, statistical reports (for average old-age pension).

Table 4.17 shows a rather noticeable drop in household equivalent income in the period 1983-1993. This is mostly due to the large decrease in real income in the late 1980s and early 1990s, the years prior to the disintegration of Yugoslavia and the first years of the transition period. Taking 1983 as our base (=100), the 1993 value of the median household equivalent income was only 86. This large drop in real income did not occur for pensioner households, though within this household group there is much diversity. Single female pensioner households experienced a decrease in real income – by 4 index points – whereas couple pensioner households experienced an increase of 6 index points. The latter can be explained by the fact that these households increasingly have two individual incomes (that is, two pensions).

That the relative income position of pensioners ought to have improved is also shown in the official statistics, since during this 10-year period the average net wage experienced a larger decrease than the average net old-age pension. Taking into account the fact that the number of pensioners increased significantly, whereas the number of employees decreased, this could have only accentuated the improved relative income position of pensioner households, since employee households now have fewer employee incomes per household.

4.5.3 *Income Sources of Pensioner Households*

We now turn our attention to the subgroup of households, which is the most relevant for our analysis, i.e. pensioner households. Table 4.18 presents the structure of their income sources. It is obvious that, apart from pensions, these households also have other income sources, including earned income.

Table 4.18 shows that in 1993 pensions accounted for 86.4% of the income of pensioner households, compared to 79.2% in 1983. For these households, income from most other sources – such as income from part-time work, self-employment income, and social benefits – has decreased in importance.

Table 4.18: Income Sources of Pensioner Households, by Income Deciles (percentage)

Decile	Income sources, 1983								
	A	B	C	D	E	F	G	H	I
1	7.3	0.6	79.3	6.7	0.5	3.7	0.1	1.8	0.0
2	10.0	2.4	78.4	6.3	0.2	1.4	0.2	1.0	0.0
3	6.5	0.8	82.4	5.3	0.5	2.2	0.5	1.7	0.0
4	5.1	1.7	84.7	4.0	0.0	1.9	0.9	1.5	0.0
5	5.1	0.6	85.9	5.6	0.3	0.3	1.1	1.2	0.0
6	2.8	4.1	84.9	1.0	1.8	3.8	0.5	1.0	0.0
7	9.3	3.6	80.8	1.6	0.7	1.8	1.1	0.8	0.2
8	7.9	1.0	86.4	2.1	1.2	0.5	0.2	0.5	0.2
9	4.6	4.5	80.5	1.8	3.0	4.5	0.5	0.7	0.0
10	2.8	3.8	54.5	2.3	3.3	6.1	14.3	0.0	12.9
All	6.3	2.4	79.2	3.7	1.2	2.7	2.1	1.0	1.5

Decile	Income sources, 1993								
	A	B	C	D	E	F	G	H	I
1	1.8	0.6	87.4	6.1	0.7	1.7	0.4	1.3	0.0
2	1.1	0.8	88.2	4.3	0.6	2.1	0.0	2.8	0.0
3	2.4	0.9	93.3	0.7	0.5	1.4	0.1	0.5	0.0
4	3.4	0.7	88.6	5.0	0.8	0.5	0.6	0.5	0.0
5	7.5	0.5	89.2	0.2	1.2	0.7	0.0	0.5	0.0
6	6.3	3.1	83.5	4.3	1.9	0.5	0.2	0.3	0.0
7	0.3	3.0	90.9	2.6	0.6	0.5	1.3	0.5	0.3
8	6.6	2.1	81.6	3.2	2.6	1.6	0.4	1.8	0.0
9	2.2	1.8	86.7	0.4	3.0	0.8	1.6	3.6	0.0
10	1.5	0.0	80.4	0.0	9.7	3.1	3.8	1.5	0.0
All	3.4	1.5	86.4	2.5	2.5	1.3	1.0	1.4	0.0

Note: Deciles are appointed for the whole population of households, i.e. each decile contains 10% of all households.

Legend: The same as for Table 4.16.

Source: Household Expenditure Survey (1983, 1993), own calculations.

4.6   Income Distribution, Poverty and Inequality

4.6.1   *Income Distribution: Decile Analysis*

4.6.1.1 Households

We will now analyse pensioner income distribution by means of the decile analysis. As in the previous sections, income deciles are appointed for all households, meaning that each decile contains 10% of all households.

In 1983, single female pensioner households represented 9.5% of all households in the first decile; the corresponding figure for 1993 is 10.3% (Table 4.19). Single female pensioner households were particularly highly concentrated in the second decile: in 1983, they represented 19.5%, and in 1993, 18.7% of all households in that income decile. The share of single female pensioner households in the total number of households has also somewhat increased during this time period: in 1983 they represented 7.3%, whereas in 1993 they represented 9.9% of all households. Obviously, this type of pensioner household is more concentrated at the lower end of the household income distribution. This comes as no surprise, since a large proportion of these pensioners receive survivor pensions, which are much lower than old-age pensions. It must be remarked that the single female pensioner household is the dominant type of pensioner household in Slovenia.

In the 10-year period, the shares of all four types of pensioner households have increased (measured as a percentage of all households in Slovenia), resulting in an increase in the number of pensioner households from 21.5% of all households in 1983, to 26.2% in 1993. Although pensioner households in 1993 were still somewhat more concentrated in the lower income deciles, this concentration is less pronounced than in 1983. Thus, in 1983, 37.3% of all households in the first income decile were pensioner households, whereas the comparable figure for 1993 is 30.6%, which is only slightly higher than the overall share of 26.2%.

Table 4.19:   The Four Types of Pensioner Households, as a Percentage of
All Households in Each Income Decile, 1983 and 1993

Decile	Pensioner households (%)				
	Single male	Single female	Couple	Other	All
			1983		
1	(1.5)	9.5	16.5	9.8	37.3
2	(2.3)	19.5	12.5	10.5	44.9
3	(2.3)	11.5	12.5	5.0	31.3
4	(1.5)	8.5	10.0	4.8	24.8
5	(1.0)	4.3	6.0	2.8	14.0
6	(0.8)	6.0	7.3	2.0	16.0
7	(0.5)	6.3	7.5	2.8	17.0
8	(0.5)	3.3	6.3	1.0	11.0
9	(1.3)	1.5	6.8	1.8	11.3
10	(0.3)	2.8	3.8	1.0	7.8
All	1.2	7.3	8.9	4.1	21.5
Decile			1993		
1	(3.0)	10.3	7.4	9.9	30.6
2	(2.9)	18.7	9.2	8.0	38.8
3	(1.7)	13.4	9.7	8.1	32.9
4	(3.0)	13.1	10.8	2.6	29.5
5	(1.8)	19.7	7.7	3.5	23.6
6	(1.6)	8.4	13.2	4.3	27.6
7	(1.2)	8.8	11.5	3.8	25.3
8	(2.5)	6.2	10.3	3.5	22.5
9	(0.5)	4.6	8.7	1.9	15.7
10	(2.4)	5.1	5.8	1.9	15.2
All	2.1	9.9	9.4	4.8	26.2

Notes: 1. Deciles are appointed for the whole population of households, i.e. each decile contains 10%
of all households.

2. Individual figures indicate the share of households of a certain type, as a percentage of all
households in a given income decile.

Source: Household Expenditure Survey (1983, 1993), own calculations.

4.6.1.2 *Persons*

Just as we have done for households, we performed a decile analysis taking persons as income units: each decile (decile group) contains 10% of all persons, and each person is taken with his or her equivalized household income. The shares, by income deciles, of three different categories – pensioners, pensioners in pensioner households and persons aged 60 and over – are presented in Table 4.20.

We have already seen – from Table 4.12 – that the relative income position of pensioners improved considerably in the 10-year period between 1983 and 1993. Although Table 4.20 uses a different unit for the income analysis – it uses a person and not a household – it could hardly produce results differing from Table 4.12. Thus, we can only repeat our previous conclusion that the relative income position of pensioners improved significantly during this ten-year period.

Table 4.20: Pensioners, Pensioners in Pensioner Households and Persons Aged 60 and Over, as a Percentage of All Persons in an Income Decile, 1983 and 1993

Decile	1983			1993		
	Pens.	Pens. in pens. households	Persons aged 60+	Pens.	Pens. in pens. households	Persons aged 60+
1	20.0	13.7	31.2	19.3	13.0	30.5
2	22.4	16.7	26.8	20.7	13.6	24.4
3	17.6	11.1	18.8	22.6	14.6	20.5
4	17.5	10.5	16.3	19.4	12.2	16.2
5	12.5	5.5	12.6	19.6	10.8	15.0
6	14.1	6.4	11.0	21.7	12.7	17.8
7	13.6	7.5	11.2	22.3	13.5	15.3
8	12.2	5.4	9.1	23.0	12.1	15.5
9	12.4	6.0	9.1	16.2	8.1	12.0
10	12.2	4.2	9.6	14.3	7.7	9.9
All	15.5	8.7	15.6	19.9	11.8	17.7

Note: Deciles are appointed by taking the whole population of persons, i.e. each decile contains 10% of all persons.

Source: Household Expenditure Survey (1983, 1993), own calculations.

Proceeding in a similar manner, the decile analysis of a subgroup of pensioners, i.e. pensioners living in pensioner households, shows that essentially there is no new additional evidence with regard to the decile analysis based on households. This subgroup of pensioners is, relatively speaking, worse off than the group of all pensioners, although it has improved its relative income position over this 10-year period. In 1983, pensioners living in pensioner households accounted for 8.7% of all persons, whereas they accounted for 13.7% of all persons in the first decile. In 1993, these pensioners accounted for 11.8% of all persons, and they were only slightly overrepresented in the lower deciles; their shares in the first and second income decile were 13.0% and 13.6%, respectively.

Table 4.21:   Persons Aged 60 and Over, as a Percentage of All Persons in an Income Decile, by Gender, 1983 and 1993

Decile	1983			1993		
	Males	Females	All	Males	Females	All
1	13.3	17.9	31.2	11.5	19.0	30.5
2	10.2	16.7	26.9	8.4	16.0	24.4
3	7.4	11.4	18.8	8.0	12.6	20.6
4	6.8	9.6	16.4	6.4	9.8	16.2
5	5.1	7.5	12.6	6.3	8.6	14.9
6	4.7	6.3	11.0	7.6	10.2	17.8
7	5.0	6.2	11.2	6.2	9.0	15.2
8	3.9	5.1	9.0	6.7	8.8	15.5
9	3.8	5.3	9.1	5.1	6.9	12.0
10	4.1	5.5	9.6	5.0	4.9	9.9
All	6.4	9.1	15.5	7.1	10.6	17.7

Note: Deciles are appointed by taking the whole population of persons, i.e. each decile contains 10% of all persons.

Source: Household Expenditure Survey (1983, 1993), own calculations.

Turning our attention to persons aged 60 and over, we see that this subgroup of persons is more concentrated at the lower end of the income distribution and that, unlike the previous two groups, this has not changed much in the 10-year period. In 1983, 15.6% of all persons were 60 years and over, compared to 17.7% in 1993. In 1983, the share of persons aged 60 and over in the first decile was 31.2%, and in 1993 it was 30.5%. The quite divergent conclusions of the decile analysis of pensioners and persons aged 60 and over is obviously due to the fact that these two groups do not overlap. A sizeable share of pensioners is younger than 60 years, and also a large number of persons aged 60 and over do not receive pensions.

Due to longer life expectancy, women represent the larger part of all persons aged 60 and over, as shown in Table 4.21; and in 1993 women represented 10.6% of all persons in this population subgroup, whereas men represented 'only' 7.1%. For this age group, we observe that both men and women were more concentrated at the lower end of the income distribution. In 1993, women aged 60 and over represented 19.0%, while men aged 60 and over represented 11.5% of all persons in the first decile.

Proceeding a bit further with the decile analysis, Table 4.22 provides a breakdown of the age group 60 years and over into three groups. Age group 50-59 is included for comparative purposes.

Table 4.22:   Persons of a Given Age Group, as a Percentage of All Persons in an Income Decile, 1983 and 1993

Decile	1983				1993			
	Age group				Age group			
	50-59	60-69	70-79	80+	50-59	60-69	70-79	80+
1	12.6	13.0	13.7	4.5	9.5	15.3	10.3	4.9
2	12.1	14.3	9.2	3.3	9.7	12.0	8.4	4.0
3	13.6	10.0	6.6	2.2	11.0	11.2	6.6	2.7
4	11.0	7.6	6.8	2.0	10.5	9.7	5.1	1.4
5	12.1	6.5	5.0	1.2	12.1	8.7	4.7	1.5
6	10.9	6.1	3.7	1.2	11.2	11.2	4.9	1.8
7	12.8	7.4	2.8	0.9	13.9	10.2	3.1	1.9
8	13.7	4.4	3.7	0.9	15.2	9.8	4.1	1.6
9	14.2	5.4	3.0	0.7	11.3	8.0	2.5	1.5
10	19.7	6.7	1.8	1.1	14.7	6.8	2.7	0.5
All	13.3	8.1	5.6	1.8	11.9	10.3	5.2	2.2

Note: Deciles are appointed by taking the whole population of persons, i.e. each decile comprises 10% of all persons.

Source: Household Expenditure Survey (1983, 1993), own calculations.

From Table 4.22, it appears that older age groups have a higher probability of being situated in the lower income deciles. Thus, in 1993, persons in the age group 60 to 69 represent 10.3% of all persons, but 15.3% of all persons in the first decile: persons in the age group 80 and over represent only 2.2% of all persons, but 4.9% of all persons in the first decile.

In other words, in 1993 persons in the age group 60 to 69 were 'overrepresented' in the first decile by a factor of 1.49 (=15.3/10.3), whereas persons in the age group 80 and over were 'overrepresented' by a factor of 2.23 (=4.9/2.2). One could say that the older the age group, the greater the concentration of persons in the lower income deciles. True, the relative income position of all three elderly age groups (60-69, 70-79, 80 and over) has improved during the 10-year period 1983-1993, but this improvement has not been uniform. Larger relative gains were achieved by younger age groups, thus the relative income position of persons in the age group 60 to 69 improved the most, whereas the age group 80 and over achieved only modest gains.

164   Several factors may influence the income position of the elderly population, and these can have a very differentiated effect on the various age groups. These factors are:
a)   social security coverage of the elderly population,
b)   the value of the social security entitlement (pension),
c)   longevity and mortality,
d)   the composition of households in which the elderly live.
It is virtually impossible to disentangle and quantify the effect of each of these factors on the relative income position of the elderly – in particular since they are not mutually independent. Also, some changes – such as changes in the value of the social security entitlements – are concentrated in a particular age group, and this change is then gradually propagated through a time period. These effects could be analysed using a cohort analysis, but this is not possible with our data set. In spite of these limitations, some conclusions may still be drawn. Thus factor (a) did result in an improved income position of the elderly, since the number of elderly dependants decreased over time. In 1983, 19.1% of all persons aged 60 and over were dependants, while in 1993 the share decreased to 10.6%. Factor (a) also influenced factor (d), i.e. the composition of households in which the elderly live. This is presented in Table 4.23.

Table 4.23:   The Socio-economic Structure of Household Members, by Age Group

Socio-economic status	Age			
	50-59	60-69	70-79	80+
	1983			
Employee	45.8	23.9	20.6	27.9
Other active person	5.9	6.5	6.6	5.3
Pensioner	19.3	39.8	40.4	36.3
Dependant	27.6	28.7	31.5	29.4
Other	1.4	1.1	0.9	1.1
Household size	3.2	2.80	2.71	3.12
	1993			
Employee	34.7	17.1	16.4	20.1
Other active person (1)	6.4 (4.2)	4.6 (3.7)	4.5 (3.8)	7.6 (6.0)
Pensioner (2)	30.4 (1.9)	54.0 (4.8)	51.1 (6.6)	44.7 (9.8)
Dependant	21.8	20.8	24.1	23.1
Other	6.7	3.5	3.9	4.5
Household size	3.30	2.73	2.58	3.00

Notes: 1.   Figures in brackets refer to persons active in agriculture.

2.   Figures in brackets refer to recipients of farmer pensions. Their number has increased dramatically in 1984, following a new pension law, which integrated farmers into the general social insurance scheme. This was implemented at extremely favourable conditions for farmers.

Source: Household Expenditure Survey (1983, 1993), own calculations.

In 1993, a person in the age group 60-69 years lived in a household whose average size was 2.73. A share of 54% of all household members were pensioners, and 17.1% were employees. While the share of dependants decreased in all household types, the decrease was largest for households where persons aged 60-69 lived; in these households, the share of dependants dropped from 28.7% to 20.8% of all household members. The elderly aged 80 and over tend to live in somewhat larger households than the 'younger' age groups (aged 60-69 and 70-79). In 1993, in households with persons of the eldest age, a considerable number of household members (9.8%) were recipients of farmer pensions[7] and a somewhat larger share of household members were active in agriculture (6%). It thus appears that the very old (80 years and over) are more highly concentrated in rural households; of course, one must bear in mind that the urban population of very old people is 'overrepresented' in various old-age and long-term care institutions, so it cannot be captured by the survey.

The socio-economic status of household members is not the only defining feature of household composition; also relevant is the gender composition. The gender composition of all persons and of pensioners within the individual age groups is presented in Table 4.24.

Table 4.24:   The Gender Structure of All Persons and All Pensioners, by Age Group, 1983 and 1993

| Gender | | | Age | |
Gender	50-59	60-69	70-79	80+
			1983	
All persons	100.0	100.0	100.0	100.0
Males	45.2	40.3	44.2	36.7
Females	54.8	59.7	55.8	63.3
All pensioners	100.0	100.0	100.0	100.0
Males	36.1	51.4	50.4	40.6
Females	63.9	48.6	49.6	59.4
			1993	
All persons	100.0	100.0	100.0	100.0
Males	48.1	44.8	35.2	30.9
Females	51.9	55.2	64.8	69.1
All pensioners	100.0	100.0	100.0	100.0
Males	38.9	49.6	39.2	37.1
Females	61.1	50.4	60.8	62.9

Source: Household Expenditure Survey (1983, 1993), own calculations.

Of course, for the age group 50-59, the share of men as a percentage of all persons is higher than their pensioner share; many men are still active in the labour force. For all the other age groups, the share of men is lower in the total population than their pensioner share, and consequently, the share of women in the total population is higher than their pensioner share. In other words, quite a number of women in the elderly age groups still do not receive a pension. The gap between the gender share in all population and share in all pensioners has narrowed in the 10-year period. Thus for women in the age group 60-69, the gap in 1983 was 11 percentage points (59.7-48.6), whereas in 1993 the gap for this age group was only some 5 percentage points (55.2-50.4). We can only reiterate the fact that the share of female dependants decreased considerably in this time period. Also, starting from the age group 60-69, women exhibit a more or less regular increase in both shares – share in population and share in pensioners. This is of course due to the differential mortality rates; and since women have lower pensions than men, the income position of older age groups in general has worsened.

As for the value of the social security entitlement (pension), we have already observed that this contributed to the improved relative income position of pensioners. Different age cohorts enter the pension system with different 'entrance' pensions, and this 'entrance' pension may be influenced not only by the pension system parameters, but also by the defining characteristics of each age cohort. In a Bismarckian system, pensions depend on past wages, i.e. on one's 'wage history'. Wages are related to the amount of human capital one possesses; the more human capital a person accumulated in his or her active work period, the larger his or her income stream was and consequently his or her pension. Though years of schooling are an admittedly imperfect proxy for the amount of individual human capital, it seems quite plausible to assume that a greater number of years of schooling would imply a higher pension.[8]

Table 4.25 clearly shows that the average number of years of schooling decreases with each pensioner age group, i.e. younger age cohorts have more human capital.

Table 4.25: **Average Number of Years of Schooling of Pensioners, by Age Group, 1993**

| | Age of pensioners | | | |
Gender	50-59	60-69	70-79	80+
Males	9.7	9.6	9.1	8.3
Females	9.3	8.8	8.2	7.2
All pensioners	9.4	9.2	8.6	7.6

Note: Due to the change in the school system, the data for 1983 are not presented, since they are not comparable to those for 1993.

Source: Household Expenditure Survey (1993), own calculations.

As the pensioner age cohort progresses through time, factor (c) exerts its influence; pensioners with lower pensions (and lower education) tend to live shorter lives, i.e. mortality rates are definitely related to income and education.[9] This factor therefore tends to increase the average pension of the elderly age groups, though in quantitative terms it is certainly not very high. The effects of differential mortality rates are shown in Table 4.26, which uses data from the National Pension Administration; pensioners with lower educational attainment (and thus presumably lower pensions) tend to live shorter.

Table 4.26: **Average Number of Years of Schooling of Pensioners, by Age Group, 1996**

	Age groups		
Gender	50-59	60-69	70+
	All pensioners		
Males	9.4	9.5	8.8
Females	9.4	8.6	7.5
All pensioners	9.4	9.1	8.2
	Pensioners deceased in 1996		
Males	8.8	8.9	8.5
Females	9.1	8.0	7.3
All pensioners	8.9	8.6	7.9

Note: Only old-age and disability pensioners are included. Different age grouping than the one used in Table 4.25 is necessitated by the existing grouping of the NPA.

Source: National Pension Administration data.

4.6.2 Poverty Incidence

For the analysis of poverty incidence, poverty lines were set at 0.4, 0.5, 0.6 and 0.7 of median equivalent household current monetary income. Poverty incidence is assessed for individuals using their household equivalent income.[10] The results are presented in Table 4.27, which shows the four poverty incidence measures for the total population and the various population subgroups, in particular pensioners and the elderly. Emphasis is on pensioners living in pensioner households and on different types of these households.

Overall, in the period 1983-1993, there was remarkably little change in the poverty incidence for the whole population regardless of the chosen value of the poverty line. On the other hand, the poverty incidence for pensioners, as well as the subgroup of pensioners living in pensioner households, decreased considerably over the 10-year period. This also holds true for persons aged 60 and over, though the decrease for this age group is somewhat less pronounced. Thus, in 1993, 31.4% of all persons aged 60 and over lived in households whose equivalent household income was less than 0.7 of the median household equivalent income, whereas the comparable figure for 1983 is 38.2%. Also, this age group has certain gender characteristics, which we have already observed in Table 4.21; in 1993, 33.6% of all women of this age group lived in households with an equivalent household income below 0.7 median equivalent household income; the comparable figure for men is 28.3%.

169

Table 4.27: Poverty Incidence Measures

Population	*Percentage of population with equivalent household income below:*							
	0.4 median		0.5 median		0.6 median		0.7 median	
	1983	1993	1983	1993	1983	1993	1983	1993
All persons	3.6	3.7	7.3	7.1	12.9	13.1	20.5	20.6
Pensioners	4.6	2.6	9.2	6.7	17.4	13.4	28.5	20.5
Pensioners in pensioner hh.	5.3	2.9	10.7	7.3	21.2	15.3	36.4	22.7
– single male pensioners	(6.4)	(3.4)	(12.8)	(12.7)	(21.3)	(19.0)	(38.3)	(28.7)
– single female pensioners	5.1	2.3	7.5	7.8	24.7	18.4	41.8	29.3
– in couple pensioner hh.	4.0	1.5	10.2	4.7	17.5	9.8	28.1	14.0
– in other pensioner hh.	8.4	6.6	15.2	11.2	25.3	22.8	48.1	31.8
All persons aged 60+	8.1	6.4	15.8	12.6	25.5	22.4	38.2	31.4
– men aged 60+	8.2	5.9	17.1	11.9	25.2	20.3	37.5	28.3
– women aged 60+	8.0	6.7	14.9	13.1	25.6	23.9	38.8	33.6

Source: Household Expenditure Survey (1983, 1993), own calculations.

Table 4.27 also exhibits certain regularities: the ranking of poverty incidence for pensioners with regard to the four types of pensioner households is fairly stable over time. In 1983 and 1993, pensioners living in couple pensioner households had almost uniformly the lowest poverty incidence; the only deviation was the poverty incidence in 1983 with the poverty line set at 0.5 of the median equivalent household income. For this threshold, the poverty incidence was 10.2%, whereas for single female pensioners it was 7.5%. The large decrease in the poverty incidence for couple pensioner households between 1983 and 1993, which was larger than for other categories of pensioners (single female, single male), can be explained by the increase in the average number of pension incomes for this group. Thus, in 1983 couple pensioner households had on average 1.48 pension incomes, compared to 1.77 in 1993. Pensioners living in 'other pensioner households' also experienced a sharp decrease in poverty incidence, and here also part of the explanation is provided by the increase in the average number of pension incomes for this household type.

170

4.6.3 Income Inequality

In section 4.6.1 income distribution by income deciles was presented and analysed in a qualitative manner. In Table 4.28 we present three aggregate measures of income inequality:
- the Gini coefficient,
- 90/10-percentile ratio, and
- 75/25-percentile ratio.

In computing these measures, each member of a given population group or subgroup (all persons, pensioners, pensioners living in pensioner households, persons aged 60 and over) was included with his or her household equivalent income.

Income inequality (as computed by the three measures) of the total population of Slovenia increased considerably during the 1983-1993 period. To make matters worse, this happened during a period of declining real incomes.

On the other hand, there have been no marked changes in income inequality for the three subgroups observed (pensioners, pensioners living in pensioner households, persons aged 60 and over). This is not really surprising, since pensions have not displayed any shifts in distribution; pensions distribution has remained fairly stable over this 10-year period. It is true that in using the equivalent income for the relevant subgroups we are, of course, also introducing other income sources; but their relative importance for these subgroups is not as pronounced as that of pensions.

Table 4.28:   Income Inequality Measures

Population	Gini coefficient		90/10		75/25	
	1983	1993	1983	1993	1983	1993
All persons	0.2367	0.2747	2.94	3.32	1.74	1.82
Pensioners	0.2420	0.2405	3.01	3.00	1.80	1.76
Pensioners living in pensioner households	0.2357	0.2408	2.97	3.02	1.82	1.74
Persons aged 60+	0.2651	0.2633	3.42	3.40	1.83	1.89

Source: Household Expenditure Survey (1983, 1993), own calculations.

The income inequality measures tell a similar story as our decile analysis and poverty incidence measures. Thus, the category 'all persons aged 60 and over' has a relatively high poverty incidence, regardless of the poverty measure (0.4, 0.5, 0.6 or 0.7 of median equivalent household income), and high values of all measures of income inequality – the Gini coefficient, the 75/25 and 90/10-ratios. These high values appear to be stable in this 10-year period. Part of the explanation lies in the fact that this subgroup is very heterogeneous with regard to income sources.

The large increase in the 90/10-ratio and comparatively more modest increase in the 75/25-ratio for the category 'all persons' are a vivid testimony to the fact that the income distribution has undergone a big change at the very upper end. This is not surprising in view of the turbulent transition period in which very large income and wealth gains were achieved by a small share of the population.

4.7 Home Ownership, Quality of Housing and Ownership of Consumer Durables

4.7.1 Home Ownership

Slovenia has one of the highest levels of home ownership in Europe; in 1993 some 87.2% of all households owned an apartment or house, as shown in Table 4.29. Table 4.29 also shows that in 1983 home ownership in Slovenia was not really the domain of the wealthy, but more of those who did not qualify for social rentals. They met their housing needs by taking up loans, or through family help, etc. The large increase in ownership levels in 1993 as compared to 1983, was mostly due to the Housing Act of 1991, which enabled the sale of the social housing stock from 1991 to 1993. The biggest winners were the wealthier households that obtained high-quality housing for a fraction of their market price.[11]

Table 4.29: Tenure Status of Various Households, by Income Deciles, 1983 and 1993

Decile	All households					
	1983			1993		
	Owner of apartment	Owner of house	Tenant	Owner of apartment	Owner of house	Tenant
1	7.8	68.5	23.8	9.6	74.1	16.2
2	8.5	54.6	36.6	21.6	60.5	17.8
3	6.8	50.4	42.4	23.1	61.1	15.8
4	7.0	40.9	51.9	27.5	59.2	13.3
5	9.5	43.6	46.9	30.8	56.9	12.3
6	5.3	39.1	55.6	34.0	54.0	12.0
7	7.5	38.8	53.6	36.5	51.7	11.7
8	6.5	33.8	59.6	41.1	48.6	10.3
9	9.5	34.6	55.6	38.8	54.0	7.2
10	12.0	29.3	58.8	36.9	52.1	11.0
Total	8.0	43.4	48.5	30.0	57.2	12.8

Table 4.29 (continuing)

Decile	Pensioner households					
	1983			1993		
	Owner of apartment	Owner of house	Tenant	Owner of apartment	Owner of house	Tenant
1	8.7	61.1	30.2	13.5	74.1	12.4
2	10.1	40.2	49.2	24.6	54.0	21.4
3	9.6	37.6	52.0	26.1	52.6	21.3
4	7.1	29.3	63.6	21.8	62.4	15.7
5	16.1	32.1	51.8	28.1	51.6	20.3
6	6.3	35.9	57.8	41.6	45.6	12.8
7	10.3	36.8	52.9	40.2	47.2	12.6
8	13.6	22.7	63.6	48.2	43.2	8.5
9	20.0	37.8	42.2	42.2	49.1	8.7
10	9.7	38.7	51.6	36.8	56.3	6.9
Total	10.2	40.0	49.5	30.6	54.3	15.1

Decile	Non-pensioner households					
	1983			1993		
	Owner of apartment	Owner of house	Tenant	Owner of apartment	Owner of house	Tenant
1	7.2	72.9	19.9	7.9	74.2	17.9
2	7.3	66.4	26.4	19.7	64.7	15.6
3	5.5	56.2	38.0	21.7	65.2	13.1
4	7.0	44.7	48.0	29.8	57.8	12.3
5	8.5	45.5	46.1	31.6	58.5	9.9
6	5.1	39.7	55.2	31.1	57.2	11.7
7	6.9	39.3	53.8	35.3	53.3	11.4
8	5.6	35.2	59.2	39.0	50.2	10.8
9	8.2	34.2	57.3	38.2	54.9	7.0
10	12.2	28.5	59.3	37.0	51.3	11.7
Total	7.4	44.3	48.2	29.8	58.3	12.0

Source: Household Expenditure Survey (1983, 1993), own calculations.

4.7.2 Quality of Housing and Ownership of Consumer Durables

An important dimension of the economic well-being of pensioners is the quality of their housing and ownership of consumer durables. A comparison of these measures of well-being for three types of households, i.e. all households, pensioner households and non-pensioner households, is presented in Table 4.30.

The selected indicators of housing quality are central heating, running water, sewage and telephone. It is shown that the housing quality of pensioner households was not very different from the quality of housing of all households. A somewhat lower level of central heating for pensioner households may be due to the fact that houses owned by pensioners are, on average, older than those owned by others.

All three household types experienced a rise in the ownership levels of consumer durables. A colour TV set has become pervasive, as well as a washing machine. Dishwasher ownership level is still low, and the much lower level for pensioner households can be explained by differing preferences and not by differences in household income (Table 4.31). Similarly, lower car ownership among pensioner households can be explained by the impact of age on the pensioners' ability to drive. The general conclusion is that pensioner households do not differ significantly in their ownership levels from non-pensioner households.

Table 4.30: Consumer Durables Ownership Levels (percentage), by Household Types, 1983 and 1993

Consumer durables	All households		Pensioner households		Non-pensioner households	
	1983	1993	1983	1993	1983	1993
Central heating	48.0	70.9	40.0	63.0	50.2	73.7
Running water	95.5	97.7	96.0	98.0	95.3	97.7
Sewage	89.1	95.5	88.8	94.1	89.2	96.0
Telephone	34.7	68.2	33.5	63.1	35.0	70.0
Car	56.4	68.2	21.7	36.2	65.9	79.6
Colour TV	39.6	83.5	29.1	76.1	42.5	86.1
Washing machine	89.7	94.3	77.6	91.0	93.0	95.5
Dish washer	5.0	15.5	1.4	7.0	6.0	18.5

Source: Household Expenditure Survey (1983, 1993), own calculations.

174

Table 4.31: Cars' and Dish Washers' Ownership Levels (percentage), by Household Types and by Income Deciles, 1983 and 1993

Income deciles	All households			
	Car		Dish washer	
	1983	1993	1983	1993
1	21.0	28.4	0.5	2.7
2	26.3	49.0	0.0	4.4
3	36.6	60.2	1.0	5.1
4	45.6	63.8	0.3	7.0
5	56.6	70.6	3.3	11.6
6	64.9	74.8	3.0	14.3
7	70.7	76.3	5.8	15.1
8	74.2	83.3	9.5	22.5
9	80.7	86.8	11.0	29.5
10	87.5	89.2	16.0	42.8
Total	56.4	68.2	5.0	15.5

Income deciles	Pensioner households			
	Car		Dish washer	
	1983	1993	1983	1993
1	6.7	5.7	0.0	2.0
2	9.5	15.7	0.0	2.0
3	14.4	28.4	0.8	2.7
4	16.2	30.0	0.0	2.6
5	16.1	36.5	1.8	4.9
6	31.3	47.6	0.0	7.5
7	38.2	46.8	4.4	7.6
8	45.5	63.0	2.3	17.7
9	62.2	66.8	4.4	16.3
10	74.2	68.5	12.9	23.9
Total	21.7	36.2	1.4	7.0

Table 4.31 (continuing)

Income deciles	Non-pensioner households			
	Car		Dish washer	
	1983	1993	1983	1993
1	29.5	38.5	0.8	3.0
2	40.0	70.2	0.0	5.9
3	46.7	75.8	1.1	6.3
4	55.3	77.9	0.3	8.8
5	63.3	81.2	3.5	13.7
6	71.3	85.2	3.6	16.9
7	77.3	86.3	6.0	17.6
8	77.7	89.2	10.4	23.8
9	83.1	90.6	11.9	32.0
10	88.6	92.8	16.3	46.2
Total	65.9	79.6	6.0	18.5

Source: Household Expenditure Survey (1983, 1993), own calculations.

4.8 Concluding Remarks

Our analysis has shown that pensioners and the elderly in general have improved their relative income position during the transition period in Slovenia. This improvement came about almost by default: during the 1980s and 1990s, pension entitlements were being extended to various segments of the population which were hitherto not integrated in the social insurance schemes, such as farmers. Also, the seemingly innocuous indexation formula by which pensions were adjusted according to the movements in average wages, proved to be quite ill-suited for periods of economic stagnation and depression. The logic of such an indexation was that pensioners should share in productivity and output growth of the economy. Unfortunately, the productivity gains, as shown by the increases in average wages, were a statistical artefact caused by a considerable decrease in the number of employed (and concomitant rapid increase in the number of unemployed). Productivity – and average wages – increased, but output stagnated or even decreased in the early 1990s.

Our analysis is very much focused on one socio-economic group, i.e. pensioners, and the elderly in general. They were doubtlessly on the winning side. Who are the losers of transition in Slovenia? The losers are the unemployed and the low-wage earners who have been left out of the share in productivity growth. As documented by Stanovnik (1999), wage inequality experienced a large increase in the early years of transition, with low-wage earners barely managing to retain their wages in real terms.

Is this improvement in the economic well-being of the elderly a more permanent phenomenon? It is not possible to make a definite prediction. Namely, pensions from the first pillar will be decreasing relative to wages, but pensions from the second and third pillars will serve as a supplementary income source. Thus, the increasing role of these two pillars might also cause an increase in income inequality among the elderly, since pension income from the second pillar (occupational pension schemes) and the third pillar (voluntary individual saving schemes) will probably be more concentrated among the higher-income pensioners. It would thus not be completely surprising if inequality and relative income poverty among the elderly start increasing. These changes will be very gradual, and they will not be detected for some time to come.

Whatever the case may be, careful monitoring of the income position and economic well-being of the elderly is necessary in order to provide policy-relevant conclusions and also to evaluate how well the pension system performs its basic function: the maintenance of a satisfactory level of well-being of the elderly.

Notes

1   A broad overview of the pension system in Slovenia and some necessary reform measures have been presented in Stanovnik and Kukar (1995).

2   Since a number of female old-age pensioners switched to a survivor pension, the actual number of years that a female pensioner received pension benefits (old-age and/or survivor pension) is certainly greater than 15.4.

3   Including all pensions and supplements, pensioners' health insurance and administrative costs.

4   It seems that in 1993 a number of 'former' dependants, who have in the meantime received a farmers' retirement pension, declared their socio-economic category as 'other' and not as 'pensioner'.

5   This is additionally presented in Table 4.19.

6   The importance of social transfers (apart from pensions) for household income in Slovenia
        is analysed in more detail in Stanovnik and Stropnik (1998).
7   This pension is a pure solidarity measure granted to farmers who made virtually no so-
        cial security contribution payments; it amounts to some 22% of the average net wage.
8   This roundabout reasoning is necessary because we do not have data on individual
        pensions: our income data are aggregates on the household level, so what we have are
        aggregate pensions for all household members. In other words, we cannot present the
        values of average pensions for each age group.
9   Johnson and Stears (1998) review some of the more recent literature on differential
        mortality rates.
10   A fairly detailed analysis of poverty incidence, based on the 1993 HES, was performed
        by Žnidaršič (1995). Her results though are not comparable with ours, since she used the
        expenditure concept and the modified OECD equivalence scale.
11   A detailed account of the sale of the social housing stock in Slovenia is provided in
        Stanovnik (1994).

References

Johnson, P./ Stears, G. (1998) 'Why Are Older Pensioners Poorer?', *Oxford Bulletin of Economics and Statistics*, vol. 60, no. 3: 3-22.

Milanovic, B. (1998) *Income, Inequality and Poverty during the Transition from Planned to Market Economy*. Washington, D.C.: The World Bank.

National Pension Administration (1991-1997) *Poslovna poročila*. Ljubljana: Zavod za pokojninsko in invalidsko zavarovanje Slovenije.

Stanovnik, T. (1994) 'The Sale of the Social Housing Stock: What Happened and Why', *Urban Studies*, vol. 31, no. 9: 1559-1570.

Stanovnik, T. (1997) 'Dohodki in socialni položaj upokojencev', *IB revija*, vol. 31, no. 5-6: 23-39.

Stanovnik, T. (1999) 'The Analysis of Personal Income Tax Returns in Slovenia in 1991 and 1996', *IB revija*, vol. 33, no. 4.

Stanovnik, T./ Kukar, S. (1995) 'The Pension System in Slovenia: Past Developments and Future Prospects', *International Social Security Review*, no. 1: 35-44.

Stanovnik, T./Stropnik, N. (1996) 'Dohodki in dohodkovna neenakost v Sloveniji in drugih državah na prehodu', *IB revija*, vol. 30, no. 3-4: 3-23.

Stanovnik, T./Stropnik, N. (1998) *Impact of Social Transfers on Poverty and Income Inequality in Slovenia: A Comparison between the Pre-Transition and the Post-Transition Period*. Ljubljana: Institute for Economic Research.

Statistical Yearbook (1990-1998) Ljubljana: Statistical Office of the Republic of Slovenia.

Zakon o pokojninskem in invalidskem zavarovanju (Pension Act) Official Gazette of the Republic of Slovenia, 12/1992 and 106/1999.

Žnidaršič, E. (1995) Kdo so revni v Sloveniji, pp. 215-226 in "Statistics of Work, Working and Living Conditions", Proceedings of the 5th International Statistical Conference, Radenci. Ljubljana: Statistical Office of the Republic of Slovenia and Statistical Society of Slovenia.

Appendix

Table 4A1: Pensioners, Pensioners in Pensioner Households and Persons Aged 60 and Over, by Income Deciles (vertical distribution), 1983 and 1993

Decile	1983			1993		
	Pens.	Pens. in pens. households	Persons aged 60+	Pens.	Pens. in pens. households	Persons aged 60+
1	13.0	15.7	20.0	9.7	11.0	17.2
2	14.5	19.2	17.2	10.4	11.5	13.8
3	11.4	12.8	12.1	11.4	12.4	11.6
4	11.3	12.1	10.5	9.8	10.3	9.2
5	8.1	6.3	8.1	9.8	9.2	8.5
6	9.1	7.3	7.0	10.9	10.7	10.0
7	8.8	8.6	7.2	11.2	11.4	8.6
8	7.9	6.3	5.8	11.5	10.2	8.7
9	8.0	6.9	5.8	8.2	6.8	6.8
10	7.9	4.8	6.1	7.2	6.5	5.6
Total	100.0	100.0	100.0	100.0	100.0	100.0

Source: Household Expenditure Survey (1983, 1993), own calculations.

Part II

Non-Transition Economies

CHAPTER 5

Austria: Do Trends in Income Distribution Influence Policy?

Christopher Prinz

5.1 Introduction

The well-being and the income position of the elderly population in Austria is to a large extent determined by the distributional forces of the public pension scheme. This study has essentially two aims: first, to analyse income inequality, income distribution and the incidence of poverty among senior citizens, and second, to relate these findings on income distribution to the organization of the pension system and the pension reform process and debate. As regards the income position of the elderly, a particular emphasis has been put on a comparison between the different population subgroups: between men and women, between younger and older pensioners, between different types of pensioner households, and between pensioners and persons aged 60 and over. Understanding these differences considerably improves one's understanding of how the Austrian system of income support in old age functions. Concerning the relationship between income distribution and the ongoing pension reform process and debate, two major questions are raised and – at least to some extent – answered: first, whether or not and how the pension system and its recent reforms have affected and will affect the well-being of the elderly population and income inequality within this population segment, and second, whether or not and how findings on income distribution, income inequality and poverty among the elderly have affected recent pension reforms or do affect the current ongoing reform debate.

Section 5.2 describes and characterizes the Austrian pension system as background information. Section 5.3 recapitulates the data and methodology used in the income analysis. Section 5.4 gives a brief account of household trends and summarizes income distribution patterns at the household level. Sections 5.5 and 5.6 focus on income distribution at the individual level (using equivalent household incomes), and on poverty and income inequality among senior citizens. Section 5.7 adds information on wealth measured in terms of ownership of durable goods. The concluding section 5.8, discusses the relevancy of the findings within the context of the recent pension reforms, the current pension reform debate, and probable future reforms.

5.2 Background: The Austrian Pension System – Rules and Trends

5.2.1 Basic Characteristics of the Pension System

184

Austria has an archetypal pay-as-you-go financed corporatist pension scheme, which covers nearly all persons active in the economy: the employed (blue- and white-collar workers and state sector employees contracted under private law), the self-employed and farmers. Only professionals are not organized within this system; their retirement systems are managed by their own organizations (see Rosner et al., 1997). Civil servants are also covered under a different and much more advantageous system, which is slowly to be harmonized with the general system. Due to the universal coverage and the generosity of the public pension system, a second pillar (occupational pensions) hardly exists; around 93% of all pensions are paid out of the public scheme.

Since the mid-1950s, when the current system was started, the basic philosophy was (and still is) that upon retirement, the public pension system should maintain everyone's standard of living (the so-called "Lebensstandardprinzip"). For this reason, the system provides an earnings-related old-age pension with a relatively high income replacement rate and a derived survivor's pension. The survivor's pension is paid to all widows, widowers and orphans and – at a lower rate – also to divorcees with a judicial claim to alimony.

In order to be entitled to an old-age pension, a minimum contribution period of 15 years is required. There is no minimum pension. However, there is a means-tested supplement to the pension for all persons who are entitled to an old-age or to a survivor's pension. This supplement (so-called "Ausgleichszulage") increases the household income for a single person to around ATS 8,000 per month, and to around ATS 11,400 per month for couples. Around one in six pensioners receives such a supplement, the majority of recipients being women with only a survivor's pension. The means-tested minimum for singles is often used as a quasi-official poverty level.

Benefits are a function of the insurance period and the income level. For each insurance year, the retiree gets 2% of the amount used as calculation basis ("Bemessungsgrundlage"), which is equal to the revalorized average income of the best 15 income years. A pension cannot exceed 80% of the calculation basis, except for deferred claims of an old-age pension. There is a ceiling (slightly above twice the average income) above which neither contributions are paid nor benefits received. This creates an incentive for high income earners to provide for additional sources of income (e.g. savings) in their old age.

Depending on birth spacing and up to a maximum of four years per child, child care periods count as insurance years, irrespective of the employment status during such periods (these are non-contributory years, but rank equally as waiting periods if a minimum of 15 contributory years have been cumulated). However, the resulting increase in benefits for mothers is rather small because the calculation base for child care periods equals less than one third of average earnings. Survivor pensions are paid in addition to any old-age entitlements. Widows and widowers receive between 40 and 60% of the pension of the deceased, depending on the income difference between the partners (52% in case of equal incomes). Entitled divorcees cannot receive more than the alimony awarded, which is 33% at maximum. About one in seven retirees are able to claim more than one pension entitlement.

The regular retirement age for an old-age pension is 65 for men and 60 for women (the female retirement age will gradually be adjusted to that of men between 2023 and 2033). Early retirement is possible five years before (60 for men and 55 for women) in the following cases: (a) the person has been insured for 37.5 years, (b) on the grounds of a reduced ability to work or (c) because of prolonged unemployment. Retirement on the grounds of disability is not bound to any age limit.

Pensions are paid 14 times a year – as wages generally are – and are adjusted annually along with wage increases (wages net of contributions, see below). Retirees pay 3.75% of their pension into the public health system and are taxed in accordance with income tax laws. They are, however, exempt from contributions to the pension and the unemployment systems, and to the family fund. Hence, in many cases, net pensions are not much lower than net income.

Roughly 80% of overall pension expenditures are covered by contributions; the remaining 20% being a contribution from the federal budget. The contribution rate is 22.8% of gross earnings, 12.55% for the employer and 10.25 for the employee. Contributions reduce the basis for calculating income tax.

5.2.2 Major System Changes During the 1990s

The pension system has been constantly adjusted over the last decade. Changes during this period were essentially driven by budgetary considerations and justified by the necessity to strengthen the underlying insurance principle (which also meant reducing the benefit level). In 1993, a major reform that brought a number of new elements into the system was passed. Ever since Austria joined the European Union, pension insurance goals have been adapted even more to suit budgetary priorities. In 1996, in order to attain the Maastricht criteria, another pension reform was implemented, this time with clearly worsened features, followed by yet another reform in 1997 believed to be of a long-term nature. Currently, the new coalition government is considering a new round of changes motivated by budgetary constraints (to meet the Maastricht criteria by 2003), and by the anticipated changes in population age structure and on the labour market.

In the course of the past decade, a discussion on the adequacy of the Austrian pension scheme started. Major structural reform proposals were put forth that emphasized the disadvantaged position of women, the favoured position of civil servants, the issue of intergenerational burden sharing, and new labour market developments and their effects on the pension scheme (Prinz et al., 1996; Rürup and Schroeder, 1997; Prinz and Marin, 1997; Die Grünen, 1998; Prinz and Marin, 1999).

After a number of smaller changes and adaptations, such as the continuous prolongation of the assessment period from the last 5 to the best 15 years, in 1993, following the recommendations of the 'Beirat für Wirtschafts-und Sozialfragen' (1991), a broader reform package was agreed upon. It was believed that this reform would be a major step forward in guaranteeing the long-term financial stability of the system. The benefit indexation rule was changed from a gross wage adjustment to an adjustment according to wages net of contributions (modified net adjustment before taxes). Pension credits for mothers (or fathers, if they were the primary caretakers) were introduced, strictly as a supplement to the earnings-related pension claim. Partial retirement was introduced with the aim of raising the very low actual retirement age. Under this scheme it is possible to reduce working hours to 50% and receive a 70% pension, or alternatively, reduce work to 70% and receive a 50% pension (note that partial retirement has been hardly used simply because early retirement has the same requirements, but is much more attractive). Finally, survivor pensions were adjusted with the aim of reducing survivor pension expenditures in the long run (reduction to only 40% of the pension entitlement of the deceased spouse, depending on the income difference).

Only a few years later, accentuated by the need to constrain public expenditures in order to meet the Maastricht criteria, some other changes in the pension scheme were implemented. These changes had little long-term perspective and were clearly geared towards reducing benefits (or increasing the retirement age) and/or increasing contributions in the short term. These measures were also part of a broader decision process known to the public as 'Austerity Programme II', following the Structural Adjustment Act in 1995 (also known as 'Austerity Programme I'). In this year, the eligibility criteria for early retirement were tightened by raising the required insurance contribution periods (e.g. from 35 to 37.5 years for early retirement due to long insurance records). Invalidity pensions are now granted temporarily for only two years, after which the possibility of vocational rehabilitation has to be tested. School and study periods are no longer considered automatically when computing the waiting period (nor for calculating pensions for which such periods had not been considered since 1988), but may now be purchased at a fixed rate. The percentage of assessed earnings paid per year of contribution was changed in order to make later retirement more attractive. And, finally, a few minor measures were taken to harmonize the schemes for the different occupational groups (raising the contribution rates for the self-employed and farmers from 12.5% to 14.5%, and introducing a few new elements into the scheme for civil servants).

After the changes in 1993 and even more so after 1996, the pension reform debate became more heated for two reasons: First, it became clear that in order to reduce expenditures in the short run (to meet the Maastricht criteria) even more drastic changes or benefit cuts would be necessary; and second, due to the strong focus on budgetary considerations, several (interest) groups and research organizations increasingly emphasized the distributional inadequacies of the Austrian pension scheme (regarding women, occupational groups, high- and low-income groups, generations, and marital status groups). Additional reforms, partly of a structural nature, were proposed from various points of view. The Ministry for Social Affairs, which is the responsible authority, supplied an expert opinion focusing on the long-term financial stability of the scheme and the objective of sharing the burden between the generations (Rürup and Schroeder, 1997). The Ministry for Women's Affairs supplied an expert opinion emphasizing the distributive inadequacy of the system and proposing measures to establish independent pension entitlements for all persons (Prinz et al., 1996). The opposition parties are calling for radical changes in the system, ranging from a focus on granting basic benefits to an emphasis on capital-funded elements (e.g. Die Grünen, 1998).

As early as in the autumn of 1997, after a very short preparation and examination period, the government agreed upon another more far-reaching reform. With the objective of solving the problems of the Austrian pension system in mind, a number of changes were implemented. Among the experts, though, there was little hope that the reform process would be completed. On the contrary, new reforms targeting the younger generations and women are expected in the near future (see discussion in the concluding section). The following were the most important elements of the 1997 reform. With the aim of increasing contribution revenues, insurance coverage was expanded to include atypical employment contracts, such as marginal employment and contracted labour. Hoping to increase the actual retirement age, a two percentage point deduction for each year of early retirement (which is much less than actuarially required) was introduced. At the same time, however, returns for each year of insurance were raised to 2%, thereby largely compensating the potential deduction. Also, partial retirement was made more attractive (lower requirements than for early retirement). A few measures will be implemented between 2000 and 2020. By 2020, but only in case of early retirement, the average income of the best 18 income years (instead of 15 years) will be used as the calculation base. As a major step towards a real harmonization of the different schemes, by then, civil servants pensions will also be based on this calculation base, rather than on the last pay. Until 2020, however, so-called 'cushioning measures' will strongly reduce the impact of these measures, thus creating new intergenerational inequities (retiring in 2019 or in 2021 can indeed make a big difference). Together with these reform measures, several labour market policy measures were implemented (such as the introduction of educational leave or the right to reduce working time for employees over 50 or for employees with care obligations).

In the beginning of the year 2000, the discussion on a pension reform was taken up again during the negotiations to form a government coalition, first by the 'old' coalition parties (Social Democrats and Christian Democrats), then by the 'new' partners (Christian Democrats and right-wing liberals). The renewed debate is primarily a response to the tax reform of 1999 that, by generously increasing family benefits and generally reducing taxes for all income groups, renewed pressure on the federal budget. As a consequence, the new coalition contract outlines several areas of change, all of which are aimed at a reduction of around 15 billion Austrian shillings of federal subsidies to the pension system by 2003. If the planned changes are literally implemented, the early retirement age will be raised by 1.5 years in 2000, and the rate of deduction for each year of early retirement will be increased. The rule regulating the annual adjustments of pensions will be changed, and the average survivor claim will be lowered. In order to put the envisaged reform plans on a broader base, the new government has appointed an expert committee on pension reform and charged it with the task of working out proposals for short-term changes (based on the coalition contract) by end of March 2000, and to prepare recommendations for a longer-term structural reform by the end of the same year.

5.2.3 Retirement Trends and Pension Expenditures

Empirically, the process of retirement in Austria is strongly dominated by an unusually high occurrence of early retirements. Only 12% of men and one quarter of all women who entered the pension system in 1996 were regular old-age pensioners; the gender difference is largely a consequence of the difference in the legal retirement age (Table 5.1). Women mainly tend to retire early due to long insurance records (40.6%). Among men, this type of early retirement is less frequent because many retire before reaching the legal early retirement age. Men overwhelmingly retire due to disability or reduced work capacity (56.8%). Early retirement due to unemployment is much more common among women. Partial retirement is rare for both men and women. Note that the pattern of retirement has not changed very much since 1996.

Table 5.1: Newly Granted Pensions in 1996 by Type of Pension
(percentage distribution)

Type of pension	Women	Men
Regular old-age pension	24.6	12.0
Early old-age pension due to long insurance record	40.6	29.1
Early old-age pension due to unemployment	11.1	1.6
Early old-age pension due to reduced work capacity	9.9	38.2
Partial old-age pension	0.8	0.5
Invalidity pension	13.0	18.6
Newly granted pensions in 1996 (absolute figures)	41,796	45,056

Source: Wörister, 1998.

The phenomenon of early retirement can also be described from a labour market perspective: Economic activity rates above the age of 55 are indeed very low in Austria when compared with other European countries and although several measures have been taken to prolong the active working phase, as described in section 5.2.2, this rate is still not increasing (Table 5.2). This low activity rate among older workers is generally seen as the principal problem of the Austrian pension scheme and reversing the trend towards early retirement is the main challenge. At age 60-64, for instance, only 1 in 18 women and 1 in 8 men are still in the labour force. Twenty-five years ago, even in Austria, almost every second man in this age group was economically active.

As a consequence of the widespread practice of early retirement, the distribution of the stock of pensioners has also changed. Note that this distribution is influenced by the fact that invalidity pensioners above the age of 60 (women) and 65 (men) respectively, remain classified in this group. Among men, old-age and invalidity pensions increased by 39% from 1975 to 1996 (Table 5.3). Invalidity pensions below the regular retirement age have increased the most rapidly (177%), followed by early old-age pensions (43%) and regular old-age pensions (17%). Note that widower's pensions were only introduced in 1981.

Table 5.2: Labour Force Participation Rates for Men and Women Above Age 50, 1971-1996

	Age group 50-54		Age group 55-59		Age group 60-64		Age group 65+	
Year	Women	Men	Women	Men	Women	Men	Women	Men
1971	48.5	92.8	35.8	83.8	13.2	44.9	3.5	7.1
1981	48.0	93.3	30.0	74.9	8.8	27.5	1.8	4.0
1991	54.0	90.8	25.8	63.2	4.9	14.3	0.9	2.5
1996	57.3	81.9	22.1	61.5	5.6	12.2	0.6	2.0

Source: 1971-1991 Census, 1996 Microcensus.

Table 5.3: Stock of Male Pensioners (000): Distribution and Trend, 1975-1996

Type of pension	1975	1980	1985	1990	1995	1996
Regular old-age pensions	263	276	259	278	303	307
Early old-age pensions[1]	46	44	77	76	69	66
Invalidity pensions below age 65[2]	60	70	114	144	160	166
Invalidity pensions above age 65	91	82	66	71	97	102
Widower's pensions below age 65	-	-	4	7	9	9
Widower's pensions above age 65	-	-	7	15	22	23
All old-age and invalidity pensions	460	472	516	569	629	641
All pensions including survivor's	460	472	527	591	660	673

Notes: 1. Early old-age pensions due to long insurance record and due to unemployment

2. Including early old-age pensions due to reduced working capacity

Source: Wörister, 1998.

Among women, old-age and invalidity pensions increased much more significantly than among men – 61% from 1975 to 1996, largely due to increasing economic activity rates – while widow's pensions remained nearly constant over this 20-year period (Table 5.4). The early retirement old-age pensions grew the most rapidly (825% !), followed by invalidity pensions below the regular retirement age (134%) and regular old-age pensions (53%).

Table 5.4: Stock of Female Pensioners (000): Distribution and Trend, 1975-1996

Type of pension	1975	1980	1985	1990	1995	1996
Regular old-age pensions	292	310	365	407	441	447
Early old-age pensions[1]	8	30	40	39	63	74
Invalidity pensions below age 60[2]	23	37	43	46	52	54
Invalidity pensions above age 60	110	109	119	121	124	124
Widow's pensions below age 60	76	78	70	66	63	63
Widow's pensions above age 60	351	370	388	390	387	386
All old-age and invalidity pensions	433	486	567	613	680	699
All pensions including survivor's	860	934	1025	1069	1130	1148

192   Source and notes as above.

Nonetheless, the recent decade was characterized by relatively stable developments. After a period of rapid decline until 1985, the actual average retirement ages in the public pension scheme remained more or less constant at around 58 for men and 57 for women (Table 5.5). Similar age trends were observed for civil servants. Note that, notwithstanding a 5-year gender difference in the legal retirement age, the difference in the actual retirement age has been relatively small due to the fact that many women simply do not have enough insurance years at the age of 55 and, because the proportion of invalidity pensions is much higher among men. It should also be mentioned that the steady decline in the female retirement age is likely to be halted by the recent pension reform measures.

Due to a favourable age structure development, the support ratio, which is the number of contributors supporting one retiree, has also changed very little since 1985, while it had declined from 1970 to 1985 mainly because of the increasing eligibility among women (Table 5.5). As a consequence, the contribution rate to the pension system could be held constant since 1985 at 22.8% of gross earnings (12.55% for the employer, 10.25% for the employee). The contribution from the federal budget stabilized at around one quarter of total pension expenditure, while the increase in the contribution rate from

1970 to 1985 led to a decline in the state's contribution during that period (Table 5.5). On the other hand, in the future, the support ratio is projected to decline drastically as a consequence of accelerating population ageing, falling below 1.0 around 2030 (Beirat für Wirtschafts- und Sozialfragen, 1991).

Table 5.5: Selected Pension Scheme Parameters: 1970-1996 (public pension scheme for blue- and white-collar workers, farmers and the self-employed, excluding civil servants)

Year	Average male retirement age (in years)	Average female retirement age (in years)	Support ratio: contributors per retiree	Contribution rate (in % of gross earnings)	Contribution by the state (in % of total)
1970	61.9	60.4	2.05	15.5	31.3
1975	61.8	60.1	1.98	17.5	33.9
1980	59.2	58.3	1.92	20.5	22.3
1985	58.3	57.9	1.71	22.7	27.7
1990	58.3	57.5	1.69	22.8	25.9
1995	58.1	56.7	1.66	22.8	25.1
1996	58.2	56.7	1.62	22.8	25.1

Source: BMfAGS, 1997.

Expressed in terms of GDP, total pension expenditure (including expenditures for civil servants) has increased by one percentage point from 1980 to 1985, but by only 0.4 percentage points during the recent decade. In 1995, pension expenditure was equal to 14.3% of GDP (Table 5.6). The pension reforms of the 1990s aim, among other things, at stabilizing that ratio during the next century. However, the rapid ageing of Austria's population, in particular between 2015 and 2030, will certainly lead to a significant increase in expenditure if current benefit levels remain unchanged (Table 5.8).

Table 5.7 shows that the net replacement rates of the pension scheme are very high on average, in particular for men in which case they reach around 80%. The 1993 pension reform has clearly led to a significant improvement in benefit levels for women, in particular among blue-collar workers (this is due to the fact that the recognition of child care periods is relatively more effective at lower incomes). Effects of the 1996 and 1997 reforms are not yet known, but the gender gap is likely to increase rather than decrease further. Among civil servants, net replacement rates are significantly higher (and usually close to or even above 100%), because their benefits are calculated on the basis of their last pay.

Table 5.6: Pension Expenditure in Per Cent of GDP: 1980-1995 (including civil servants)

Year	Gross domestic product (in billion ATS)	Old-age pensions (% of GDP)	Survivor pensions (% of GDP)	Invalidity pensions (% of GDP)	Total pension expenditure (% of GDP)
1980	996	8.39	3.30	1.16	12.86
1985	1350	9.24	3.26	1.41	13.91
1990	1803	9.31	3.03	1.42	13.76
1995	2356	9.71	3.00	1.59	14.30

Source: BMfAGS, 1997.

Table 5.7: The Net Replacement Rate of New Old-age/Invalidity Pensions: 1987 and 1993-1995

Year	Women: Blue-collar workers	Women: White-collar workers	Men: Blue-collar workers	Men: White-collar workers
1987	64.6	70.1	78.0	82.8
1993	66.0	68.0	77.9	80.5
1994	71.3	72.3	78.1	81.2
1995	73.0	72.6	78.4	81.2

Source: BMfAGS, 1997.

Although the replacement rates of those covered in the system are relatively high, a significant proportion of the population still does not receive any pension. Among women, in 1993-94 this was true for roughly 18% of women above the age of 60 (around 180,000 women in total), for men this was true only for a very small minority (see Prinz et al., 1996). Among these 180,000 women, the large majority or 97% were married; hence, these women were provided for through their husband's wage or pension and they could become survivor pension recipients at a later stage in their life. Only 4,000 women and 1,500 men above the age of 60, corresponding to 0.4% and 0.26%

of the respective population group, depend on social assistance. Among them, an disproportionate share is divorced and only a relatively small proportion is married.

Table 5.8: Age Structure Trends for Austria: 1970-2030
(medium variant 1995-2030)

Year	Total population of Austria (000)	Proportion of children below age 15	Proportion of working age population	Proportion of young elderly age 60-74	Proportion of elderly above age 75
1970	7,467	24.4	55.5	15.4	4.7
1975	7,579	23.2	56.4	15.2	5.2
1980	7,549	20.4	60.4	13.1	6.0
1985	7,578	18.3	61.9	13.2	6.6
1990	7,729	17.4	62.5	13.2	6.9
1995	8,046	17.5	62.7	13.5	6.2
2000	8,084	16.7	62.6	13.5	7.2
2015	8,052	13.3	60.9	16.7	9.1
2030	8,067	13.3	52.0	22.6	12.1

Source: ÖSTAT (1996), forecast ÖSTAT (1998).

In contrast to the recent decade, which had been characterized by stability, in the future the Austrian pension scheme will face a number of difficulties, largely due to demographic patterns (Table 5.8): the working age population will decline both in absolute terms (minus 17%) and in relative terms, while the elderly population will sharply increase (plus 68% in absolute terms between 1995 and 2030) according to the medium variant estimated by the Austrian Statistical Office (ÖSTAT, 1998). Two major reasons for this development are very low and steadily declining fertility rates, which hit an all-time low of 1.32 children per woman on average in 1998 and 1999, and rapid improvements in life expectancy since 1970, also at an older age, improvements which are generally believed to continue (Table 5.9). Given the current demographic and economic situation, most authors agree that there are basically two possibilities for the system to survive in the long run (compare, for example, Guger, 1997, or Prinz, 1994): raising the factual retirement age or reducing income replacement rates. In reality, both of these options or aims may be achieved through a number of very different reform measures. Increasing the contribution rate is not seen as a sensible option for reasons of international competitiveness. The following analysis sheds more light on the income situation of the elderly, thus answering the question of whether or not there is indeed room for a reduction of pension benefit levels.

Table 5.9: Total Fertility Rate and Gender-specific Life Expectancies: 1970-1998

Year	Total fertility rate (children per woman)	Male life expectancy at birth	Female life expectancy at birth	Male life expectancy at age 60	Female life expectancy at age 60
1970	2.29	66.5	73.4	14.9	18.8
1975	1.83	67.7	74.7	15.6	19.6
1980	1.65	69.0	76.1	16.3	20.3
1985	1.47	70.4	77.3	17.0	21.0
1990	1.45	72.4	78.9	17.9	22.2
1995	1.40	73.5	80.1	18.7	22.9
1998	1.32	74.7	81.0	19.3	23.6

Source: ÖSTAT (1996) and ÖSTAT (1998).

5.3 The Data

Income data used in this study are taken from the Austrian Microcensuses 1985 and 1995 (with a few facts added from other Microcensus surveys). The Microcensus is a regularly-taken household survey with a relatively large sample size (around 65,000 persons or 0.8% of the population are interviewed). It is taken quarterly and asks questions regarding income once every two years. Once selected as part of the sample, answering the questionnaire is a civic duty; for this reason, there is practically no non-response to the general questions. However, questions on income are exempt from this obligation, hence there is a non-response rate of nearly 30% to these questions. Notwithstanding this high rate of non-response, comparisons with other data sets (such as data derived from tax on wages statistics) have demonstrated a reasonable quality and reliability of the Microcensus income data. Two major advantages of this data set, in addition to its sample size, are a rather complex weighting procedure (guaranteeing high representativeness) and the availability of a large number of socio-demographic background variables. Alternative income data that is reasonably reliable and has an equally rich set of background variables are scarce. The European Community Household Panel, for which the first results for Austria for the year 1994 became accessible during 1998, is another alternative, although the sample size is of course much smaller. Once several data waves become available, the Household Panel will provide the means for a longitudinal income analysis, which is, however, of less relevance for the analysis of senior citizens than for that of other population groups, because pensioners are relatively less likely to change their income status over time.

The income analysis covers exactly one decade, from the mid-1980s to the mid-1990s. Income according to the Microcensus shows an individual's regular monthly net income (labour income plus social transfers such as pensions, including family allowances and occupational pensions). Since all individuals in a household are interviewed, household incomes and equivalent household incomes can be reconstructed.

197

5.4 Pensioner Households: Composition, Size, and Income

After two decades of stability, between 1985 and 1995 unforeseen immigration waves led to an increase in the total population size by half a million (see Table 5.8). However, the number of households has been increasing continually since World War II due to declining fertility, increasing life expectancy and changing family formation and dissolution patterns, which have contributed to the gradual decline in the average household size. The average household size declined from 2.92 to 2.82 for non-pensioner households between 1985 and 1995 (Table 5.10), which is, in fact, less than would have been expected without immigration. The number of households increased by more than 300,000 during this decade. The size of pensioner households has increased, because more couples jointly survive beyond retirement age; this is also clear from the decline in the proportion of pensioners living in one-person households (from 41 to 37%) and the corresponding increase of those living in two-person households (from 50 to 55%). By contrast, the main trend in the recent decade for non-pensioner households has been a decline in the proportion of persons living in larger households, i.e. five or more persons. In short, the large majority (or 92%) of pensioners live in one- or two-person households, which is obviously not the case among the child and working-age population (for which the corresponding proportion is 24%). This household size distribution must be kept in mind with regard to its relation to the relatively steep equivalence scale used in this analysis. Note that a pensioner household is defined as a household with at least one pensioner, and no active earners, entrepreneurs or unemployed; a pensioner is a person over 50 who declares him or herself as a pensioner. Following this definition, a non-pensioner household may also include one or more pensioners.

Table 5.10: **Distribution of Persons in Pensioner and Non-pensioner Households by Household Size, and Average Household Size, 1985 and 1995**

Persons ...	Proportion of persons in households with ... persons					Average
	One person	Two persons	Three persons	Four persons	Five plus persons	House-hold size
... in pensioner households						
1985	41.4	50.4	6.5	1.5	0.2	1.45
1995	37.1	55.2	5.7	1.3	0.7	1.49
... in non-pensioner households						
1985	5.9	17.2	24.7	29.9	22.3	2.92
1995	7.2	17.2	24.8	30.9	19.9	2.82

Source: Own calculations based on Microcensus data.

The large majority (more than 80%) of one-person pensioner households are single females, although the proportion of single males has increased since 1985 (Table 5.11). In 1995, around 55% of both pensioners and non-pensioners lived in couple households. However, while this household composition has rapidly declined among non-pensioners (from 64 to 56% within a decade), it has increased among pensioners.

Before switching to the detailed analysis of equivalent household incomes (which is then related to the issue of pension reform), this section looks at income sources, the income position and the income distribution at the household level. Pensioner and non-pensioner households are distinguished, and to the extent necessary, four broad household groups are compared: single females, single males, couples with one or two incomes, and other households.

Table 5.11: **Distribution of Persons in Pensioner and Non-pensioner Households by Household Composition, 1985 and 1995**

Persons ...	*Proportion of persons in households with ... composition*				
	Single males	Single females	Couples	Other types	Total
... in pensioner households					
1985	6.0	35.3	50.4	8.2	100
1995	6.3	30.7	54.8	8.1	100
... in non-pensioner households					
1985	3.0	3.0	63.8	30.3	100
1995	4.0	3.2	55.9	38.9	100

Source: Own calculations based on Microcensus data.

Information on income sources is not included in the Microcensus because it only asks for monthly net individual incomes. Such information is available from the ECHP, however, even this data set only provides the income composition and the main source of income but not the exact contribution of each source to total household income (Table 5.12). Pensioner households rely almost exclusively on public pension income, although one in four of these households also have some sort of capital income, mostly some sort of private savings or pensions.

Among non-pensioner households, the income composition is naturally very different, with a dominance of wages or salaries. One in two of these households also receive some other social benefits, in many cases family allowances. One in four indicate some additional capital income, and one in six mention income from other sources, such as private (inter-generational) transfers – but none of these incomes are classified as the main income source. Every third non-pensioner household also states income from public pensions, and for one in two of these households this is even the main source of income.

Table 5.13 gives an overview of the average total household income by type of household. Among pensioners, caused by differences in wage levels and the length of insurance records, single males have 30% higher incomes than single females. A couple-pensioner household has almost twice the income of a single female pensioner. The reported increase between 1985 and 1995 was larger among couples and other household types than among singles, which is a consequence of the increasing proportion of married women entitled to an employment-related old-age pension. This rise in turn being caused by the increase in female labour force participation. Among non-pensioners, income differences between single males and single females are smaller and declined further between 1985 and 1995.

Table 5.12: Income Sources of Pensioner and Non-pensioner Households in 1994

Type of household	Proportion of households indicating the following sources of income (in parentheses: proportion for which this is the main source of income)						
	Wages or salaries	Self-employ-ment	Public pensions	Unem-ployment benefits	Other social benefits	Capital income (savings)	Income from other sources
Pensioner households	0 (0)	0 (0)	100 (99)	0 (0)	2 (0)	24 (1)	7 (0)
Non-pensioner households	78 (69)	20 (8)	32 (16)	7 (2)	48 (1)	26 (1)	16 (3)

Source: European Community Household Panel for Austria (ECHP, second wave).

Table 5.13: Median Household Income for Pensioner and Non-pensioner Households by Household Composition, 1985 and 1995 (in ATS, 1995 prices)

Persons ...	Household composition			
	Single males	Single females	Couples	Other types
... in pensioner households				
1985	9850	7700	12960	12960
1995	13000	9840	18300	19500
Index (1985=100)	132	128	141	151
... in non-pensioner households				
1985	13330	11010	20210	22760
1995	15000	13714	26000	29410
Index (1985=100)	113	125	129	129

Note: 100 ATS = 7.2673 EURO (1 January 1999) or 7.4846 ECU (1 January 1995).

Source: Own calculations based on Microcensus data.

The income distribution of pensioner households over household income deciles – each decile containing 10% of all households – is given in Table 5.14 (and also in the Appendix, Table 5A1). Taking all pensioner households together (which formed 35% of all households in 1985, but only 30% in 1995), two out of ten were found in the three highest and almost four out of ten in the three lowest income deciles. Single male pensioners, who represented around 3% of all households both in 1985 and 1995, were clearly underrepresented in the lower and overrepresented in the upper income deciles. In 1995, only one in five single male pensioner households were found in the three lowest deciles, but almost two in five in the three highest deciles. During the last decade, however, the relative income position for this population group has worsened. Single female pensioner households are also underrepresented in the first decile, but they are very much concentrated in the second and third decile. Obviously, although they have low incomes on average, the means-tested supplement to low pensions guarantees that few single (female) pensioners are found in the first income decile. Due to the disproportionate increase in this supplement between 1985 and 1995, this effect has even been more accentuated. Nevertheless, in 1995 almost one in two single female pensioner households were found in the three lowest income deciles.

In higher income deciles, the proportion of single female pensioners gradually declines. Only one in seven pensioner households of this type are found in the upper three deciles (again, see also Appendix, Table 5A1). Just as among single males, between 1985 and 1995 the relative income position of single female pensioners has worsened. Note that the proportion of single female pensioner households has declined by four percentage points during the last decade. This decline is mainly a consequence of a continual decline in the proportion of widows; a proportion which – still as a consequence of World War II – was atypically high in Austria in 1985.

Though not as pronounced as among single females, pensioner couples are also very much underrepresented in the upper and overrepresented in the lower income deciles. They are, however, more often found in the first decile. Other pensioner households are more equally distributed over income deciles in general, except for a disproportionate count in the first decile. Between 1985 and 1995, the relative income position improved for both couple and 'other' pensioner households, though much more for 'other' pensioner households, bearing in mind that the category of 'other' pensioner households comprises only around 5% of all pensioner households.

Table 5.14: **Proportion of Different Types of Pensioner Households as Per Cent of All Households in Each Income Decile, 1985 and 1995 – horizontal distribution**

Year	Type of pensioner household				
	Single males	Single females	Couples	Other types	All types
1985					
1	1.2	15.7	17.8	4.2	38.9
2	2.1	32.7	12.4	1.8	49.0
3	2.0	25.4	15.6	1.5	44.4
4	1.7	15.4	18.8	3.6	39.4
5	4.8	28.3	11.6	1.9	46.6
6	3.6	19.4	11.3	1.5	35.8
7	3.0	12.9	10.9	1.9	28.7
8	4.5	9.8	8.0	1.5	23.9
9	3.5	10.0	8.1	1.2	22.9
10	4.2	8.6	6.7	0.2	19.7
Total	3.1	17.8	12.1	1.9	34.9
1995					
1	1.3	10.1	15.4	2.8	29.6
2	1.7	28.7	12.8	1.3	44.6
3	2.8	23.9	14.5	1.3	42.5
4	2.9	19.1	13.4	1.1	36.5
5	2.0	14.6	14.6	2.4	33.5
6	3.4	11.5	13.0	1.8	29.7
7	3.8	10.1	10.5	1.7	26.2
8	3.0	8.7	10.3	1.5	23.5
9	3.8	6.5	8.9	1.4	20.6
10	4.0	6.1	6.2	1.3	17.5
Total	2.9	13.9	12.0	1.6	30.4

Note: Figures in this table indicate the proportion of households of a certain type as percentage of all households in a given income decile. Similar information, but totalled over each household type (vertical distribution), is given in the Appendix, Table 5A1.

Source: Own calculations based on Microcensus data.

5.5 Equivalent Income Distribution among the Elderly

In order to obtain a realistic picture of the income position of the different groups of senior citizens, equivalent household incomes (calculated as described in section 5.2) are needed. Note that the equivalent scale used in this study (1.0 for the first adult, 0.7 for other adults and 0.5 for each child under the age of 16) is almost identical to the one usually used in Austria, but considerably steeper than the scale used by EUROSTAT (1.0 for the first adult, 0.5 for other adults and 0.3 for each child) and most recently also by the OECD. The consequence of a steep scale, which infers relatively less economies of scale for larger households, is a lower equivalent household income for persons in larger households and hence a relatively lower income for children in general as compared to persons in one-person households (see for instance Förster, 1994). This should be kept in mind when interpreting the following tables.

Table 5.15 gives equivalent income deciles for 1985 and 1995 in 1995 prices. During this decade, equivalent incomes increased about 2.9% annually, with slightly lower increases in the higher deciles. In 1995, the median equivalent monthly gross income was 11,000 ATS or 823 ECU. Compared with household incomes, equivalent incomes are distributed considerably more equally and, between 1985 and 1995, they have increased much less than the household incomes for all deciles.

Table 5.15: **Equivalent Household Incomes by Income Decile, Real Increases between 1985 and 1995 (in ATS, 1995 prices)**

Year	Income decile in ATS								
	10%	20%	30%	40%	50%	60%	70%	80%	90%
1985	4715	5674	6477	7345	8239	9301	10558	12009	14483
1995	6240	7590	8760	9890	11000	12180	13700	15500	18420
index (1985=100)	132	134	135	135	134	131	130	129	127
annual increase	2.8%	2.9%	3.0%	3.0%	2.9%	2.7%	2.6%	2.6%	2.4%

Note: 100 ATS = 7.2673 EURO (1 January 1999) or 7.4846 ECU (1 January 1995).

Source: Own calculations based on Microcensus data.

By contrast to the previous section, the following decile investigation uses persons as the unit of analysis: each decile contains 10% of all persons, and each person is considered with his or her equivalent household income. Just as in the household section, the following tables show the horizontal income distribution, while the vertical distribution is given in the corresponding appendix tables.

The proportion of three different population groups (pensioners older than 50 years, pensioners in pensioner households, and all persons older than 60 years) in each income decile is given in Table 5.16 and in the Appendix, Table 5A2. Total percentages have changed very little between 1985 and 1995. The group of pensioners aged 50 and over is just as large as the group of persons aged 60 and over, in both years comprising around 21% of the population. The proportion of pensioners living in pensioner households declined slightly, from 17 to 16% of the population or from 82 to 75% of all pensioners.

Table 5.16: **Proportion of Pensioners, Pensioners in Pensioner Households and Persons Aged 60 and Over as a Percentage of All Persons in Each Income Decile, 1985 and 1995 – horizontal distribution**

Income decile	1985			1995		
	Pensioners aged 50 and over	Pensioners in pensioner households	All persons aged 60 and over	Pensioners aged 50 and over	Pensioners in pensioner households	All persons aged 60 and over
1	16.2	14.3	19.0	12.1	10.8	14.0
2	21.0	19.5	23.0	21.0	18.9	22.9
3	19.6	17.2	22.2	20.7	17.5	22.3
4	23.2	20.1	24.8	20.8	16.6	20.8
5	25.6	21.6	26.7	23.2	17.3	22.4
6	25.0	20.8	25.6	26.9	20.2	26.4
7	19.9	14.9	18.8	22.2	14.9	21.4
8	18.7	13.3	17.8	23.1	15.8	21.2
9	20.4	15.5	19.5	22.5	14.3	20.5
10	18.5	13.4	18.0	19.4	12.6	18.1
Total	20.8	17.1	21.5	21.2	15.9	21.0

Note: Figures in this table indicate the proportion of persons in a certain group as percentage of all persons in a given income decile. Similar information, but totalled over each population group (vertical distribution), is given in the Appendix, Table 5A2.

Source: Own calculations based on Microcensus data.

All groups of pensioners and the elderly improved their income position significantly between 1985 and 1995. For all three groups, there is a particularly pronounced decline in the proportion found in the first (lowest) income decile, e.g. from 16 to 12% among pensioners and from 19 to 14% among all persons aged 60 and over. Also for all groups, the observed maximum shifted upwards by one income decile from the fifth to the sixth decile. The sixth decile now contains 26-27% pensioners and persons aged 60 and over, and 20% pensioners in pensioner households.

There are, however, significant differences between these groups. Pensioners experienced the fastest improvement during the recent decade. While they were overrepresented in the 4th-6th income decile in 1985, they are now overrepresented in the 5th-9th decile. Pensioners in pensioner households are worse off than pensioners in general and also improvements in the last decade were less pronounced. The group of senior citizens, including pensioners as well as elderly – largely women – that are not eligible for a pension, also experienced smaller improvements. They are mainly still overrepresented in the 2nd-6th income decile.

205

Table 5.17: **Proportion of Pensioners and Persons Aged 60 and Over as a Percentage of All Persons in Each Income Decile, by Gender, 1985 and 1995 – horizontal distribution**

Income decile	1985				1995			
	Female pensioners	Male pensioners	Women over 60	Men over 60	Female pensioners	Male pensioners	Women over 60	Men over 60
1	8.7	7.5	12.2	6.8	5.8	6.3	8.4	5.6
2	13.8	7.2	16.6	6.4	13.4	7.6	16.4	6.5
3	11.7	7.9	15.2	7.1	12.2	8.5	14.5	7.8
4	14.1	9.2	16.8	8.0	12.3	8.5	13.4	7.4
5	15.6	10.0	17.9	8.8	13.8	9.4	14.3	8.1
6	14.9	10.1	16.7	8.9	15.8	11.1	16.3	10.2
7	11.7	8.2	12.0	6.8	12.0	10.1	12.4	9.0
8	10.3	8.4	10.8	7.0	13.0	10.1	12.3	9.0
9	12.3	8.1	11.7	7.8	12.4	10.1	11.4	9.1
10	10.6	7.9	9.8	8.2	10.4	9.0	9.5	8.6
Total	12.4	8.5	14.0	7.6	12.1	9.1	12.9	8.1

Note: Figures in this table indicate the proportion of persons in a certain group as a percentage of all persons in a given income decile. Similar information, but totalled over each gender group (vertical distribution) is given in the Appendix, Table 5A3.

Source: Own calculations based on Microcensus data.

It is also interesting to look at men and women separately, which is done in Table 5.17 (and in Table 5A3 in the Appendix), both for the categories of persons older than 60 and pensioners. From these calculations it becomes obvious that it is the group of women aged 60 and over – that still includes a significant proportion without a pension entitlement – which is in the most difficult position and could hardly improve its income position in relative terms. In both years they were overrepresented in the 2nd-6th decile. Only the disproportionate increase in the means-tested supplement to a pension clearly affected women more than men, thus reducing the proportion of elderly women found in the first income decile from 12 to 8% (among men, there was only a one percentage point reduction). Male and female pensioners, who were usually concentrated around the median in 1985, are now mostly overrepresented above the median equivalent income. Men are found in higher groups than women. Note that primarily as a consequence of demographic developments half a century ago, the proportion of women aged 60 and over among the total population declined while the corresponding proportion of men aged 60 and over increased.

206

Table 5.18: **Proportion of Persons in Different Age Groups as Per Cent of All Persons in Each Income Decile, 1985 and 1995 – horizontal distrib.**

Income decile	1985				1995			
	Age group 40-59	Age group 60-69	Age group 70-79	Age group 80 plus	Age group 40-59	Age group 60-69	Age group 70-79	Age group 80 plus
1	14.4	7.3	8.4	3.3	15.8	6.6	5.3	2.1
2	12.5	8.9	11.0	3.1	15.7	9.7	8.6	4.6
3	13.8	8.5	10.3	3.4	17.3	9.6	7.7	5.0
4	18.7	10.8	10.0	4.0	20.5	9.5	7.2	4.0
5	20.1	11.8	10.5	4.4	22.2	10.1	8.1	4.2
6	24.5	11.5	10.1	3.9	24.6	12.2	9.6	4.6
7	26.2	9.1	7.6	2.1	26.4	10.7	7.4	3.3
8	26.5	9.0	6.6	2.2	30.1	10.7	6.5	4.0
9	30.0	9.7	7.5	2.3	33.6	10.5	6.3	3.7
10	37.0	11.1	4.7	2.2	36.1	8.8	6.6	2.7
Total	22.4	9.8	8.7	3.1	24.2	9.9	7.3	3.8

Note: Figures in this table indicate the proportion of persons in a certain group as a percentage of all persons in a given income decile. Similar information, but totalled over each age group (vertical distribution), is given in the Appendix, Table 5A4.

Source: Own calculations based on Microcensus data.

Equally telling is a more detailed comparison of the different age groups; this time looking at persons only and not at pensioners (Table 5.18 and Table 5A4 in the Appendix). Again, note the demographic discontinuities in the past, leading to uneven age structure trends during the period from 1985 to 1995, with an increase in the proportions of age 40-59 and age 80+, a decline in the proportion of age 70-79, and a steady trend in the proportion of age 60-69. As may be expected from the existing age-wage profile, both in 1985 and in 1995 the proportion of the mature working-age population (the age group 40-59) increases with income decile. They are by far under-represented in the lower deciles (around one in five are found in the three lowest deciles) and overrepresented in the upper deciles (more than two in five classified in the three highest deciles). Between 1985 and 1995, however, the relative income position of this population group did not change significantly.[1]

Among the elderly population, young elderly aged 60-69 are significantly better off than those above the age of 70. This difference, which strongly correlates to the gender structure of these groups (with a much higher proportion of women above age 70), has become significantly smaller over the last decade. There are only small differences in income patterns between persons at age 70-79 and persons over the age of 80. The 70-79 age group, however, experienced more pronounced income improvements during the observed decade than the oldest segment of the population, which is again largely a consequence of shifts in the gender structure.

The following figures show the vertical income distribution over certain subgroups of the population (but only for one year), i.e. totalling percentages for each group (as is done in all the appendix tables). This gives a better picture of the concentration of the different population, pensioner, age and marital status groups across equivalent household income deciles. As mentioned repeatedly, the means-tested pension supplement guarantees that senior citizens in general are rarely found in the first income decile, irrespective of age, gender or status. Income distributions for men over the age of 60 and male pensioners of any age are very similar. The large majority – approximately 57% – has incomes above the median (Figure 5.1). Among women, on the contrary, differences between younger and older pensioners are large. The latter, who overwhelmingly live alone (compare also Figure 5.3), are very much concentrated in the second and third decile, and a majority (52%) is found below the median. On the other hand, the income position of younger female pensioners resembles that of men, while the

207

income distribution for the entire group of women above age 60 mirrors that of the older female pensioners.

Figure 5.1: Income Distribution for Selected Population Groups by Equivalent Household Income Decile, 1995

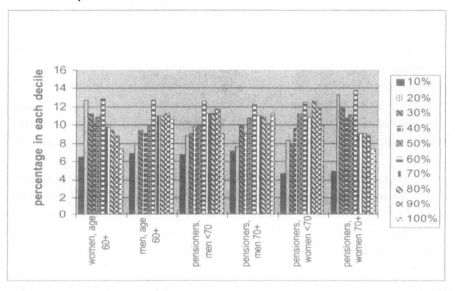

Source: Own calculations based on Microcensus data.

Looking more closely at educational and occupational groups of senior citizens provides a more differentiated picture (Figure 5.2) although even according to these characteristics few pensioners are found in the lowest income decile. Among pensioners with primary education or blue-collar status, only a few were found in the higher income deciles and the majority – 55% taking men and women together – were below the median equivalent income. Note that more than three out of four current pensioners belong to these lower education groups. On the other hand, one in five white-collar pensioners, one in four civil servants and one in three tertiary educated pensioners belong to the highest income decile. Among civil servants, more than 80% have incomes above the median equivalent income, notwithstanding the fact that even in this group the majority has only primary education, which gives rise to pension reform measures aiming at harmonizing the different pension schemes. Among white-collar pensioners, the respective proportion is 68%.

Between 1985 and 1993, the situation improved for blue-collar pensioners and especially for civil servants. It has deteriorated, though, for white-collar pensioners, which is largely a consequence of the changing gender composition of this group (with a rapidly increasing proportion of women).

Figure 5.2: Income Distribution for Selected Pensioner Groups by Equivalent Household Income Decile, 1993

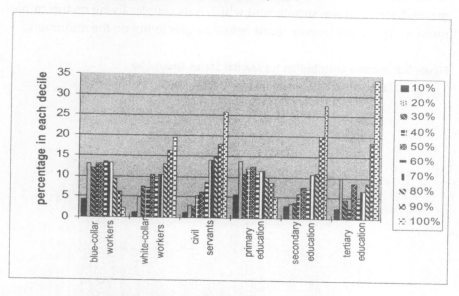

Source: Own calculations based on Microcensus data.

Strong differences in income position are also found when comparing marital status groups by gender. Much of these differences are explained by the peculiarities of the Austrian pension system, with a distinct emphasis on marriage and the maintenance of survivors, and entitlements which are directly proportional to the length of insurance and the level of income. Given those explanations, marital status differentials are strikingly different among men and women. Men above the age of 60 who live alone as singles, as divorcees or as widowers are much better off than those who are married. Among widowers, who have their full earnings-related pension plus, for some of them, a survivor pension, as few as 2% are found in the lowest income decile and still only 13% in the three lowest deciles. Every second widower is found in the highest three deciles. Single and divorced men above the age of 60 are also in a good position with almost two thirds of them above the median, but they lack a survivor pension. Married men, who make up for 80% of the male population above the age of 60 and who share income with their spouse, are quite equally distributed over all deciles with a certain concentration around the median. This is equally true for married women. Note that married men and women in general are more often found in the first income decile; a direct consequence of the functioning of the means-tested pension supplement which puts couples living on this minimum in equivalent income terms below singles living on the minimum.[2]

Figure 5.3: Income Distribution for Marital Status Groups by Equivalent Household Income Decile, 1995

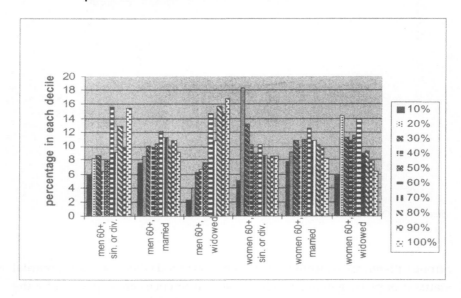

Source: Own calculations based on Microcensus data.

Among women, marital status differentials are almost the opposite. Married women are in the best position because they benefit from their husband's income; while the majority of women living alone is found below the median. Single and divorced women (13% of the female population over age 60), who live from their own earnings-related pensions, are concentrated mostly in the second decile. These are women living on a minimum pension. Widowed women (46% of the female elderly population) are slightly better off. They have lower individual entitlements than single or divorced women, if any (because more than 50% of those widows are not entitled to any individual claims), but they all have derived survivor claims. Claims which on average are as high as the average women's individual entitlement.

It is telling to compare senior citizens with other population age groups, as is done in Figure 5.4. Children below age ten (whose parents are usually very young and who also tend to live in larger households) are in the worst position, with 20% in the lowest income decile and 75% below the median equivalent income. The situation changes and finally turns around with increasing age. Among teenagers (age 10 to 19), 62% are found below the median, among young adults (age 20 to 39) 47% and among mature adults (age 40 to 59) only 38%. Among the latter, 15% belong to the highest income decile. Among senior citizens (above age 60), the income distribution is more balanced, somewhat comparable to the income distribution among young adults except for the lowest and highest income deciles. Note that the flatter EUROSTAT equivalence scale would tell a slightly different story (essentially worse for one-person households and better for persons in larger households).

Figure 5.4: Income Distribution for Selected Age Groups by Equivalent Household Income Decile, 1995

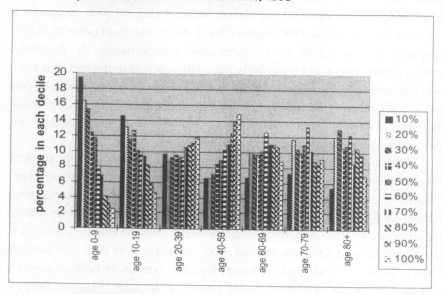

Source: Own calculations based on Microcensus data.

5.6 Poverty and Income Inequality among Senior Citizens

The income distribution of senior citizens in 1995 was characterized by a low proportion in the lowest decile, and correspondingly a relatively high proportion in the second decile (since pensioners living on the means-tested pension supplement fall into this income group), and a flat distribution otherwise. Moreover, between 1985 and 1995 the income position of senior citizens has generally improved. As a consequence, poverty among the elderly is likely to be low and to have declined recently. This result is found in various poverty studies (Steiner and Giorgi, 1997; Steiner and Wolf, 1996; Lutz et al., 1993) and confirmed by our own calculations. Note that in this study poverty is measured in terms of relative income poverty, presupposing that persons in such defined poor households are in a difficult economic, social and psychological position. These people are not necessarily poor. A recent Austrian study has demonstrated that adding information on the absence of accepted social standards reduces the number of the actually poor to around one third (Steiner and Giorgi, 1997). Hence, we can only claim to talk about the 'potentially poor'.

Naturally, different poverty lines result in very different proportions of the population being income poor. At 40% of the median equivalent income, an infinitely small proportion of pensioners appears at risk of poverty (Table 5.19). If the total population above the age of 60 is compared at the most frequently used 50% median level, the incidence of poverty in 1995 was only 5.5%, and 4.6%, if only pensioners are compared. The difference between pensioners and the elderly population is due to the fact that a certain proportion of the elderly are not entitled to any pension. At this threshold, poverty among the elderly has declined substantially (by three percentage points) within just one decade in comparison to a decline of only one percentage point among the total population.

Taking 60 or even 70% of the median equivalent income as the poverty threshold, increases the proportion of potentially poor senior citizens considerably. In Austria, the means-tested pension supplement ('Ausgleichszulage' or AZL) is generally used as a quasi-official poverty line. By coincidence, this level (the AZL for a single person) is almost exactly identical to the above defined 70% poverty line, both in 1985 and in 1995. The last column in Table 5.19 may thus not be appropriate to measure relative poverty among senior citizens in the Austrian context, as it rather measures the percentage of persons living on the means-tested minimum pension. Under this definition, as much as 28% of all women and 22% of all men aged 60 and over, as well as 20% of the younger pensioners and 25% of the older pensioners were relatively income poor in the year 1995, as compared to 26% of the total population. At the 60% median level, 11-14% of the elderly population appear income poor in 1995, compared to 16% of the total population. Note that the proportion of potentially poor persons is always higher for the total population than for the elderly population (and the decline since 1985 is smaller for the total than for the elderly), except at the 70% median level. Though not shown in the table, there are considerable differences in educational and occupational status. The lowest proportion of potentially poor – less than 6% at the 70% poverty threshold – is found among civil servant pensioners.

Table 5.19:   **Poverty Incidence among Senior Citizens: Four Alternative Poverty Lines**

Population group	Four poverty lines: proportion below ... % of the median equivalent income							
	40%		50%		60%		70%	
	1985	1995	1985	1995	1985	1995	1985	1995
All persons	3.7	4.0	9.6	8.5	18.5	16.3	29.1	26.3
Persons aged 60+	2.8	2.4	8.6	5.5	17.4	13.6	28.8	25.3
Women aged 60+	2.9	2.3	8.6	5.2	17.8	14.2	30.4	27.5
Men aged 60+	2.6	2.4	8.7	5.9	16.8	12.8	25.9	21.7
All pensioners	2.5	2.0	7.6	4.6	15.7	11.7	26.4	22.6
Pensioners aged 50-69	2.3	2.0	6.5	4.7	13.2	11.0	21.7	20.4
Pensioners aged 70+	2.6	2.0	8.6	4.5	18.1	12.4	30.8	24.9
Pensioners in pensioner households	2.6	2.4	8.2	5.5	17.3	14.0	29.0	26.8

Source: Own calculations based on Microcensus data.

Table 5.19 shows that among the elderly in general, the risk of being poor had considerably declined between 1985 and 1995. This decline is much more significant among older than among younger pensioners. Exceptions to this trend are those groups, where the proportion of women has rapidly increased (pensioners with secondary or tertiary education and pensioners with white-collar status).

It is indeed surprising that the AZL-level coincides with the 70% poverty line both in 1985 and in 1995, because the AZL-level increased disproportionately several times over the last decade. As a matter of fact, between 1985 and 1995 the AZL-level increased by 71% in nominal terms (from ATS 4,514 in 1985 to 7,710 in 1995) and 32% in real terms, compared to an increase in per capita GDP by only 20% during the same period. Interestingly enough, influenced by changes in household composition and in female labour force participation, between 1985 and 1995 the median equivalent household income increased at the same rate as the AZL-level was raised (the exact increase was 34% in real terms and 73% in nominal terms, i.e. from ATS 6,360 to 11,000).

Trends and levels in income inequality more adequately characterize the income distribution of the elderly population and distributional effects of the pension system as well as of recent pension reforms. In Table 5.20, three income inequality measures are used to describe income differentials between different sub-groups of the elderly population: the 90/10-decile ratio which measures inequality at the extremes, the 75/25-quartile ratio which measures inequality around the median, and the widely used Gini coefficient which captures all income groups. Further, two income definitions are used and compared in this table: (i) equivalent household income on the basis of total household incomes (as above), and (ii) individual pension income. Making this difference is necessary in order to isolate income effects that are due to the pension system from other effects, which are a consequence of e.g. the changing household composition or the increasing number of women with incomes and pensions. Note that for men, equivalent household income is significantly lower than individual pension income, while for women, naturally then, the opposite relationship holds true.

Several conclusions may be derived concerning income inequality among senior citizens in Austria. Between 1985 and 1995, equivalent incomes increased much faster than individual incomes, which is largely due to the increasing proportion of (married) women entitled to their own employment-related pension. For the same reason, income inequality on the basis of equivalent household incomes declined during the last decade, for men more than for women. Still looking at equivalent incomes, inequality is higher (though declining) among men than among women; a fact that is again caused by women's employment behaviour.

Table 5.20: **Income Differentials within and between Different Sub-groups of Senior Citizens**

Population group	Income definition	Income differential indicator			
		median income	Gini coefficient	90/10 decile ratio	75/25 quartile ratio
All persons					
1985	equivalent		0.250		
1995	income		0.234		
Persons 60+					
1985	equivalent	6040	0.240	2.9	1.7
1995	income	11000	0.215	2.5	1.7
Women 60+					
1985	equivalent	6000	0.231	2.8	1.8
1995	income	10670	0.210	2.5	1.7
Men 60+					
1985	equivalent	6470	0.251	3.1	1.8
1995	income	11670	0.221	2.7	1.7
Pensioners 50+					
1985	equivalent	6280	0.233	2.8	1.7
1995	income	11180	0.210	2.6	1.7
Pensioners 50-69					
1985	individual	7000	0.265	3.5	1.9
1995	income	11000	0.258	3.7	1.9
Pensioners 70+					
1985	individual	6000	0.241	2.8	1.8
1995	income	10000	0.248	3.0	1.8
Pensioners 50+					
1985	individual	6400	0.256	3.3	1.9
1995	income	10600	0.253	3.0	1.8
Female pens. 50+					
1985	individual	5300	0.241	3.1	1.7
1995	income	9000	0.247	3.2	1.7
Male pens. 50+					
1985	individual	8000	0.221	2.6	1.6
1995	income	13000	0.210	2.5	1.6
Persons 60+					
1985	individual	6000	0.361	n.a.	2.1
1995	income	10000	0.325	n.a.	2.0

Note: 100 ATS = 7.2673 EURO (1 January 1999) or 7.4846 ECU (1 January 1995).

Source: Own calculations based on Microcensus data.

Conclusions on the basis of individual pension incomes are very different. Here, inequality measured in terms of Gini coefficients has changed very little (with a small increase among female pensioners and a small decline among male pensioners). This is an effect of the pension scheme itself which rewards the (positively correlated) coincidence of high(er) incomes and long(er) insurance records, thus, largely ignoring the value of unpaid work and implicitly rewarding men more than women. Income inequality is higher among women, on the other hand, because the multiplication of income with the length of insurance tends to increase the difference between women with 'male' work careers and 'family-oriented' women with relatively few insurance years and, hence, relatively low pension benefit entitlements. The latter effect has increased since 1985. Pension income inequality also used to be higher among younger pensioners (age 50-69) in 1985, but this difference has become smaller over the past decade. By far the highest Gini coefficient – 0.36 in 1985 and 0.33 in 1995 – resulted in the group of all persons above age 60, driven by the fact that there was a significant proportion of women aged 60 and over without any pension entitlement, neither an old-age pension (if less than 15 contributory years) nor a survivor pension (if still married).

In Figures 5.5 and 5.6 the reproduction of the corresponding Lorenz curves characterizes the difference between the two income concepts. Looking at pensioners, the difference in income distribution between an individual pension income and an equivalent household income is very small. Looking at the group of senior citizens as a whole, as is necessary for the analysis of the adequacy of the pension system, shows that the relatively large inequalities produced by the individual pension incomes are significantly tempered by the household composition patterns.

Table 5.21 takes yet another look at income distributions by comparing ratios between various sub-groups of senior citizens, again using both income concepts. The main conclusions from these calculations are that (1) it does make a big difference whether we use one or the other income concept, (2) that the income indicator itself (e.g. median, quartiles, deciles) matters, (3) that the gender issue is highly relevant, (4) that the age of the group under consideration cannot be ignored, and (5) that it is crucial to differentiate between pensioners and the elderly population.

Figure 5.5: Lorenz Curves – Income Distribution of Pensioners

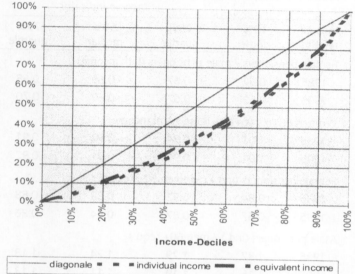

Lorenz Curves:
Income distribution of pensioners

Figure 5.6: Lorenz Curves – Income Distribution of Persons Aged 60 and Over

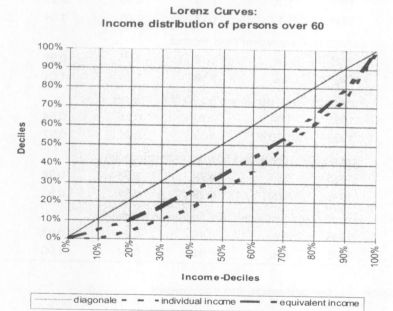

Lorenz Curves:
Income distribution of persons over 60

Table 5.21: Selected Income Relations between Different Sub-groups of Senior Citizens

	Income indicator				
Income relation	10% decile	25% quartile	50% median	75% quartile	90% decile
Female pensioners / male pensioners (ind. income)					
1985	0.62	0.67	0.66	0.68	0.74
1995	0.59	0.67	0.69	0.70	0.75
Women 60+ / men 60+ (equivalent income)					
1985	1.01	0.94	0.93	0.91	0.90
1995	1.01	0.91	0.91	0.92	0.92
Female pensioners (ind.) / women 60+ (equ.)					
1985	0.84	0.92	0.88	0.88	0.94
1995	0.67	0.87	0.84	0.86	0.87
Male pensioners (ind.) / men 60+ (equ.)					
1985	1.37	1.29	1.24	1.18	1.15
1995	1.15	1.19	1.11	1.13	1.07
Pensioners 50+: equivalent / ind. income					
1985	1.10	1.04	0.98	0.93	0.95
1995	1.17	1.13	1.05	1.04	1.00
Persons 60+: equivalent / ind. income					
1985	n.a.	1.18	1.01	0.99	0.96
1995	n.a.	1.18	1.10	1.01	0.99
Pensioners 70+ / pensioners 50-70 (ind. income)					
1985	1.04	0.90	0.86	0.84	0.85
1995	1.20	1.03	0.91	0.97	0.96
Persons 60+ / pensioners 50+ (equivalent income)					
1985	0.95	0.98	0.96	0.98	0.97
1995	1.00	0.95	0.98	0.97	0.99
Persons 60+ / pensioners 50+ (individual income)					
1985	n.a.	0.86	0.94	0.93	0.96
1995	n.a.	0.91	0.94	1.00	1.00

Source: Own calculations based on Microcensus data.

On the level of individual pension incomes, women reach only around two thirds of the income of men (compare also results reported by Wolf and Wolf, 1991, on this issue), with small improvements since 1985. The difference is the largest (and increased) at the lowest decile. On the basis of equivalent incomes, however, women attain more than 90% of men's income, and the difference is the lowest at the 10% decile. This discrepancy is explained by a high proportion of housewives married to men with a high (pension) income.

There is also a large difference in the income distribution between younger and older pensioners. By contrast to all other deciles/quartiles, older pensioners have higher pension incomes at the 10% decile; another indication of the relatively flatter income distribution. One explanation could be differences in life expectancy by socioeconomic status (i.e. lower life expectancy for the poorest segment of the population). In relative terms, older pensioners improved their position between 1985 and 1995, and quite significantly so.

Comparing the two income concepts for pensioners above the age of 50 and for persons above the age of 60 shows that equivalent incomes are significantly higher at the lower income stratum (in particular when looking at all persons; not just pensioners), while at the highest deciles individual incomes are slightly higher. Finally, the comparison between persons and pensioners shows a lower difference on the basis of equivalent incomes, in particular at or below median income.

5.7 Wealth Measured in Terms of Ownership of Durable Goods

The analysis in Section 5.6 only focuses on relative income poverty and inequality, more or less assuming that low income is related to a difficult economic and/or social and/or psychological position. This is a clear restriction, especially since the Microcensus data used in this study are unlikely to cover income from sales, rental of property and similar sources. The factual economic position of a household could be very different, e.g. depending on household ownership status. To shed some light on the changes in the well-being of elderly households in Austria, this section summarizes the results of wealth measured in terms of the ownership of certain durable goods since 1974, again based on Microcensus data. The lack of such goods is often used as an indication of factual poverty (e.g. Lutz et al., 1993, where the lack of at least four out of seven relevant goods is defined as a poverty threshold).

Table 5.22: Ownership of Durable Goods: Long-term Trends for Selected Groups since 1974

Durable goods	Year	All households	Status of head of household		
			blue-collar employee	white-collar employee	pensioner
Telephone	1974	42	25	62	32
	1979	62	49	79	53
	1984	79	69	89	75
	1989	87	81	93	85
	1993				86
Washing machine	1974	64	74	71	46
	1979	72	78	80	57
	1984	80	84	85	71
	1989	83	87	84	79
	1993				81
Dish washer	1974	4	1	6	1
	1979	10	5	17	3
	1984	18	13	31	7
	1989	28	26	44	12
	1993				15
Colour TV	1974	11	7	17	8
	1979	44	42	57	35
	1984	61	61	65	59
	1989	88	90	91	85
	1993				90
Car	1974	49	56	71	13
	1979	55	68	78	18
	1984	61	73	82	23
	1989	63	78	82	28
	1993				33

Source: ÖSTAT (1991), Wolf (1995).

In the period from 1974 to 1993, households equipped with telephones, washing machines, dish washers, colour TVs and cars increased remarkably (Table 5.22). Indeed, several of these durable goods, like telephones or colour TVs, have lost their discriminating effect in poverty research, since almost every household has access to them. Among these goods, today dish washers seem to discriminate the best. In general, pensioner households are only a little worse equipped than employee households. There is no difference in telephone, washing machine and colour TV ownership anymore. Pensioners tend to own dish washers much less often than other groups, but this has behavioural rather than economic reasons. Moreover, only every third pensioner household has a car, compared to four in five employee households. While a car is indeed a heavy economic investment, also this difference does not simply have economic reasons. In fact, only about 60% of men and less than 20% of women above the age of 65 have a driving licence. In addition, the proportion of actual drivers among the population with a driving licence declines with age.

The arguments relating to car ownership are confirmed by Table 5.23. Car ownership is extremely low among one-person pensioner households (mainly single women) but has reached 60% among two-person pensioner households by 1993. Hence, the large majority of elderly persons with a driving license does have a car. One-person pensioner households are significantly more often at risk of poverty when looking at poverty in terms of durable goods. However, the trend over the last decade indicates an eradication of poverty at old age. The proportion of one-person pensioner households with running water only has decreased from 23 to 10% (among two-person households even down to only 2%), while the proportion with a bath and central heating has doubled from 23 to 43% (from 38 to 62% among two-person pensioner households). Pensioners living on the minimum pension are not worse off in terms of durable goods, however, they do tend to live in lower quality housing. Notwithstanding major improvements in the economic position of senior citizens, only a minority goes on holiday every year (e.g. one third of all pensioners living alone).

Table 5.23: Ownership of Durable Goods: Pensioner Households 1984, 1989 and 1993

Durable goods	Year	All pensioner households	Type of pensioner household		
			one person	two persons	minimum pension
Telephone	1984	73	69	79	54
	1989	83	75	88	73
	1993	86	82	89	87
Washing machine[1]	1984	62	52	76	52
	1989	88	82	96	78
	1993	91	86	97	88
Dish washer	1984	6	3	9	1
	1989	9	5	13	3
	1993	15	8	23	8
Colour TV	1984	59	53	68	38
	1989	83	76	88	67
	1993	90	86	96	84
Car	1984	23	8	40	7
	1989	28	10	52	11
	1993	33	16	60	26
Bath and central heating	1984	30	23	38	16
	1989	43	32	50	23
	1993	52	43	62	39
running water only	1984	17	23	9	32
	1989	11	17	4	27
	1993	7	10	2	14
No holidays	1984	–	–	–	–
	1989	65	71	60	82
	1993	65	67	61	79

Note: 1. Data for 1989 and 1993 include those, who have a washing-machine in the house.

Source: ÖSTAT (1991), Wolf (1995).

Table 5.24 confirms the results on differences by occupational status found elsewhere (e.g. Lutz et al., 1993). The two groups of pensioners that are at a relatively high risk of living under economic hardship are farmers and, to a lesser degree, blue-collar workers. Since the share of these two groups among the total population of pensioners will gradually decline in the future, (potential) poverty among senior citizens is likely to decline further, even if disproportionate increases in means-tested pension supplements are not implemented.

Table 5.24: Ownership of Durable Goods: Pensioner Households in 1993

Durable goods	Type of pensioner household				
	farmer pensioner	self-employed pensioner	blue-collar pensioner	white-collar pensioner	civil servant pensioner
Telephone	76	89	85	90	88
Washing machine	90	94	92	90	93
Dish washer	10	29	11	23	20
Colour TV	78	92	92	92	96
Car	25	46	29	39	53
Bath, central heating	49	66	49	59	62
Running water only	9	1	6	4	2
No holidays	87	63	71	50	49

Source: Wolf, 1995.

5.8 Conclusion: Income Distribution and Pension Reform

The income analysis lends itself to a number of conclusions on the well-being of senior citizens in Austria. The income position of pensioners (though not to the same extent for all persons above the age of 60) improved remarkably between 1985 and 1995. One reason for this is the increased proportion of women entitled to a pension; in the lower income stratum, the improvement is largely due to the increase in the means-tested supplement. As a result, poverty among the elderly is no longer an issue in Austria. Today, there are by far fewer elderly than there are children at risk of being income poor. In this respect, the pension policy was quite successful. Only when the poverty line is set exactly at the current level of the means-tested supplement – which is equal to 70% of the median equivalent income – is there a significant proportion of elderly that may be considered relatively income poor.

223

The income distribution among senior citizens is overall very flat. This is a result of the pension system having supplements for those at the lower end and a threshold on contributions and benefits at the upper end. There are, however, considerable inequalities by gender, marital status and occupational group. Women have generally lower incomes, which is a direct result of the earnings-related pension scheme with its inadequate recognition of unpaid care work. Women experienced less improvements during the last decade in terms of average incomes, however, there was a significant increase in the proportion of women entitled to a pension. Also, the income distribution among women was flatter on the basis of equivalent incomes, though steeper on the basis of individual pension incomes. Gender differences are accentuated when looking at marital status groups. Married men and women are, by definition, in a similar position when equivalent incomes are compared. Women who live alone are in a particularly bad income position on average, while men who live alone are particularly wealthy. Again, such differences result from a system largely ignoring the value of unpaid care work. As far as occupational groups are concerned, farmers and blue-collar workers seem underprivileged (which is a consequence of their low active incomes), while civil servant pensioners are particularly well-off. This is the direct consequence of a significantly different (i.e. more beneficial) pension scheme for civil servants. Finally, younger pensioners are more wealthy than older ones. This is partly related to the different gender composition of these two groups and partly a consequence of improved education, rather than a characteristic of the pension system, since – at least until 1993 – pensions were indexed according to gross wage increases.

Some of the pension reform measures of the 1990s will have an effect on the income distribution of senior citizens, both regarding income inequality between different groups of elderly and in relation to other population groups; effects which were not yet observable in 1995. For example, the change of the indexation method from gross wage to net wage increase adjustments in 1993 will – over a longer period – lead to relatively lower incomes for older pensioners as compared to younger pensioners. In other words, there will be a gradual decline in the level of pension income between retirement and death (though not nearly as much as with price increase adjustments, which are quite common in several European countries). While this does not sound desirable, it was a necessary step to achieve higher intergenerational fairness. With gross wage increase adjustments, a higher burden on the working age population in the future (higher taxes or higher social security contributions), e.g. caused by population ageing, would have led to much higher increases in pension incomes relative to the increases in wages and salaries.

The introduction of pension credits for child care periods in 1993, as another example, has improved the situation of mothers (though not so much in absolute terms), but only if they have contributed a minimum of 15 years of work or have a 25-year insurance record. Insofar, the issue of valuing unpaid care work has only been dealt with partially. Eventually, to give a third relevant example, steps taken towards the harmonization of the pension system of civil servants in the 1997 reform package will significantly reduce income inequality between occupational groups in the very long run. This was indeed a major achievement towards abolishing privileges. However, the transition period 2000-2020 was not very well designed. In fact, due to far-reaching cushioning measures, this accomplishment will hardly be effective before 2020.

Pension reforms before the mid-1980s, to a large degree – and quite successfully so – aimed at improving the income position for pensioners, a group that for a long time belonged to the poorest segment of the population. The mid-1980s marked the turning point when reforms suddenly focused on short- and medium-term reductions of overall public pension expenditures, though not at a reduction of inequalities. Due to the disproportionate increase of the means-tested supplement, also in this most recent decade, poverty among senior citizens could be reduced further. The mid or late 1990s (are likely to) mark another turning point in Austrian pension reform policy. While the income position of the elderly has improved, income inequalities between senior citizens have increased, because pension income distribution has hardly been challenged.

In the future, two issues are critical. First, the system still excludes a significant proportion of women, because unpaid care work is given little attention or value. The large gender differences in income distribution among senior citizens are well documented in this analysis. Extending the mandatory individual pension insurance to all persons irrespective of their employment status, introducing a basic pension for all, or adding pension splitting for couples would be three alternative variants to deal with or solve this problem. These three options would have very different distributional consequences (see Prinz et al., 1996). In essence, these options aim at replacing derived or missing entitlements with individual entitlements. In this respect the discussion process has already started, but with no result yet.

The second important issue is the distribution between generations. Given the unavoidable shift in age structures, particularly between 2015 and 2030, if there are no further pension reforms, an increased economic burden will inevitably be borne by the younger generations. To avoid such a situation, current and soon-to-be pensioners must be included in the reform process, and one way or other, their benefit entitlements will have to be reduced. This income distribution analysis shows that pensioners are by and large no longer disadvantaged in economic terms (though we should not forget about those groups which are still under-supplied) and that certain groups are obviously very well off; this is a strong argument for reforms to distribute the future burden of population ageing equally on all age groups. The generations above age 40 can be included into the reform process in a number of ways, e.g. by adjusting benefits regularly for increases in life expectancy at retirement age, by considering actually fair premiums and deductions for late or early retirement after or before the regular age, and by taking total lifetime earnings as the basis for calculating benefit levels. Essentially, all these measures merely aim at increasing contribution equivalence and reducing contribution-free entitlements.

A third significant issue in the Austrian context is the harmonization of the system of civil servants, which started already with the 1997 reform. This analysis has verified that this harmonization is unlikely to lead to economic hardship.

Notes

1   Note that although not documented in Table 5.18, the relative income position of children and of young adults deteriorated during that decade (compare also Figure 5.3).
2   In 1995, the minimum was ATS 7,710 for singles and ATS 11,000 for couples, the latter resulting in an equivalent income of ATS 6,470 on the basis of the equivalence scale used in this project.

References

Beirat für Wirtschafts- und Sozialfragen (ed.) (1991) *Soziale Sicherheit im Alter.*

BMfAGS (1997) *Bericht über die soziale Lage 1996. Datenband* sowie *Analysen & Ressort-aktivitäten.* Wien: Bundesministerium für Arbeit, Gesundheit und Soziales.

Die Grünen (1998) *Das grüne Pensionsmodell.* Wien: Die Grünen.

Förster, M. (1994) *Measurement of Poverty and Low Incomes in a Perspective of International Comparisons,* OECD Labour Market and Social Policy Occasional Paper no.14. Paris: OECD.

Guger, A. (1997) 'Perspektiven der österreichischen Altersvorsorge im internationalen Vergleich', *WIFO Monatsberichte,* vol. 70, no. 9.

Lutz, H./ Wagner, M./ Wolf, W. (1993) *Von Ausgrenzung bedroht,* Forschungsberichte aus Sozial- und Arbeitsmarktpolitik no. 50. Wien: Bundesministerium für Arbeit und Soziales.

ÖSTAT (1991) *Personen- und Haushaltseinkommen von unselbständig Beschäftigten; Ausstattung der Haushalte,* Beiträge zur österreichischen Statistik, no. 1.013. Wien.

ÖSTAT (1996) *Demographisches Jahrbuch Österreichs 1993/94/95,* Beiträge zur österreichischen Statistik, no. 1.207. Wien.

ÖSTAT (1998) *Bevölkerungsprognose 1998-2050.* ÖSTAT-Schnellbericht. Wien.

Prinz, Ch. (1994) 'Zukünftige Altersstrukturveränderungen und das Pensionsproblem am Beispiel Österreichs', *Journal für Sozialforschung,* vol. 34, no. 3.

Prinz, Ch./ Rolf-Engel, G./ Thenner, M. (1996) *Neue Wege der eigenständigen Alterssicherung von Frauen – Ausgangslage und Reformmodelle.* Wien: Bundesministerin für Frauenangelegenheiten.

Prinz, Ch./ Marin, B. (1997) *Pensionsreformen ab 1999 – Einige Vorschläge für einen langfristig nachhaltigen Generationenvertrag.* Wien: Bundeskanzleramt.

Prinz, Ch./ Marin, B. (1999) *Pensionsreformen – Nachhaltiger Sozialumbau am Beispiel Österreichs.* Frankfurt/New York: Campus.

Rosner, P./ Url, T./ Wörgötter, A. (1997) 'The Austrian Pension System', in Rein, M./ Wadensjö, E. (eds.), *Enterprise and the Welfare State.* Cheltenham: Edward Elgar.

Rürup, B./ Schroeder, I. (1997) *Perspektiven der Pensionsversicherung in Österreich.* Wien: Bundesministerium für Arbeit, Gesundheit und Soziales.

Steiner, H./ Wolf, W. (1996) *Armutsgefährdung in Österreich,* Schriftenreihe "Soziales Europa", no. 3. Wien: Bundesministerium für Arbeit und Soziales.

Steiner, H./ Giorgi, L. (1997) 'Armut und Armutsbekämpfung in Österreich', in BMfAGS (ed.), *Bericht über die soziale Lage 1996. Analysen & Ressortaktivitäten.* Wien: Bundesministerium für Arbeit, Gesundheit und Soziales.

Wolf, I./ Wolf, W. (1991) *Wieviel weniger ...? Einkommensunterschiede zwischen Frauen und Männern in Österreich.* Wien: Bundesministerium für Arbeit und Soziales.

Wolf, W. (1995) 'Personen- und Haushaltseinkommen von Pensionisten; Ausstattung von Pensionistenhaushalten', *Statistische Nachrichten,* no. 7: 509-519.

Wörister, K. (1998) Statistische Information (Oktober 1998). Wien: Bundeskammer für Arbeiter und Angestellte, Abteilung Statistik.

Appendix

Table 5A1: Distribution of Different Types of Pensioner Households by Income Decile, 1985 and 1995 – vertical distribution

Year	Type of pensioner household				
	Single males	Single females	Couples	Other types	All types
1985					
1	3.8	8.8	14.7	21.6	11.1
2	6.9	18.5	10.3	9.5	14.1
3	6.3	14.2	12.8	7.8	12.6
4	5.5	8.6	15.5	18.5	11.3
5	15.8	15.9	9.6	9.8	13.3
6	11.9	10.9	9.3	8.1	10.3
7	9.9	7.3	9.2	10.0	8.3
8	14.4	5.4	6.4	7.6	6.7
9	11.3	5.5	6.5	6.2	6.4
10	14.3	5.0	5.8	1.0	5.9
1 – 3	17.0	41.5	37.8	38.9	37.8
4 – 7	43.0	42.6	43.5	46.3	43.2
8 – 10	40.0	15.9	18.7	14.8	19.0
Total	100.0	100.0	100.0	100.0	100.0
1995					
1	4.6	7.2	12.9	16.8	9.7
2	6.1	20.6	10.7	7.8	14.7
3	9.6	17.2	12.2	7.7	14.0
4	10.0	13.7	11.2	6.5	12.0
5	6.8	10.5	12.2	14.4	11.0
6	11.9	8.3	11.0	10.8	9.8
7	13.3	7.3	8.8	10.6	8.6
8	10.5	6.2	8.6	9.2	7.7
9	13.4	4.7	7.4	8.5	6.8
10	13.7	4.4	5.2	7.6	5.7
1 – 3	20.3	45.0	35.8	32.3	38.4
4 – 7	42.1	39.7	43.0	42.4	41.4
8 – 10	37.6	15.3	21.2	25.3	20.2
Total	100.0	100.0	100.0	100.0	100.0

Note: Figures in this table indicate the proportion of households of a certain type in each income decile.

Source: Own calculations based on Microcensus data.

Table 5A2: **Distribution of Pensioners, Pensioners in Pensioner Households and Persons Aged 60 and Over by Income Decile, 1985 and 1995 – vertical distribution**

Income decile	1985			1995		
	Pensioners aged 50 and over	Pensioners in pensioner households	All persons aged 60 and over	Pensioners aged 50 and over	Pensioners in pensioner households	All persons aged 60 and over
1	7.8	8.4	8.8	5.7	6.8	6.7
2	10.1	11.4	10.7	9.9	11.9	10.9
3	8.7	9.3	9.6	9.8	11.0	10.6
4	12.0	12.7	12.3	9.8	10.4	9.9
5	12.3	12.7	12.4	10.8	10.7	10.5
6	12.0	12.1	11.8	12.9	12.9	12.7
7	9.6	8.7	8.7	10.5	9.4	10.2
8	9.0	7.8	8.3	10.9	9.9	10.1
9	9.6	8.9	8.9	10.6	9.0	9.7
10	9.0	8.0	8.5	9.2	7.9	8.6
Total	100.0	100.0	100.0	100.0	100.0	100.0

Note: Figures in this table indicate the proportion of persons in each income decile.

Source: Own calculations based on Microcensus data.

Table 5A3: Gender-specific Distribution of Pensioners and Persons Aged 60 and Over by Income Decile, 1985 and 1995 – vertical distribution

Income decile	1985				1995			
	Female pensioners	Male pensioners	Women over 60	Men over 60	Female pensioners	Male pensioners	Women over 60	Men over 60
1	7.1	8.8	8.7	9.0	4.8	6.9	6.5	6.9
2	11.1	8.5	11.9	8.5	11.1	8.4	12.7	8.0
3	8.7	8.7	10.1	8.6	10.0	9.4	11.3	9.5
4	12.2	11.6	12.9	11.3	10.2	9.4	10.4	9.1
5	12.6	11.8	12.8	11.6	11.2	10.2	10.9	9.9
6	12.0	12.0	11.9	11.7	13.2	12.4	12.8	12.7
7	9.5	9.7	8.6	8.9	9.9	11.2	9.7	11.0
8	8.3	10.0	7.7	9.3	10.7	11.2	9.5	11.0
9	9.8	9.4	8.3	10.1	10.2	11.1	8.8	11.2
10	8.7	9.5	7.1	10.9	8.6	9.9	7.4	10.6
Total	100.0	100.0	100.0	100.0	100.0	100.0	100.0	100.0

Note: Figures in this table indicate the proportion of persons in each income decile.

Source: Own calculations based on Microcensus data.

Table 5A4: Distribution of Persons in Different Age Groups by Income Decile, 1985 and 1995 – vertical distribution

Income decile	1985				1995			
	Age group 40-59	Age group 60-69	Age group 70-79	Age group 80 plus	Age group 40-59	Age group 60-69	Age group 70-79	Age group 80 plus
1	6.4	7.5	9.7	10.6	6.5	6.7	7.3	5.4
2	5.6	9.1	12.7	10.1	6.5	9.9	11.7	12.0
3	5.7	8.0	11.0	10.3	7.1	9.7	10.5	13.1
4	9.0	11.8	12.3	13.9	8.5	9.7	9.8	10.6
5	9.0	12.1	12.1	14.1	9.0	10.1	11.0	10.8
6	10.9	11.7	11.7	12.6	10.3	12.5	13.3	12.3
7	11.7	9.3	8.8	6.8	10.9	10.9	10.1	8.6
8	11.8	9.2	7.7	7.1	12.4	10.9	8.8	10.6
9	13.2	9.7	8.5	7.3	13.9	10.7	8.5	9.7
10	16.7	11.5	5.5	7.2	14.9	8.9	9.1	7.0
1 – 3	17.7	24.6	33.4	31.0	20.1	26.3	29.5	30.5
4 – 7	40.6	45.0	44.9	47.4	38.7	43.2	44.1	42.2
8 – 10	41.7	30.4	21.7	21.6	41.2	30.5	26.4	27.3
Total	100.0	100.0	100.0	100.0	100.0	100.0	100.0	100.0

Note: Figures in this table indicate the proportion of persons in each income decile.

Source: Own calculations based on Microcensus data.

CHAPTER 6

Reforms in the UK: Involving the Private Sector

Carl Emmerson
Paul Johnson
Gary Stears

6.1 Introduction

State pension provision in the United Kingdom is in two tiers. The first, the basic state pension, was introduced in 1948 and is currently worth about 15% of average earnings (24% for a couple). It is the largest single government expenditure, currently costing around 30 billion pounds or just under 4% of GDP. Despite being a contributory benefit, virtually all pensioners receive the basic state pension as a result of their own contribution record, or in the case of many married or widowed women their spouses' contributions. The State Earnings Related Pension Scheme (SERPS) was introduced in 1978, and is compulsory for all employees earning above a set amount who have not opted out into an occupational pension, or from 1988 a personal pension scheme. Originally the design of SERPS was reasonably generous, but substantial reforms have been made on several occasions which have had the effect of substantially reducing its future generosity.

Private sources of income, mainly from occupation pensions are also extremely important. Around half of pensioners receive some form of private income, although this is extremely unevenly distributed. Income from private sources is set to rise in future, not because of increased membership of occupational pension schemes which have been constant for about 30 years but due to higher accrued pension rights. This is not only due to cohort effects with younger generations, on average, being richer, but also the effect of legislation giving greater protection against inflation to those who move jobs and hence leave occupational schemes early.

Compared to most of its European neighbours the United Kingdom faces a different set of problems with regard to future generations of pensioners. A combination of reforms reducing future costs already in place and much smaller levels of demographic change than is forecast for most countries means that the current system is sustainable in terms of cost. However the reductions in generosity of state schemes in future will lead to increasing pensioner inequality, with those without private sources of income being substantially poorer with respect to the working population than the present set of pensioners.

This study first looks in detail at the public and private sources of income received by pensioners before going on to look at recent trends in retirement and demographics and the implications for future contribution rates. It then looks at the changes in the levels and composition of pensioner incomes between 1989 and 1995 and how these compare to the experiences of the population as a whole. Finally the study looks at how incomes vary with age in each of the years and also assesses the levels of income inequality between different groups of pensioners.

6.2 Current Pension Provision

State provision in the UK is comprised of two tiers. The first tier is made up of the flat rate basic state retirement pension and means-tested benefits, while the second tier is comprised of SERPS. While the majority of pensioners receive the basic state pension, around half also receive income from a private pension. These are typically defined benefit occupational pensions although in the future pensioners will also receive significant proportions of income from personal pension schemes which are typically of a defined contribution nature. This is because prior to 1988 it was only possible to 'opt out' of SERPS into a defined benefit (and hence typically occupational) pension, whereas since employees could choose to take out a defined contribution scheme instead.

6.2.1 Basic State Pension

The basic state pension was introduced in 1948 and until 1982 increased in value often by more than growth in earnings, as shown in Figure 6.1 and Table 6.1. Since 1982, however, legislation has linked its value to prices, and it has already fallen as a share of average earnings from nearly 20% to around 15% today. If price indexing continues then it will be worth just 6.7% of average earnings by 2050.[1]

Figure 6.1: The Level of the Basic State Pension in Relation to Earnings and Real Prices, 1948 to 1995

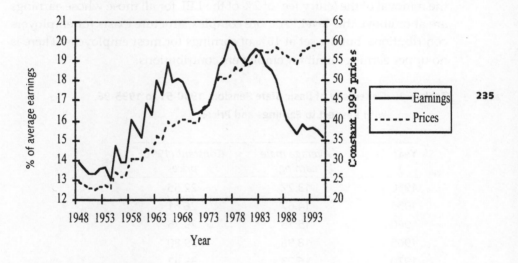

Source: HM Treasury, 1996.

Currently 95% of men and 56% of women qualify for the full basic state pension. The figure for women is distorted since nearly all widows receive a full pension on the basis of their deceased husbands' contribution record, while only 40% of non-widows receive a full state pension. This is not just due to lower contribution records by women, but also because until 1978 married women were allowed to pay a different rate of National Insurance Contribution in return for forgoing their entitlement to the Basic State Pension.[2]

The basic state retirement pension is payable to some 10 million pensioners and in 1996-97 cost around £29 billion a year (3.9% of GDP).[3] The basic state pension is not quite universal as eligibility is contingent on having made sufficient National Insurance Contributions (NICs). At present individuals have to make NICs once their income is in excess of the lower earnings limit (LEL), which is currently about 15% of average earnings (£64 per week in 1998-99), and rises annually in line with inflation. Those whose earnings are above the LEL pay contributions of 2% of the LEL and then 10% on all earnings up to the upper earnings limit (UEL), which is slightly above average earnings (£485 per week in 1998-99). No employee NICs are made on earnings above the UEL. The LEL is set approximately equal to the basic pension, while the UEL is fixed by statute to be a ratio of between 6.5 and 7.5 times the LEL. From April 1999 the structure of NICs is to be altered by the removal of the 'entry fee' of 2% of the LEL for all those whose earnings are at or above this level.[4] A more complex structure exists for employers contributions, but are set at 10% of earnings for most employees. There is no upper earnings limit for employers contributions.

236

Table 6.1: Generosity of Basic State Pension, 1950-51 to 1995-96, with Respect to Earnings and Prices

Year	Average male earnings	Constant (1995) prices
1950	13.27	22.55
1955	14.67	26.61
1960	15.15	29.75
1965	18.96	39.80
1970	16.23	39.42
1975	18.70	50.64
1980	18.81	53.51
1985	18.49	57.16
1989	15.58	55.34
1990	15.32	54.30
1991	15.76	57.44
1992	15.57	58.00
1993	15.62	59.07
1994	15.50	59.35
1995	15.15	58.85

Source: HM Treasury, 1996.

For full state pension entitlement men have to have paid NICs for 44 years, while women have to have made contributions for 39 years. The lower number of years for women results from their state pension age being 60 as opposed to 65 for men, although state retirement ages are being equalized at 65 in 2020. Upon equalization of the state retirement age women will also have to make NICs for 44 years. Individuals who have made inadequate contributions for a full pension, receive a reduced basic pension which is set at a minimum of 25% of the full basic pension.

Provisions are made for time spent out of work. For example, contribution credits are made for time spent in education or training, or for periods of unemployment or disability. The total number of years required for a full state pension may also be reduced by Home Responsibility Protection (HRP), which was introduced in April 1978 for those individuals who take time out of the labour market to look after children or sick relatives. Hence in future more women will qualify for a full basic state pension on the basis of their own contribution record.

6.2.2 *Means-tested Benefits*

Means-tested benefits, namely income support, housing benefit and council tax benefit, are payable to around three million pensioners in order to help them meet housing costs and supplement income. The total cost of means-tested benefits to pensioners is around £9.6 billion per annum (1.2% of GDP).[5] Housing benefit is paid to those on low incomes in rented accommodation. Currently around one fifth of those over the retirement age are eligible for some payment, which equates to two thirds of those living in rented accommodation.[6]

The principal benefit for those in the UK with low incomes is Income Support. One in four claimants are over the state retirement age, and of these three out of four are single women, and nearly half are aged over 80.[7] Around 15% of those over the state retirement age qualify for Income Support,[8] since it is set at a more generous level than the basic state pension, as shown in Table 6.2. This is an artefact of government policy over the 1980s and 1990s of uprating the basic state pension only in line with prices while indexing income support by more than prices. Those approaching the state retirement age with little or no savings will have no incentive to try and save for their retirement since Income Support is withdrawn with a 100% taper.

Table 6.2: Rates of Income Support and Basic Pension, 1998-99 (£ per week)

	Basic state pension	Income support	Gap (%)
Single, under 75	64.70	70.45	9
Couple, under 75	103.40	109.35	6
Single, 75-79	64.70	72.70	12
Couple, 75-79	103.40	112.55	9
Single, 80+	64.95	77.55	19
Couple, 80+	103.90	117.90	13

Source: Department of Social Security website.

6.2.3 State Earnings Related Pension Scheme (SERPS)

SERPS was introduced in 1978 with qualification for the pension based on paying NICs. It was intended for those employees who had earnings above the LEL and were not able to contribute to an occupational pension scheme. Originally it was designed so that an individual would receive 25% of their average earnings between the LEL and the UEL from the best 20 years of their working lives. This was soon reduced to 20%, with average earnings being calculated over the individuals' whole lifetime instead of their best 20 years. This, and other reforms such as halving the proportion of SERPS that a spouse can inherit have had the effect of greatly reducing the future generosity, and hence cost of SERPS in the future. The current cost of SERPS is around £2 billion a year which is payable to some four million pensioners. The cost of SERPS is however expected to grow considerably as it reaches maturity, costing some £12 billion in 2030, which is around a quarter of the cost if SERPS had been left in its original form.

The second tier in the UK is compulsory in the sense that individuals are either in SERPS or they have 'contracted out' of the state scheme into an alternative private pension scheme.[9] Contracting out foregoes entitlement to SERPS and results in the NICs paid by the employee and the employer to be reduced. The employees' NICs are reduced by 1.8 percentage points, while secondary contributions by the employer are reduced by 3 percentage points. According to the Government Actuary Department this contracting out cost the Government in 1994-95 some £7.4 billion in lost revenues.

State spending on the basic state pension and SERPS is currently just over 30 billion pounds. This is equivalent to 4.2% of GDP, and just under 10% of total government spending. Table 6.3 shows how state spending on the contributory state pension benefits has increased as a share of GDP since 1989, mainly due to lower economic growth. Faster growth in other areas of government spending such as health and social security benefits to other, primarily unwaged groups has actually led to share of government spending on pensions falling slightly over this period.

Table 6.3: State Spending on Contributory Retirement Pension Benefits, 1989-90 to 1996-97 (in real, 1996-97 prices, £ million)

	Basic state pension	Earnings related pension	Total	% of GDP	% of government spending
1989-90	26,681	696	27,377	3.94	10.04
1990-91	26,928	890	27,817	4.08	10.07
1991-92	28,137	1,257	29,394	4.39	10.35
1992-93	28,027	1,483	29,509	4.40	9.73
1993-94	28,513	1,758	30,272	4.40	9.60
1994-95	28,422	1,996	30,418	4.24	9.32
1995-96	28,539	2,286	30,825	4.20	9.10
1996-97	29,113	2,738	31,851	4.23	9.42

Note: Spending converted to real terms using the GDP deflator.

Sources: Department of Social Security, Social Security Statistics, various years; HM Treasury, 1998b.

6.2.4 Private Sources of Income

The majority of the working population has contracted out of SERPS into either a personal pension or an occupational pension. Personal pensions are defined contribution schemes, otherwise known as money purchase arrangements. Some occupational pension schemes are defined contribution, but the majority are defined benefit – that is the final benefits are determined by the number of years in the scheme with benefits being some function of salary (usually final salary). Both personal pensions and occupational schemes are financed by contribution from earnings with personal pensions contributions generally being paid solely by the employee, while occupational schemes contributions are partly or wholly made by the employer.

The proportion of pensioner income from private sources is expected to continue to grow in the future. The reason for this is not increased coverage of occupational pensions which has been steady for the last 30 years, but instead due to higher individual entitlements. This has been caused not only by the effect of younger cohorts being richer, but also by the introduction of legislation to provide better protection to accrued occupational pension rights from inflation.[10] This has been particularly important in protecting the rights of those who have moved jobs and hence left an occupational scheme 'early'.

Table 6.4: Supplementary Pension Coverage amongst Employees, by Age and Sex

	18-24	25-34	35-44	45-54	55 +	Total
Men						
Occupational pension	25	53	67	70	59	58
Personal pension	15	37	29	28	21	28
SERPS	59	9	3	2	19	14
Earnings below LEL	1	0	0	0	0	0
Women						
Occupational pension	26	44	47	45	31	41
Personal pension	10	21	17	18	13	17
SERPS	49	25	27	28	34	31
Earnings below LEL	15	10	10	9	21	12

Note: Percentages may not sum to one hundred due to rounding.

Sources: Office for National Statistics (1997b), 1995 Family Resources Survey and authors' calculations.

Around half the population are currently members of an occupational pension. This has been relatively constant for about 30 years, although recent years have seen a rise in the proportion of women members occurring at the same time as a fall in the membership of males. Table 6.4 shows second tier pension coverage amongst men and women for various age groups. It should be noted that this table excludes the self-employed who are much less likely to have made any second tier pension provision. A far larger proportion of women employees are likely to not have any second tier cover-

240

age since they are more likely to be working part-time, and hence earning below the LEL. For example, 55% of women employees working full-time are members of an occupational pension scheme compared to just 24% of those working part-time. SERPS coverage is highest amongst the oldest and youngest age groups. Amongst the oldest groups this is likely to be because the return from opting out into a personal pension plan is likely to be smaller than their expected SERPS entitlement.

6.2.5 Health Care

Government spending on health care and personal social services in 1997-98 was £53 billion (6.7% of GDP).[11] Although all UK citizens receive National Health Service treatment free at point of use, a disproportionate amount of this spending goes on the elderly. For example, a large proportion of health spending in the UK goes on Hospital and Community Health Services (HCHS), and it is estimated that 41% of this spending is on those aged 65 and over despite their population share of just 16%.[12] In addition, unlike those of a working age, pensioners automatically qualify for free prescriptions and dental treatment.

6.3 Trends in Retirement and Demographics

Currently the state pension age in the UK is 65 for men and 60 for women, although legislation has already been passed which will lead to an equalized retirement age for both men and women of 65 by 2020.[13] However, a growing and significant proportion of men in particular are retiring before they reach the state pension age. The proportion of the population aged over 65 has been increasing since the 1960s, and is forecast to continue increasing until around 2030. However, these shifts in the population structure are smaller than is forecast for most western countries.

6.3.1 Retirement

While many individuals retire at state pension age, a substantial number retire before or even after this age. Evidence from the British Retirement survey indicates that the average age of retirement for a sample aged 55-69 in 1988-89 who were re-interviewed in 1994, was 62 for men and 60 for women[14] (Tanner, 1997). Men are much more likely to retire before the state pension age than women. In fact this trend to early retirement by men has been growing over time.

Figure 6.2 plots the mean proportion of men in employment at different ages for three date-of-birth cohorts. As can be seen the employment-age profiles for each successive cohort lie under those for the previous cohort for nearly all ages, indicating that a smaller proportion of men were in employment in the later cohorts. As shown in Table 6.5, 85% of men in the cohort born between 1913 and 1917 were still in work when they were aged 60, compared to under 60% of those born between 1923 and 1927 when they were of the same age.

Figure 6.2: Proportion of Men in Employment, by Date of Birth Cohort

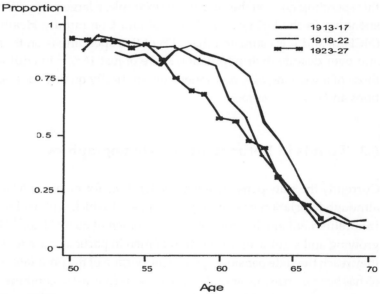

Source: Tanner, 1997.

Table 6.5: Proportion of Men in Employment (in %), by Year

	1968-1972	*1973-1977*	*1978-1982*
Age 55	86.3	89.7	91.5
Age 60	84.7	66.2	57.7
Age 65	34.8	17.7	19.1

Source: Tanner, 1997.

6.3.2 Demographics

Not only have the past few decades seen an increase in the numbers who are retiring early but the proportion of the population aged 60 or over has also been rising. Whereas in 1951 around 16% of the total UK population was aged 65 or over, today this has risen to over 20%. This will continue to rise in the next century, with 23% of the population being aged 60 and over by the year 2011 as shown below in Table 6.6. Changes in fertility rates over time are shown in Table 6.7.

Table 6.6: Age Structure of UK Population

Year	0-14	15-59	60-74	75+
1951	22.55	61.74	12.17	3.54
1961	23.42	59.59	12.82	4.17
1971	24.08	56.91	14.28	4.73
1981	20.59	59.17	14.43	5.82
1991	19.13	60.13	13.76	6.98
1995	19.39	60.12	13.50	6.99
2001	18.99	60.68	12.97	7.37
2006	18.03	60.96	13.58	7.43
2011	17.20	60.11	15.23	7.47

Note: Columns may not sum to one hundred due to rounding. Figures are mid-year estimates for 1951 to 1995 and projections for mid-year populations for 2001 onwards.

Source: Office for National Statistics, 1997a.

Table 6.7: Fertility Rates, by Age of Mother at Childbirth, 1961 to 1997

Age of mother	1961	1971	1981	1991	1997
15-19	37	50	28	33	30
20-24	173	154	107	89	75
25-29	178	155	130	120	104
30-34	106	79	70	87	89
35-39	51	34	22	32	39
40-44	16	9	5	5	7
All ages	91	84	62	64	59

Note: Number of live births per 1000 women.
Source: Office for National Statistics, 1999.

This increase in the elderly population has been caused partially by increases in life expectancy at all ages. Table 6.8 presents life expectancy rates by age and gender in 1985-87 and 1993-95. The figures indicate that the life expectancy of both genders increased over the five years, for instance life expectancy at birth for males increased from 71.9 to 73.9 years. Life expectancy at older ages also increased, for example a man aged 60 in 1985-87 would have been expected to live another 16.8 years, whereas eight years later a man of a similar age would be expected to live a further 18.2 years. Interestingly the percentage increase in the life expectancy over the six-year period was higher for males than females for all of the age groups.

Table 6.8: Life Expectancy in the UK, by Sex and Age

Age	Males			Females		
	1985-87	1993-95	% increase	1985-87	1993-95	% increase
0	71.9	73.9	2.78	77.6	79.2	2.06
60	76.8	78.2	1.82	81.2	82.2	1.23
65	78.4	79.5	1.40	82.3	83.2	1.09
70	80.5	81.4	1.12	83.7	84.5	0.96

Sources: Office for National Statistics, 1990, 1997a.

The next section looks at the generosity of the state pension arrangements towards current pensioners in terms of replacement rates. It goes on to consider forecasts for future changes in demographics and the reforms made to state provision on future state expenditures, in terms of both affordability and also generosity.

6.4 Recent Trends

As discussed in section 6.2, the basic state pension is currently worth around 15% of male average earnings, compared to around 20% before it was formally linked to prices in the early 1980s. However due to the generosity of the original SERPS calculations[15] and the fact that average earnings of those close to retirement are below the average of the working population as a whole, the effective replacement rates provided by the state are, in practice, much higher than 15%. The gross and net replacement rates for a single male retiring at 65 in 1998 who earned half, average and twice median earnings (in that year for both his age and gender) is shown below in Table 6.9.

Table 6.9: How the UK State Pension Varies with Lifetime Earnings, Individual Retiring in 1998

Annual earnings related to median	1/2	1	2
Basic weekly pension	62.45	62.45	62.45
SERPS weekly pension	17.22	49.95	104.88
Gross total weekly pension	79.67	112.40	167.33
Gross pension as % of current gross male average earnings	18.7	26.4	39.4
Gross replacement rate	62.5	44.1	32.8
Net total weekly pension	79.67	110.00	153.94
Net pension as % of current net male average earnings	24.9	34.4	48.1
Net replacement rate	71.9	50.0	34.7

Note: References to average earnings refer to the median full-time earnings amongst men of the same age for each year of the individual's working life. It is assumed that the individual has made enough contributions to qualify for the full basic state pension. All prices are at 1997 levels. Replacement rate is income-relevant to the individual's income at age 55 up-rated by inflation.

Source: Emmerson and Johnson, 1998.

So a male retiring in 1998 who had median earnings would receive a basic state pension of £62.45 and SERPS pension of £49.95. This is equivalent to 26% of current male gross average earnings and 44% of this individual's gross earnings at 55, up-rated for inflation. The net replacement rate is even higher – around 50% of his net earnings at 55, reflecting the progressivity of the UK income tax system. Table 6.10 shows the state pension entitlement for the same individual, but with a non-working spouse. The only change is that the couple will receive a higher basic state pension (an additional £37.55 a week), regardless of their level of earnings.

Table 6.10:   Same as Table 6.9, but with a Non-working Spouse

Annual earnings related to median	1/2	1	2
Basic weekly pension	99.80	99.80	99.80
SERPS weekly pension	17.22	49.95	104.88
Gross total weekly pension	117.02	149.75	204.68
Gross pension as % of current gross male average earnings	27.5	35.2	48.2
Gross replacement rate	91.8	58.7	40.1
Net total weekly pension	117.02	149.06	192.24
Net pension as % of current net male average earnings	36.6	46.6	60.0
Net replacement rate	103.2	65.7	42.4

Note: As Table 6.9.

Source: Emmerson and Johnson, 1998.

As we noted earlier the population of the UK is ageing, but will an older population place an additional burden upon the state? A common measure of this burden is the support ratio, that is the ratio of the number of people of working age to the number of pensioners. This support ratio plus projections is presented in the third row of Table 6.11. The support ratio is projected to remain fairly constant up until 2020, but thereafter it declines as the population ages as a result of the 'baby boom' generation retiring. However, in order to ascertain more clearly the burden of state pension provision one has to look at the ratio of those who are of working age and who contribute to the number of recipients of the state pension. This ratio for 2000 and beyond is given in the fourth row of Table 6.11 and follows a similar trend as seen with the support ratio.

Many of the recent reforms to the UK pension system have had the effect of substantially reducing its future generosity, and hence cost to the taxpayer. These reforms include the equalization of the state retirement age, the indexing of the basic state pension to prices and not earnings as well as numerous alterations to SERPS.[16] The future costs of the basic state pension and SERPS in both constant prices and as a percentage of GDP are shown in Table 6.12. This also gives the implied National Insurance Contribution rates (as a total of employee and employer contribution levels).

Table 6.11:   Support and Contributors/pensioners Ratios, 1980 to 2050

	1980	1991	2000	2010	2020	2030	2040	2050
Working age	32.5	34.4	35.2	36.0	37.5	35.8	34.4	33.8
Pension age	9.4	10.4	10.5	11.7	11.5	13.5	14.3	13.5
Support ratio	3.5	3.3	3.4	3.1	3.3	2.7	2.4	2.5
Contributors/ pensioners	–	–	2.1	1.9	2.0	1.6	1.5	1.5

Note: Support ratio is the number aged over 16 and below the state retirement age divided by the number over the state retirement age (65 for men and 60 for women until 2010, 65 for both from 2020). The ratio of contributors to pensioners differs from the support ratio due to those of working age but not contributing, and those receiving a state pension but living abroad. Future real GDP growth of 2% a year has been assumed.

Sources: Government Actuary (1994, 1995), Retirement Income Inquiry (1996).

Table 6.12:   Future Cost of State Pension under Current Legislation

	2000	2010	2020	2030	2040	2050
Basic State Pension (£ bn)	29.8	33.6	35.2	41.9	44.5	42.3
SERPS (£ bn)	4.2	8.4	10.9	12.0	10.2	9.9
Total state pension cost (£ bn)	34.0	42.0	46.1	53.9	54.7	52.2
Cost as percentage of GDP (%)	4.35	4.86	4.83	5.12	4.71	4.07
Required N.I. contribution rate (%)	17.7	17.4	16.8	17.2	15.8	14.0

Note: Future National Insurance Contributions assume real earnings growth of 1%. GDP growth of 2% a year has been assumed for the proportion of GDP forecasts. All prices in 1994-95 levels.

Source: Government Actuary (1994 and 1995), Retirement Income Enquiry (1996).

Despite SERPS not maturing until 2030, and the rising costs of the basic state pension due to increases in the population aged over the state retirement age, the increase in cost as a percentage of GDP is very small. This is due mainly to the policy of only up-rating the basic state pension in line with prices and not earnings, which are expected to grow at a faster rate. Indeed those individuals who retire in 2045 having constantly earned twice median male earnings (for their age and that year) will receive a state pension (i.e. basic state pension plus SERPS) of under 20% of gross male average earnings (Emmerson and Johnson, 1998). This is in contrast to the 33% shown in Table 6.9.

6.5 Household Composition and Incomes

The data used in this work is drawn from the UK Family Expenditure Surveys (FES) of 1989 and 1995. Both these surveys contain around 7,000 households who were asked a variety of questions on their incomes, expenditures, socio-economic status, household composition and other personal characteristics. This data series has been used extensively in the UK by both government departments and private institutions for the analysis of income. The size of the sample plus the depth and richness of its data means that this data set lends itself quite readily to this analysis.

The income definition used in the analysis is net household income before housing costs. It is the same definition as that used by the UK's Department of Social Security (DSS) in its Households Below Average Income (HBAI) publications. All incomes are in January 1997 prices and are equivalized using the standard OECD scale unless otherwise indicated.

248   **Table 6.13:   Composition of Households**

Number of people in household [1]	% of pensioners		% of all persons[2]	
	1989	1995	1989	1995
1	22.49	24.26	9.88	10.96
2	54.44	53.40	28.13	28.26
3	12.83	12.75	19.54	20.36
4	4.79	5.46	25.12	24.72
5	3.30	2.35	11.40	10.62
6 +	2.15	1.79	5.94	5.08

Note: (1) Including children. (2) All persons includes pensioners and children.

Columns may not sum to one hundred due to rounding.

6.5.1 Composition of Households

The composition of households in the UK is shown in Table 6.13. It suggests that between 1989 and 1995 there has been a slight shift towards smaller households. For example, the proportion of persons living in households with three or less people decreased from 59.6% in 1989 to 57.6% in 1995. Amongst pensioners the shift is less clear, though unlike non-pensioners the vast majority of pensioners live in households of three or less people. Over a longer period however there has been a shift towards pensioners being increasingly less likely to live with non-pensioners, from around one third at the start of the 1960s to under one sixth by the 1990s (Johnson and Stears, 1995).

6.5.2 Household Durables

The composition of pensioner households does not differ from non-pensioner households just in terms of the number of people within these households. Given that they contain fewer people it is not surprising that their houses tend to be physically smaller, with the average number of rooms being 5.1 compared to 5.7 amongst non-pensioner households. The most important difference in assert ownership between pensioners and non-pensioners is in housing tenure. Fifty per cent of pensioner households are owned outright, compared to just over 10% amongst non-pensioner households, as shown in Table 6.14. This is important when considering the incomes of pensioners and non-pensioners since those who own their properties outright should really be assigned with an imputed rental income. Looking at other durable goods we find that pensioners are less likely to have a video recorder, washing machine, car or central heating but are just as likely to have a phone.

249

Table 6.14: **Percentage of Pensioner and Non-pensioner Households with Certain Durable Items, 1995**

	Pensioner households	Non-pensioner households	All households
Housing tenure: mortgage	9	55	42
Housing tenure: own outright	51	13	24
Video recorder	57	90	81
Washing machine	84	94	91
Car	48	79	70
Phone	92	93	93
Central heating	81	87	86

Source: 1995 Family Expenditure Survey.

6.5.3 Pensioner Incomes

We now turn our attention to pensioner incomes. The average pensioner income in 1989 and 1995 for the different types of pensioner households is shown in Table 6.15. This shows real growth in household incomes of each of the four categories of pensioner households. Those households containing either non-pensioners or more than one pensioner benefit unit experienced considerably lower levels of income growth. This is likely to be caused by a change in the type of households in this category, with richer pensioners from the younger cohort being more likely to live alone. It should also be noted that for the United Kingdom the chosen years (1989 and 1995) are not from similar points on the economic cycle, with 1989 being at the peak of a boom and 1995 after recovery from a recession. The likely impact of this is to indicate lower levels of income growth for those more reliant on earnings compared to those whose income comes from other sources.

250   **Table 6.15:   Mean Pensioner Household Income in 1989 and 1995, by Household Type (£ per week)**

Household type	1989	1995	% increase
Single male pensioner household	106.85	143.00	33.8
Single female pensioner household	103.54	125.47	21.2
Pensioner couple household	115.42	140.81	22.0
Other pensioner household	169.55	185.57	9.4
All pensioner households	110.02	134.13	21.9
All households	155.25	166.06	7.0

Note: Equivalized household incomes at January 1997 prices.

Sources: 1989 and 1995 Family Expenditure Surveys; authors' calculations.

The real increase in pensioner incomes has been driven by an increase in the level of private pension income received (as opposed to the coverage), and real increases in the levels of social security benefits. There has been no difference in the real level of income received from either the basic state pension, which is unsurprising since it is indexed to prices and coverage has not increased significantly over the period.

The composition of household income of pensioner households is shown in Table 6.16, and is compared to the composition of incomes of the population as a whole. Unsurprisingly, pensioner households are more reliant on unearned forms of income. Looking at changes between the two years, the share of income from the state pension has fallen, which is due to real growth in total incomes, but no real increase in the generosity of the basic state pension. Investment income now also forms a smaller part of income which is an effect of the economic cycle, with much lower nominal interest rates in 1995 compared to 1989.

Table 6.16: **Composition of Household Incomes, 1989 and 1995**

	All pensioner households		All households[1]	
	1989	1995	1989	1995
Self-employment	3.7	2.6	10.4	8.6
Private pension	21.5	25.6	5.2	7.0
Investment income	15.2	13.6	5.4	5.2
Earnings	2.2	3.4	62.1	58.9
State pension	41.8	33.9	7.8	7.7
Other state benefits	15.5	20.8	9.1	12.5

Notes: (1) Includes pensioner households. Columns may not sum to 100% due to rounding.

Sources: 1989 and 1995 Family Expenditure Surveys; authors' calculations.

Table 6.17 shows how the composition of income varies between different types of pensioner households. Pensioner couples receive higher proportions of income from self-employment and earnings than single pensioners who on average are older. Pensioner couples are also less reliant on the state with income from both the basic state pension and other state benefits making up a smaller fraction of their total incomes. Other pensioner households are much more reliant on other state benefits, mainly because they receive a smaller share from the basic state pension.

Not only have the average real incomes of pensioners grown between 1989 and 1995, but this increase occurred across the entire income distribution of pensioners. Table 6.18 shows that growth in incomes between each of the deciles of pensioner households has been between 13.5 and 28.3% for all deciles. The first and tenth deciles are found to have experienced lower real growth in incomes than those in deciles four to seven.

251

Table 6.17: Composition of Pensioner Household Incomes, 1989 and 1995

	Single male pensioner household		Single female pensioner household		Pensioner couple household		Other pensioner household	
	1989	1995	1989	1995	1989	1995	1989	1995
Self-employment	0.7	1.1	0.8	0.3	6.2	4.1	1.7	2.5
Private pension	21.2	28.7	15.0	17.0	26.5	31.2	15.8	15.5
Investment income	13.0	12.5	16.1	12.8	15.4	15.0	13.7	9.8
Earnings	0.3	0.3	0.3	0.3	3.0	4.0	3.9	9.7
State pension	45.9	32.4	51.4	45.7	38.6	30.1	31.9	28.0
Other state benefits	18.8	25.1	16.4	24.0	10.3	15.6	33.1	34.5

Note: Columns may not sum to 100% due to rounding.

Source: 1989 and 1995 Family Expenditure Surveys; authors' calculations.

Table 6.18: Incomes of All Pensioner Households

Income decile	1989		1995		Percentage increase	
	Mean	Median	Mean	Median	Mean	Median
1	51	55	58	64	14.3	15.2
2	65	66	78	78	19.8	19.5
3	73	72	89	89	22.8	23.2
4	79	79	99	99	25.2	25.1
5	86	86	109	109	27.0	26.9
6	93	93	119	118	28.3	27.4
7	105	104	134	134	28.1	29.2
8	125	123	156	155	25.5	26.0
9	160	160	192	191	19.8	19.8
10	283	248	321	268	13.5	8.1
All	112	89	136	113	21.2	27.7

Note: All figures in January 1997 pounds per week of equivalized incomes.

Source: 1989 and 1995 Family Expenditure Surveys; authors' calculations.

The average real increase in incomes experienced by the whole population over this period is much lower than that experienced by pensioner households, although pensioners still on average have much lower levels of income. This is in fact a continuation of a trend seen over the last 30 years. Average pensioner incomes have grown proportionally faster than the rest of the population, especially during the 1980s (Johnson and Stears, 1995). The real income growth experienced by pensioners between 1989 and 1995 is not only greater than that experienced by the population as a whole, but also more evenly shared across the income distribution. Table 6.19 shows that the incomes of all households grew on average by 8%, with most growth occurring in the second, third and tenth income deciles. The first decile did relatively poorly, as a result of the relatively large increase in unemployment that occurred over the period.

Table 6.19: Incomes of All Households

Income decile	1989		1995		Percentage increase	
	Mean	Median	Mean	Median	Mean	Median
1	48	55	49	60	1.1	8.9
2	74	74	82	82	10.5	10.5
3	89	89	100	100	11.9	12.2
4	107	107	116	116	9.0	9.0
5	126	126	135	135	7.5	7.5
6	147	146	157	157	7.1	7.2
7	171	170	181	181	6.2	6.4
8	199	199	212	211	6.3	6.2
9	241	239	259	256	7.5	7.0
10	384	331	421	361	9.6	9.0
All	159	135	171	145	8.0	7.4

Note: Includes pensioner households. All figures in January 1997 pounds per week of equivalized incomes.

Source: 1989 and 1995 Family Expenditure Surveys; authors' calculations.

Table 6.20 looks at the proportions of pensioner households by equivalized income deciles in both 1989 and 1995. For instance in 1989, 39% of households in the poorest income decile were pensioner households, compared to 31% in 1995. The figures indicate that in 1995 pensioner households were less likely to be found in the lowest four income deciles than they were in 1989. This is to be expected given the larger increases in household incomes experienced by pensioners compared to the rest of the population over this period. Indeed this trend has been occurring since the start of the 1970s with the growing number of unemployed tending to replace the poorest pensioners in the bottom income deciles (Goodman and Webb, 1994).

Table 6.20: Percentage of Pensioner Households, by Equivalized Household Income Deciles

Decile	1989	1995
1	38.66	30.92
2	59.96	46.15
3	59.62	52.43
4	36.37	49.37
5	22.57	37.61
6	17.87	27.03
7	14.84	22.89
8	10.63	17.97
9	10.72	13.45
10	8.62	12.16
All	29.38	31.25

Note: Columns may not average last cell due to rounding.

Source: 1989 and 1995 Family Expenditure Surveys; authors' calculations.

An important question is not only what has happened to pensioners in the income distribution, but also have the experiences of different types of pensioners been varied. Tables 6.21 and 6.22 give a more detailed breakdown by the different household types. These show that the main group of pensioners who have moved up the income distribution from the first three income deciles has been single female pensioners. Pensioner couples have also experienced some movement up the income distribution, while a larger proportion of the top four deciles are now single male pensioners. Other pensioner households appear to have done relatively worse over the period, possibly caused by a composition effect, with richer pensioners from younger cohorts now being more likely to live independently.

Table 6.21: **Percentage of Households by Equivalized Household Income Deciles, in 1989**

Income decile	Single male pensioner household	Single female pensioner household	Pensioner couple household	Other pensioner household	Non-pensioner household
1	3.9	17.2	14.0	3.5	61.3
2	5.6	21.6	26.8	6.0	40.0
3	8.2	30.8	16.5	4.1	40.4
4	4.3	14.2	14.7	3.2	63.6
5	2.7	6.4	11.9	1.6	77.4
6	2.9	4.8	7.5	2.7	82.1
7	1.1	4.6	8.2	1.0	85.2
8	0.4	3.7	5.5	1.0	89.4
9	1.5	2.3	5.8	1.2	89.3
10	0.8	2.7	4.1	1.0	91.4
All	3.3	11.5	11.9	2.6	70.6

Note: Rows may not sum to 100% due to rounding.
Source: 1989 Family Expenditure Survey; authors' calculations.

Table 6.22: **Percentage of Households by Equivalized Household Income Deciles in 1995**

Income decile	Single male pensioner household	Single female pensioner household	Pensioner couple household	Other pensioner household	Non-pensioner household
1	3.2	11.4	12.6	3.8	69.1
2	5.3	16.3	20.1	4.4	53.9
3	9.1	21.3	17.5	4.6	47.6
4	6.3	21.6	17.9	3.6	50.6
5	4.7	13.5	15.5	3.9	62.4
6	2.9	10.6	11.8	1.7	73.0
7	4.2	7.4	9.6	1.8	77.1
8	2.5	4.9	9.3	1.2	82.0
9	2.1	3.4	7.2	0.8	86.5
10	2.5	2.2	6.4	1.1	87.8
All	4.3	11.4	12.9	2.7	68.8

Note: Rows may not sum to 100% due to rounding.
Source: 1995 Family Expenditure Survey; authors' calculations.

This section has shown how incomes have changed between 1989 and 1995 for both pensioner and non-pensioner households. The next section goes on to look at how household incomes vary by age of the household head in both of the years of our study.

6.6 Income between Different Age Groups

Figure 6.3 shows the age-income profiles for pensioner households and all households in 1989 and 1995.[17] The general trend seen is that household income rises up until the fifties, with quite rapid growth in the twenties, thereafter incomes remain fairly constant until retirement when incomes drop. Households in 1995 tended to have higher levels of income than households with the same age of head in 1989, despite the fact that the economic cycle would have increased incomes of the same age group in 1989 compared to 1995. The reason for this is that later date-of-birth cohorts tend to be richer than earlier cohorts. This fact also helps to explain why the age-income profiles decline in retirement as older pensioners have come from earlier and therefore poorer cohorts compared to younger pensioners. The two age-income profiles do however give some indication of what happens to incomes in retirement for any given cohort. A pensioner cohort in 1989 would be six years older in 1995 thus a 60-year-old in 1989 would be 66 in 1995. Comparing incomes for pensioners in 1989 with pensioners' incomes six years later we see that generally incomes have grown (e.g. 65-year-olds in 1989 had around £120 per week, while 71-year-olds in 1995 received £130). The main reason for this growth is differential mortality, as poorer pensioners tend to die earlier than richer pensioners.

Figure 6.4 presents more closely the 1989 and 1995 age-income profiles for pensioner households and all households with one or more pensioners. Not surprisingly, the 1989 age-income profiles are largely indistinguishable, as are the 1995 profiles, although there is some divergence at the earlier ages. Also, as noticed above, the 1989 profiles lie below the 1995 profiles. Looking at incomes for pensioner households we see that average household income seems to rise with age for those retiring before 65 (the sudden drop between 50 and 52 for pensioner households in 1995 should be treated with caution given the small cell size). Part of the explanation for this is that some of these households are single female households, who as we saw earlier tend to be the poorest pensioner households, who are retiring at or just before state pension age. Another possible explanation is that some of those who retire before state pension age are doing so involuntarily, either because of ill-health or involuntary redundancy etc. and as such have lower incomes than those who retire voluntarily. Of course this same effect could be achieved if people are retiring voluntarily, but those who are able to command a higher wage have more incentive to stay in work longer and retire later. After 65 retirement incomes start to decline, although there is some indication in the figure that incomes start to rise again for the older pensioners. This last trend should however be treated with caution given the small sample size but is likely to be caused by strong effects from differential mortality.

Figure 6.3: Average Equivalized Weekly Income, by Age, All Households vs. Pensioner Households (in £ per week)

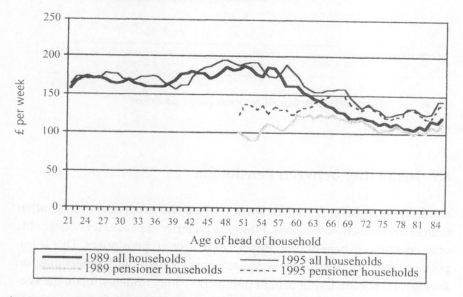

Source: 1989 and 1995 Family Expenditure Surveys; authors' calculations.

So far we have looked at the household incomes of pensioners, and seen that not only have these risen by more than for the population as a whole, but unlike the rest of the population this rise in incomes has been shared fairly equally across the income distribution. The next section goes on to assess whether this has led to unchanged inequality amongst pensioner households and also whether the incomes amongst some groups of pensioners are more unequal than others.

Figure 6.4: Average Equivalized Weekly Income; Pensioner Households vs. All Households with One or More Pensioners (in £ per week)

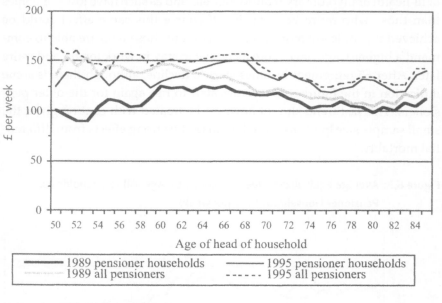

Source: 1989 and 1995 Family Expenditure Surveys; authors' calculations.

6.7 Inequality between Pensioners

Unlike the analysis so far this section uses the incomes of benefit units, rather than entire household incomes. While the majority of pensioner households only contain one benefit unit, this is not true of all pensioners. This is important since (for example) those pensioners who live with others may, on average, be poorer. Using benefit unit income may underestimate the economic well-being of pensioners if they share the income of non-pensioner household members, but is more likely to highlight the effects of changing patterns of accrued private pension rights and changes in the generosity of income from the state. This is particularly true of the UK since eligibility for means-tested benefits is based on benefit unit income, rather than the income of the household as a whole.

Tables 6.23 and 6.24 show which income deciles different categories of pensioner benefit units are in. All categories of pensioners are disproportionately found in the lower income deciles, with – as found in section 6.5 – this being more likely among single pensioners than pensioner couples.

Table 6.23: Percentage of Individuals, by Equivalized Benefit Unit Deciles, in 1989

Decile	Single pensioners	Pensioner couples	All pensioners	Pensioners in pensioner households	All persons aged 60+
1	17.8	16.6	34.4	29.0	32.2
2	25.1	37.4	62.6	54.4	58.6
3	21.3	24.9	46.2	37.1	42.9
4	7.0	19.1	26.2	19.0	23.6
5	4.2	12.3	16.5	10.5	15.2
6	3.5	10.5	14.0	8.8	14.1
7	2.4	7.6	10.0	6.5	9.7
8	1.9	5.2	7.1	4.2	7.1
9	1.6	6.5	8.1	5.0	8.6
10	1.8	5.4	7.1	4.2	7.2
All	8.7	14.6	23.2	17.9	21.9

Note: Columns may not average last cell due to rounding. Table 6A1 in the Appendix presents the same table, but instead the percentage of pensioners within each class falling into each decile.

Source: 1989 Family Expenditure Survey; authors' calculations.

By 1995 the proportion of the first decile that was single pensioners had fallen to 13% from 18% in 1989. However this still represents a higher proportion than their population share of around 9%.

Table 6.25 looks at position of pensioners in the income distribution by age rather than whether they are single or not. It shows that while pensioners are over-represented in the lower income deciles, the first income decile does not have a disproportionate share of pensioners whose head is aged 60-69. Indeed by 1995 only 8% of the first decile came from pensioners in this category compared to their population share of 10%. It is clear from Table 6.25 that it is older pensioners who are typically poorer, with for example an extremely small proportion of those aged over 80 found in the top *four* income deciles, especially in 1989. This is of course consistent with the earlier finding that single pensioners tended to have lower levels of equivalized income than pensioner couples.

Table 6.24: Percentage of Individuals, by Equivalized Benefit Unit Deciles, in 1995

Decile	Single pensioners	Pensioner couples	All pensioners	Pensioners in pensioner households	All persons aged 60+
1	13.0	19.0	32.0	27.1	26.1
2	21.1	32.3	53.4	46.8	48.3
3	21.1	27.6	48.8	42.0	41.5
4	10.9	21.5	32.4	26.4	28.5
5	6.7	13.7	20.4	15.4	17.6
6	5.4	11.3	16.7	11.6	14.7
7	3.3	13.1	16.5	10.2	13.9
8	2.9	9.0	11.8	8.5	9.0
9	2.3	5.4	7.7	4.5	6.2
10	1.9	7.8	9.7	6.3	8.6
All	8.9	16.1	24.9	19.9	21.4

Note: Columns may not average last cell due to rounding. Table 6A2 in the Appendix presents the same table, but instead the percentage of pensioners within each class falling into each decile.

Source: 1995 Family Expenditure Survey; authors' calculations.

Table 6.25: Percentage of Individuals, by Age of Head and Equivalized Benefit Unit Income Deciles in 1989 and 1995

Decile	Age of head of benefit unit					
	60-69		70-79		Over 80	
	1989	1995	1989	1995	1989	1995
1	11.2	8.4	12.5	11.8	8.5	6.0
2	24.1	19.2	25.4	19.7	9.0	9.4
3	20.8	16.8	15.1	16.7	7.1	7.9
4	13.1	14.9	8.3	8.7	2.3	4.9
5	10.6	9.4	3.7	5.4	0.8	2.8
6	9.5	8.3	3.3	4.9	1.3	1.6
7	7.1	9.3	2.0	3.5	0.6	1.2
8	5.1	5.7	1.7	2.3	0.3	0.9
9	5.9	4.3	2.2	1.1	0.5	0.7
10	5.1	5.3	1.2	2.0	0.9	1.3
All	11.3	10.2	7.5	7.6	3.1	3.7

Note: Columns may not average last cell due to rounding.

Source: 1989 and 1995 Family Expenditure Surveys; authors' calculations.

We have shown that pensioner benefit units were less likely to be in the poorer income deciles in 1995 than they were in 1989. In Table 6.26 we look more closely at the incidence of poverty by examining the proportion of pensioners below certain fractions of overall median equivalized benefit unit income. The proportion of pensioners below these 'poverty lines' fell between 1989 and 1995; for instance in 1989 nearly 60% of all pensioner benefit units had less than 70% of median income, by 1995 this had fallen to 44%. This is to be expected since the incomes of pensioner households at the bottom of the income distribution were found to have increased by substantially more than the increase in median income of the entire population over the period.

Table 6.26:   Share of Pensioners Below Various Percentages of Median Income

Type of pensioner household	Level relative to median equivalized household income							
	40%		50%		60%		70%	
	1989	1995	1989	1995	1989	1995	1989	1995
Single male pensioner	5.1	2.2	18.4	10.5	35.0	22.8	61.1	43.6
Single female pensioner	6.9	2.2	23.4	14.4	41.0	27.6	69.7	46.1
Pensioner couple	4.1	4.0	19.2	13.7	40.8	28.3	54.8	41.8
All pensioners in pensioner households	5.1	4.2	20.9	14.2	40.7	28.7	59.9	44.0
All pensioners	4.7	4.0	16.8	12.1	32.3	24.5	49.3	38.1
All persons aged 60+	4.7	3.1	15.5	11.1	31.9	24.2	48.6	38.0
All persons	6.1	6.4	14.0	15.6	22.8	24.3	32.0	33.6

Source: 1989 and 1995 Family Expenditure Surveys; authors' calculations.

Table 6.27 shows different measures of income inequality for different groups of pensioners. Between 1989 and 1995 pensioner inequality, as measured by the Gini coefficient was fairly unchanged. This is fairly unsurprising given the fact that real increases in pension incomes were found to be evenly spread across the income distribution, and the slightly higher growth found for household incomes amongst the first decile relative the tenth decile not being found once *benefit unit* income is used.

Looking at difference between the various pensioner groups it is found that inequality was unchanged amongst all pensioner groups, with the exception of single female pensioners, amongst whom inequality fell. Inequality is higher amongst pensioner couples and single male pensioners than single female pensioners. This is unsurprising since single female pensioners are more concentrated around the bottom of the income distribution. This is partially due to lower levels of income from occupation pensions and also due to cohort effects, since single female pensioners are on average older.

Table 6.27:   Measures of Inequality

Pensioner type	Gini coefficient		90 / 10		75 / 25	
	1989	1995	1989	1995	1989	1995
All pensioners	0.30	0.29	3.21	3.27	1.81	1.82
All pensioners in pensioner households	0.28	0.27	3.10	3.13	1.73	1.76
Pensioner couple	0.30	0.29	3.40	3.37	1.89	1.96
Single male pensioner	0.26	0.28	2.79	3.29	1.71	1.70
Single female pensioner	0.30	0.26	3.08	2.85	1.62	1.62
All persons aged 60+	0.29	0.28	3.41	3.22	1.88	1.86
All persons	0.35	0.35	4.67	4.45	2.31	2.17

Note: Benefit unit incomes (equivalized for the purpose of comparisons between single pensioners
            and pensioner couples).

Source: 1989 and 1995 Family Expenditure Surveys; authors' calculations.

While pensioner inequality has been relatively unchanged over the period 1989 to 1995 this is not the case over a longer period. Inequality amongst pensioners fell almost continuously from 1960 to 1981 before rising sharply until 1990. The fall in pensioner inequality until 1971 results from increasing coverage and generosity of social security benefits, little change in earnings inequality and high levels of inflation reducing returns from investment mainly for the richest pensioners. The increase in inequality amongst pensioners throughout the 1980s occurred mainly because of an unequally shared increase in private pension income and high levels of real interest rates increasing investment income disproportionality amongst the wealthy (Johnson and Stears, 1995).

6.8 Conclusions and Future Policy Options

Pensioner incomes grew substantially in real terms between 1989 and 1995, with the population as a whole experiencing a much lower growth in real income. Although inequality amongst pensioners rose sharply throughout the 1980s, this was not found to be the case for the period 1989 to 1995. This is likely to have been caused by the downturn in the economic cycle having a greater effect on those pensioners with investment income then those reliant on means-tested benefits which have increased in real terms.

The UK pension system has been in a state of almost continual reform over the last 25 years.[18] Since coming to power in May 1997 the current government has proposed further reforms.[19] While the basic state pension will continue to be price-indexed the Government has stated that its intention is to increase the generosity of means-tested benefits to pensioners in line with earnings. This will, in the short term at least, lead to an increase in the number of pensioners on means-tested benefits. The government has also announced the replacement of SERPS with the new State Second Pension (SSP). This will be more generous to lower earners, and unlike SERPS also has credits for those caring for a dependant under five.[20]

A key part of the government's proposals is for an increase in the proportion of pension income from private sources. The government is hoping to achieve this with the introduction of Stakeholder pensions which are a low-cost, flexible personal pension aimed at middle earners (defined as those earning between £9,000 and £18,500). The success of these pension schemes is extremely important for the government's proposals to work. One problem may be the fact that the majority of the individuals who are in the government's target group already have a private pension arrangement. Those who do not are much more likely to have fluctuating earnings and experience periods of unemployment. In addition they tend to have very low levels of savings – suggesting that they may want to start saving in a more flexible form than in a pension.

The increase in pensioner income from private sources that is being proposed by the government is essentially a continuation of government policy since the early 1980s. This will leave the UK state pension system in a sustainable position, at least in terms of affordability. Whether the system remains sustainable in terms of equity remains to be seen. Further increases in the generosity of the State Second Pension may eventually be required – particularly if means-tested benefits do continue to rise with earnings – in order to increase incentives for individuals to save for their own retirement.

Notes

1 Assuming real earnings growth of 1% a year.
2 Currently 445,000 women are still paying this reduced rate since they were allowed to continue with lower contributions. In 1978 however, 4.1 million married women had chosen this reduced rate of contribution.
3 Source: Department of Social Security (1997).
4 Source: HM Treasury (1998a).
5 Source: Social Security Departmental Report (1998).
6 Source: 1995 Family Resources Survey.
7 Source: Department of Social Security (1997).
8 Source: 1995 Family Resources Survey.
9 The self-employed and those earning below the LEL (which is mainly part-time women) are the only groups who are not compelled to have some form of second tier provision.
10 Early leavers are now protected against inflation of up to 5% a year.
11 Source: HM Treasury (1998b).
12 Source: Department of Health (1998).
13 As a result of the 1995 Pension Act the state retirement age is to be increased by six months every year between 2010 and 2020.
14 Based on self-reported retirement age.
15 The reforms to the SERPS formula which have reduced its generosity are due to be phased in from the start of the next century.
16 Originally the SERPS formula considered 25% of individual average earnings from the best 20 years of their life. This has been reduced to 20% of average earnings across their whole working life. In addition a spouse can now only inherit half of his/her deceased partner's SERPS pension compared to 100% originally. There have also been other more technical adjustments to the calculations which have also had the effect of reducing its generosity.
17 All households includes those in the pensioner household category.
18 For more details of these pension reforms and alternative options, see for example Dilnot and Johnson (1992), Disney (1996), Disney (1998) and Johnson (1999).
19 The government's proposals are contained in Department of Social Security (1998). For an analysis of these reforms see Disney, Emmerson, and Tanner (1999).
20 For more details of the impact of the State Second Pension see Agulnik (1999).

References

Agulnik, P. (1999) 'The Proposed State Second Pension', *Fiscal Studies*, vol. 20, no. 4: 409-421.

Department of Health (1998) *Departmental Report 1998*. London: The Stationary Office.

Department of Social Security (1997) *Social Security Statistics 1997*. London: The Stationary Office.

Department of Social Security (1998) *A New Contract for Welfare: Partnership in Pensions*. London: DSS.

Dilnot, A./Johnson, P. (1992) 'What Pension Should the State Provide?', *Fiscal Studies*, vol. 13, no. 4: 1-20.

Dilnot, A./Disney, R./Johnson, P./Whitehouse, E. (1994) *Pensions Policy in the UK: An Economic Analysis*. London: Institute for Fiscal Studies.

Disney, R. (1996) *Can We Afford to Grow Older? A Perspective of the Economics of Ageing*. Cambridge: MIT Press.

Disney, R. (1998) 'Crises in Public Pension Programmes in OECD: What Are the Reform Options?', University of Nottingham discussion paper No. 98/20.

Disney, R./Emmerson, C./Tanner, S. (1999) *Partnership in Pensions: An Assessment*, Commentary no. 78. London: Institute for Fiscal Studies.

Emmerson, C./Johnson, P. (1998) 'Pension Provision in the United Kingdom', Institute for Fiscal Studies Working Paper (forthcoming), London.

Goodman, A./Webb, S. (1994) *For Richer, for Poorer: The Changing Distribution of Income in the United Kingdom, 1961-91*, Commentary no. 42. London: Institute for Fiscal Studies.

Government Actuary (1994) *Pensions Bill (1994): Report by the Government Actuary on the Financial Provisions of the Bill on the National Insurance Fund*. London: HMSO.

Government Actuary (1995) *National Insurance Fund Long Term Financial Estimates*. London: HMSO.

HM Treasury (1996) *Tax Benefit Reference Manual, 1995-96 Edition*. London: HM Treasury.

HM Treasury (1998a) *Financial Statement and Budget Report, March 1998*. London: The Stationary Office.

HM Treasury (1998b) *Public Expenditure Statistical Analyses 1998-99*. London: The Stationary Office.

Johnson, P. (1999) *Older Getting Wiser*. Sydney: Institute of Chartered Accountants in Australia.

Johnson, P./Stears, G. (1995) 'Pensioner Income Inequality', *Fiscal Studies*, vol. 16, no. 4: 69-93.

Office for National Statistics (1990) *Annual Abstract of Statistics, 1990 edition*. London: HMSO.

Office for National Statistics (1997a) *Annual Abstract of Statistics, 1997 edition*. London: HMSO.

Office for National Statistics (1997b) *Living in Britain: Results from the 1995 General Household Survey*. London: The Stationary Office.

Office for National Statistics (1999) *Social Trends 29, 1999 edition*. London: The Stationary Office.

Retirement Income Enquiry (1996) *Pensions 2000 and beyond*, volume 1. London: Retirement Income Enquiry.

Social Security Departmental Report (1998) *The Government's Expenditure Plans 1998-99*. London: The Stationary Office.

Tanner, S. (1997) 'The Dynamics of Retirement Behaviour', in Disney, R./Grundy, E./Johnson, P., *The Dynamics of Retirement*, Department of Social Security Report No. 72, London.

265

Appendix

Table 6A1: Percentage of Individuals, by Equivalized Benefit Unit Deciles, in 1989

Decile	Single pensioners	Pensioner couples	All pensioners	Pensioners in pensioner households	All persons aged 60 and over
1	20.6	11.4	14.8	16.2	14.7
2	29.0	25.7	27.0	30.4	26.7
3	24.6	17.1	19.9	20.8	19.6
4	8.1	13.2	11.3	10.7	10.8
5	4.9	8.5	7.1	5.9	6.9
6	4.0	7.2	6.0	4.9	6.4
7	2.8	5.2	4.3	3.6	4.4
8	2.1	3.6	3.0	2.4	3.2
9	1.9	4.4	3.5	2.8	3.9
10	2.0	3.7	3.1	2.4	3.3

Note: Columns may not average 10% due to rounding.

Source: 1989 Family Expenditure Survey; authors' calculations.

Table 6A2: Percentage of Individuals, by Equivalized Benefit Unit Deciles, in 1995

Decile	Single pensioners	Pensioner couples	All pensioners	Pensioners in pensioner households	All persons aged 60 and over
1	14.6	11.8	12.8	13.6	12.2
2	23.8	20.1	21.4	23.5	22.5
3	23.8	17.2	19.6	21.2	19.4
4	12.3	13.4	13.0	13.3	13.3
5	7.6	8.6	8.2	7.8	8.2
6	6.1	7.0	6.7	5.9	6.9
7	3.7	8.2	6.6	5.1	6.5
8	3.3	5.6	4.7	4.3	4.2
9	2.6	3.3	3.1	2.2	2.9
10	2.2	4.9	3.9	3.2	4.0

Note: Columns may not average 10% due to rounding.

Source: 1995 Family Expenditure Survey; authors' calculations.

Table 6A3: Percentage of Individuals, by Equivalized Benefit Unit Deciles, in 1989

Decile	All male pensioners	All female pensioners	All males aged 60 and over	All females aged 60 and over
1	12.8	16.4	12.4	17.4
2	26.2	27.7	25.5	29.9
3	18.8	20.6	18.4	21.2
4	12.3	10.2	11.9	9.4
5	7.7	6.4	7.8	5.7
6	6.9	5.5	7.4	4.9
7	4.6	4.1	4.8	3.8
8	3.3	2.9	3.5	2.4
9	4.1	3.1	4.5	2.6
10	3.3	3.0	3.7	2.8

Note: Columns may not average 10% due to rounding.

Source: 1989 Family Expenditure Survey; authors' calculations.

Table 6A4: Percentage of Individuals, by Equivalized Benefit Unit Deciles, in 1995

Decile	All male pensioners	All female pensioners	All males aged 60 and over	All females aged 60 and over
1	12.3	13.3	11.3	13.6
2	21.1	21.9	21.8	24.1
3	18.0	20.3	17.8	21.1
4	13.0	13.0	13.6	12.8
5	8.2	8.5	8.1	8.5
6	7.1	6.3	7.2	5.9
7	7.2	6.2	7.4	5.2
8	5.3	4.3	4.9	3.3
9	3.5	2.7	3.3	2.1
10	4.3	3.4	4.7	3.3

Note: Columns may not average 10% due to rounding.

Source: 1995 Family Expenditure Survey; authors' calculations.

List of Contributors

Carl Emmerson, Senior Research Economist at the Institute for Fiscal Studies, London

Paul Johnson, former Deputy Director of the Institute for Fiscal Studies, now with the Financial Services Authority, London

Christopher Prinz, Programme Director of the Social Policy Modelling Unit at the European Centre for Social Welfare Policy and Research, Vienna, currently Project Co-ordinator at the OECD Social Policy Division, Paris

Zsolt Spéder, Director of the Demographic Research Institute of the Hungarian Statistical Office, Budapest

Tine Stanovnik, Senior Research Fellow at the Institute for Economic Research and Associate Professor of Economics at the Faculty of Economics, Ljubljana

Gary Stears, former Research Economist at the Institute for Fiscal Studies, now Senior Economist at the Association of British Insurers, London

Nada Stropnik, Senior Research Fellow at the Institute for Economic Research, Ljubljana

Adam Szulc, Assistant Professor at the Institute of Statistics and Demography of the Warsaw School of Economics

For Product Safety Concerns and Information please contact
our EU representative GPSR@taylorandfrancis.com Taylor & Francis
Verlag GmbH, Kaufingerstraße 24, 80331 München, Germany

T - #0176 - 270225 - C0 - 238/163/15 - PB - 9780815382362 - Gloss Lamination